THE VICTORIAN
GARDENER

THE VICTORIAN GARDENER

THE GROWTH OF GARDENING & THE FLORAL WORLD

ANNE WILKINSON

FOREWORD BY BOB FLOWERDEW

SUTTON PUBLISHING

First published in the United Kingdom in 2006 by
Sutton Publishing Limited · Phoenix Mill
Thrupp · Stroud · Gloucestershire · GL5 2BU

British Library Cataloguing in Publication Data
A catalogue record for this book is available from the British Library.

ISBN 0-7509-4043-3

Typeset in 11/13.5 pt Garamond.
Typesetting and origination by
Sutton Publishing Limited.
Printed and bound in England by
J.H. Haynes & Co. Ltd, Sparkford.

To
Richard Allfrey
1947–2004

Contents

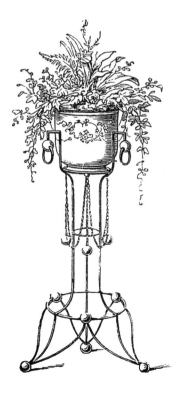

List of Colour Plates

List of Black and White Illustrations

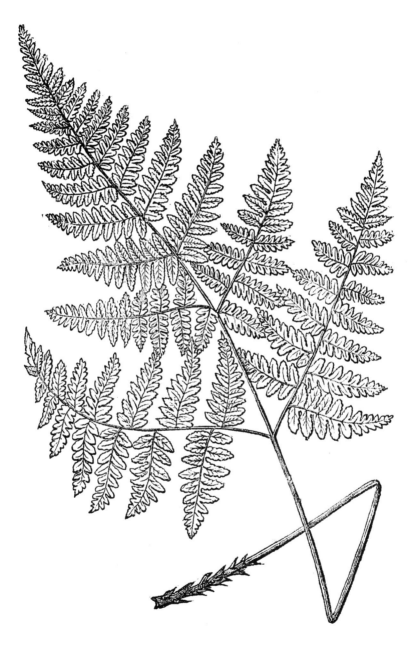

Foreword

The Victorian gardeners created our modern gardens. Little we now do horticulturally was not already being done back then, and back then it was often being done better. We probably grow fewer varieties of plants than they did, and we certainly no longer need to crop our gardens over such extended seasons, thanks to transport and refrigeration. We have other advantages, especially with modern clothing, electric heating and ventilation, legally enforced seed purity and germination rates, and health and safety regulations! But in all the basics we are continuing exactly as they did, though to our minds usually on a much more humble scale than what was so often perceived as 'Victorian gardening'.

And that is what is so fascinating about this book: Anne Wilkinson has painstakingly collated scattered fragments of evidence to re-create the early evolution of our gardens. Not of those of the grand and stately homes and great botanical institutions, but of those gardens belonging to us, the real gardeners. Extracting pertinent snippets from the books and magazines of the time, Anne has carefully built up a cohesive history not only of how we gained gardening both as a hobby and as a profession, but also of how we gained our various sorts and types of gardens. From the early cottage and town house beginnings through to such refinements as the Water, Rose and Exotic, she traces each theme and its development. Of course I was particularly interested in the Vegetable and Fruit Gardens but was drawn in by all the other sections, especially the second part, 'Learning to Garden'.

But let me leave you now to enjoy it all for yourself, reminding you only that this book explains how we derived our knowledge of plants and methods from the hard work and tenacity of just a few generations of far-sighted men and women. It is humbling to realise how much we owe them. As someone once said, truly, we stand on the shoulders of giants.

Bob Flowerdew
Dickleburgh
Norfolk
July 2005

Preface

This book is a different approach to Victorian gardening. I have chosen to emphasise the work of amateur gardeners and show how they came to be the primary focus of both the retail market and horticultural publishing. Along with the main text, readers will find mini-biographies of some of the most important players in the story. Many well-known names, however, such as Loudon, Robinson, Jekyll, Paxton and Lindley, do not feature in these, as their lives have already been covered elsewhere. I have chosen to focus on lesser-known gardeners, from wealthy landowners to working people, who all had extraordinary enthusiasm and ability to persevere in their ambitions and encourage others to do the same. There are many people mentioned in the text on whom I would like to have given more information, but I looked for it in vain. They produced a book or two and then, like their gardens, they disappeared for ever. The exception is the most important amateur of all, Shirley Hibberd, on whom I have plenty more information and whose story deserves, I feel, to be told in full in a future book.

As well as the biographies and the main narrative, readers will find Tips and Comments from our Victorian gardeners, many of which are as relevant today as they were when they were written. I have also tried to give a good account of the Victorian gardening magazines, which are the key to any research on the subject, and I hope the details given in the Appendix will help writers in the future. There is much more to discover in their closely printed pages and they could be the basis of many more books and research projects. Finally, I have listed places to visit to see Victorian gardening re-created today, and a list of suppliers to help put into practice some of the ideas described in these pages.

Anne Wilkinson
Upminster
October 2005

Acknowledgements

This book began as a thesis for the Open University many years ago and I would therefore like to thank John Golby and Bill Purdue, my supervisors, for their guidance, interest and enthusiasm in steering me through the technicalities of academic research. I also value the co-operation and friendship of Julia Matheson, a fellow researcher at the OU, who was one of the few people I could discuss Victorian gardening with, knowing she would be interested.

My research took me to many corners of dusty archives and libraries and I never failed to marvel at the knowledge and interest shown by the curators. Both the Lindley Library and the British Library moved to new buildings during the time I was working in them, and I praise the ingenuity of the staff in never failing to find the requested documents in the apparent upheaval. I also became a regular customer at the Hackney Archives, whose help was invaluable, and in particular I would like to thank Isobel Watson of the Friends of Hackney Archives for her early support and encouragement. The Museum of Garden History also proved a fund of treasures, and I especially thank Philip Norman for his detailed assistance. Similarly, much quirky material waited to be discovered at the John Johnson Collection of the Bodleian Library in Oxford, whose staff were also generous with their help.

A huge amount of help, too, was given by Tim Rumball at *Amateur Gardening* in allowing me to plunder the magazine's archives and use its illustrations. I am also grateful to Michael Riordan at St John's College, Oxford, for information on H.J. Bidder, and to George Butters Esq., for information on the Butters family and for allowing the use of the Dommersen portraits. Similarly, I thank Louth Town Council for permission to use the Panorama, Tim Evans for Birkenhead's fern book, Gavin Weightman for good advice, and Suttons Seeds and Crowders' Nurseries for their catalogues. I could not have produced many of the illustrations without the instruction and support of Trevor Jackson, to whom I am also very grateful. Lastly, I thank Jaqueline Mitchell for her faith in agreeing to publish the book, and the unfailing support of my friends and family in believing in me, in particular my daughters, Isabelle and Florence Allfrey, whose good humour and practical support always keep me going.

Introduction

The Gardens of Heligan, Alton Towers, Biddulph Grange, Waddesdon Manor, Normanby Hall: just some of the great gardens of the Victorian age. But what about the gardens that were not so great, the gardens belonging to ordinary people? The Victorians were ambitious and the middle classes were rising classes; the working people slowly gained independence and income, and they too wanted their luxuries and their status symbols. A garden seemed to be something everyone in Britain considered essential. It was part of the home and one of the novelties of the age. As exciting plants and patent inventions were released onto a newly created retail market, it appeared that gardening held an interest for people of all classes.

But how did novice gardeners know what to do if they could not afford skilled staff to work for them? Gardening was also time-consuming, and there were few labour-saving devices in the early part of the century. There were no TV gardeners, no glossy magazines, no easy-to-follow books, no garden centres, no Internet. It was 'do it yourself' before the phrase was invented. Extraordinary though it may seem, the term 'amateur gardening' was not used before the 1850s. Certainly there were plenty of amateurs who were gardeners: florists, botanists, cottagers, allotment-holders, ladies, clergymen, all sorts of people who grew things for pleasure. However, most of them grew only certain things: florists grew florists' flowers, cottagers grew vegetables and a few decorative hardy plants, wealthy collectors grew zonal pelargoniums or cape heaths. The working classes grew gooseberries and currants and a melon on the compost heap: they would not think of grapes or nectarines; they would not even think of tomatoes. This was not just a matter of money; it was a matter of aspiration.

The difficulty of finding information amid the wealth of resources highlights another problem with the terminology of horticultural history. There is a difference between 'garden history' and 'the history of gardening'. 'Garden history' seems largely to be used to mean the history of garden design. This is an interesting and useful study, but many people who indulge in it seem to know little of either plants or the practical side of gardening. Phrases such as 'the social history of gardening' seem to be an attempt to look beyond pure design, but authors are often reluctant to go outside the great estate gardens or the walled kitchen gardens, because of course they are usually well documented and easier to research. It is now time to look further into social history to find out how amateur gardening fitted into people's lives, and discover new facts about the names we frequently hear mentioned, but so rarely connect with real people.

The 1851 census for the first time recorded more people in Britain living in towns than in the countryside. The structure of society was changing, and with those changes came new ideas and new ambitions. This is the story of how gardening became one of the things that anyone could do. People from all classes became amateur gardeners. The wealthier still employed people to work for them, but they began to take more interest in and responsibility for the design of their gardens and choice of plants. The less well off learned the skills of gardening themselves, demystifying the secrets of gardening previously retained by the professionals. In the process, gardening brought people together as equals, which was not easily accepted in the 1850s. This is the story of the writers and gardeners who had the vision to realise that gardening could be a pleasure in itself:

> This outdoor life not only keeps the blood in a healthy glow, and the brain active in its search for knowledge, but . . . the meanest tasks are elevated even to dignity by the fact of their necessity. Hence, a man who is a thorough gardener feels no shame in handling the spade, or in wheeling rubbish to the pit; for though his means may enable him to enjoy all the refinements of life, it is his pride that there is not one manipulation but that he can perform himself, and so a brown skin and hard hands give him no fear that he shall lose his claim to the title of gentleman. And the world is very forgiving on this matter – its sympathies are with a gardener![1]

Many people live in Victorian houses and carefully restore them to how they think they would have looked in the nineteenth century, but few try to re-create Victorian gardens. The perception is that they were all bedding plants and ornaments, but this is not entirely accurate. Of course the Victorians liked their formal flower beds and their standard roses, but they also loved the wild and the exotic, the hardy perennials and the florists' flowers. They enjoyed gardening a hundred and fifty years ago for the same reasons as we enjoy it in the twenty-first century, and it was their hard work and persistence against all the opposition that gives us the vastly superior opportunities we have today. We owe it to them to understand how this came about.

PART ONE

The Gardeners

CHAPTER ONE

'The Home of Taste': How Gardening Enhanced Domestic Life

Gardening became popular in Britain in the nineteenth century because it was the right place and the right time. The temperate climate, abundant rainfall and a variety of soil conditions meant that a suitable habitat could be found for almost any plant that was introduced. Skills in botany and horticulture were well established and the challenges posed by new plants were welcomed by gardeners and nurserymen alike. Britain's position as a centre of world trade meant that the people were used to new products and ideas, and they were quickly absorbed into their lives. By the mid-nineteenth century, Britain was a wealthy country; by the end of the century, even the lower middle classes took novelties for granted and were eager to show them off. But no one wanted to fall into the trap of appearing 'vulgar', and they were happy to take advice on taste and style from newly appointed experts. It was inevitable that decorative plants would become one more consumer item on the shopping lists of those with money to spend.

The Victorian home was a refuge from the outside world, a kingdom in itself, ruled over by the head of the family and inhabited by his subjects. The 'home of taste' was said to be 'an anchorage when life becomes a hurricane'.[1] Possessions showed status: a man would be judged by the clothes worn by his family, the furniture and ornaments in his drawing room and the appearance of his garden. Although nominally under the control of the man of the house, the day-to-day running of the home was undertaken by the wife. The garden, therefore, as part of the home, often came under her domain, and women's attitudes to gardening give us insights into how amateurs went about creating gardens in the nineteenth century.

The development of amateur gardening was closely related to the growth of housing, yet while there is plenty of information on how Victorian towns and suburbs developed and how gardens related to

the pattern of streets and houses,[2] there is little information on how the gardens were actually used. This has led to a belief that gardening did not take place in towns at all in the nineteenth century, and that amateur gardening did not start until much later. This view appears to be supported by the fact that the *Gardeners' Chronicle*, often regarded as the 'bible' of Victorian gardening, devoted little space to town or amateur gardening until late in the century, when forced to do so by popular demand.[3] However, the *Chronicle* was operating with its own interests in mind and, as will be seen in Chapter Three, these did not include people who had small town gardens.

Yet these small gardens did exist and became an essential part of the landscape of all towns. By the 1850s building land in towns had became scarce and houses were built closely together in a uniform pattern, on as small a scale as possible. The market gardeners and nurserymen on the edge of towns were driven out by high land prices and worsening pollution, making it impossible to grow food or keep cows for fresh milk within walking distance of the centre of town. For the first time, large urban areas became purely residential. The repeated pattern of rows of houses, topped with chimneys and

A suburban garden in the 1890s. Women were often the chief gardeners in the home and some of the earliest amateur writers. (*Museum of Garden History*)

interspersed with small gardens, stretched as far as the eye could see. The world became dark. Soot made the buildings black and fog often obscured the daylight. Industry and commerce governed a world regulated by railway time. Even the names of the new synthetic dyes invented to brighten up life reflected the world in which they were produced: Manchester Brown, London Dust and Dust of Ruins.[4] No wonder people living in these new houses wanted to retain a link with the countryside and create a little colour in the drabness.

But in cultivating a garden, the Victorians were not simply indulging in nostalgia for the countryside. British people felt a deep need to establish an 'estate' of their own, however small. If an Englishman's home was his castle, then the garden was his country estate. British social structure had developed differently from other European countries,[5] which may be what makes amateur gardening so peculiarly British.[6] Traditionally farms and estates in Britain remained intact for generations, passing in entirety to the oldest son, while younger sons left the land and sought other occupations. Landowners remained powerful and became patrons of the surrounding communities. In many European countries, however, land was divided among all children on the death of a parent, creating ever-diminishing farms and smallholdings, often barely providing a living above subsistence level. Whereas landowning in England symbolised power, in many other countries it symbolised drudgery and became a burden. When the English middle classes obtained their individual terraced houses or villas, with a rectangle of garden attached, they saw it as a miniature country estate where they could indulge their individuality and be their own masters, whereas the European who was freed from his family smallholding immediately graduated to a town apartment with no more than a balcony from which to look out over his shared urban domain.

The realities of town living in the nineteenth century were not very pleasant. There was constant pollution from soot, causing dirt and fog. There was overcrowding, and dirty, smelly streets and heavy traffic. But living in town was a necessity for being near work before cheap train fares made it possible to commute. The ideal compromise for people who could afford it was the suburb. John Claudius Loudon (1783–1843), writing in 1838, explained its attraction: 'Towns, by the concentration which they afford, are calculated essentially for business and facility of enjoyment; and the interior of the country, by its wide expanse, for the display of hospitality, wealth and magnificence, by the extensive landed proprietor: or for a life of labour and wealth, but without social intercourse, by the cultivator of the soil. The suburbs of towns are alone calculated to afford a maximum of comfort and enjoyment at a minimum of expense.'[7]

Constant washing and keeping hands smooth and soft by a never-failing use of Vaseline or a mixture of glycerine and starch, kept ready on the washstand to use after washing and before drying the hands – are the best remedies I know. Old kid gloves are better for weeding than the so-called gardening gloves; and for many purposes the wash-leather housemaid's glove, sold at any village shop, is invaluable.

Mrs C.W. Earle, *Pot-Pourri from a Surrey Garden*, p. 116

In the 1830s Loudon wrote *The Suburban Gardener* for the middle classes, who found it convenient to live in small 'satellite' settlements outside London and other large towns. They were very different from the suburbs that would surround towns without a gap of country by the end of the century: this must be borne in mind when reading books and magazines described as being 'for suburban gardeners'. The late-nineteenth-century suburb was a commuter-land of small terraced houses close to railway stations where the garden could be measured in square feet rather than the quarter or half acre common to Loudon's suburbia.

But could these terraced-house 'gardens' be used as gardens? We think there is nothing odd in calling a small yard at the back of a town house, or even a balcony with a few pots on it, 'a garden'. The space behind a Victorian terraced house, however, was unlikely to have been regarded as a garden until well into the second half of the nineteenth century. Earlier, it would have contained the privy, the only lavatory for the house, and the whole of the 'back extension' of a terraced house would have been the kitchen, scullery and washhouse. It was not an inviting place for the family to use as a 'garden', particularly as the only access would have been through the servant's quarters (and it probably was just one servant in such houses). Until the necessity for a privy disappeared with the introduction of indoor water closets, the 'garden' would never be a place of pleasure.

As to how these 'gardens' were used, once they were considered suitable, there was probably as much variety as there is now: some people enjoy cultivating them, others pave them over and use them as dog runs, and some do nothing, so they simply become patches of weeds. There would have been more scope for a real garden in the semi-detached villas which occupied wider spaces and had side access. In either case, houses were not usually owned, but held on leases for several years or months. It was not practical to invest too much money in the permanent features of a garden. This was one reason for the popularity of bedding plants: they only lasted one season, so could be bought when needed and then discarded when a family moved on. Even the more exotic subtropical plants could be regarded as temporary, as it would take a skilled gardener with access to a glasshouse to keep them alive for more than a year or so. Similarly the urns, pots and statues used decoratively could be taken away, along with the other furniture, when the family moved.

Once people had gardens, they had to learn how to look after them. In the early part of the century, those with a rural past would remember the great gardens of their family patrons, and the cottage gardens of their own parents or grandparents. But by the mid-century, with less memory to rely on, people began to copy the great gardens in towns: the parks. Municipal parks were created to provide fresh air and exercise and to appease the unrest felt when working people protested about the conditions in which they had to live.[8] The government gave working people access to open space before they took it for themselves by force. At first parks were modelled on the eighteenth-century landscape style, but as gardeners began to establish themselves as park designers, they took on their own identity, which was maintained beyond the end of the twentieth century. Park garden designs were usually based on shrubs and bedding plants, which became the dominant style for many gardens of the Victorian era.

The Victorians liked to encourage participation in self-improvement, and gardening fitted in with nature study, geology and botany as activities taught to children. Women with time on their hands (and most women in the middle classes had plenty of time on their hands) were expected to be productive in an uncommercial way. Flowers and plants could be drawn and

Topiary of a table and glasses in clipped box. The Victorians loved novelty, and labour-intensive crafts were considered suitable occupations for women. (*Amateur Gardening*, 31 January 1885, p. 474) (*Amateur Gardening*)

painted; they could be collected, dried or pressed, labelled and put into albums or displayed in frames. For many Victorian women the garden became the focus of their lives. Because it was perceived as part of the home, it was private rather than public, and women had the freedom to express themselves in it without worrying about what other people thought. Considering their clothing and their image of helplessness in the nineteenth century, it may seem extraordinary that women could have even attempted gardening in any practical way. However, nineteenth-century women were used to dealing with life in long skirts and corsets. Servants and farmers' wives had to take part in hard physical work whether they liked it or not, which shows that it could be done, and many women must have taken to gardening as a release from the formality of the rest of their lives.

One of the gardeners most admired by John Loudon in the 1830s was Louisa Lawrence (*c.* 1803–55). Although she employed six gardeners in her two-acre garden, she planned and supervised the work herself. Loudon thought she had impeccable taste and used her garden as an example of what other gardeners who may not have her means and advantages could do themselves:

> It is worthy of remark, that a good deal of the interest attached to the groups on the lawn of the Lawrencian villa depends on the plants which are planted in the rockwork. Now, though everyone cannot procure American ferns, and other plants of such rarity and beauty as are there displayed, yet there are hundreds of alpines, and many British ferns, which may be easily procured from botanic gardens, or by one botanist from another; and, even if no perennials could be obtained suitable for rockwork, there are the Californian annuals, which alone are sufficient to clothe erections of this kind with great beauty and variety of colouring.[9]

Loudon's approval of Mrs Lawrence shows that he was prepared to accept women as equals in matters of gardening taste, whether or not he expected them to go out and weed and dig themselves. When recommending how gardens should be run, he frequently refers to women as essential helpers, particularly for watering and insect-collecting. Loudon's own wife, Jane (1807–58), certainly was a practical gardener. In *Gardening for Ladies* she recommends tools and equipment which are suitable for women, including a small spade, clogs to put on over shoes, or a small plate of iron to go under the sole of the shoe, fastened with a leather strap, stiff, thick leather gloves or gauntlets, and a light wheelbarrow. She stresses the benefits to health and even describes the process of digging: 'A lady, with a small light spade may, by taking time, succeed in doing all the

JANE WELLS LOUDON (1807–58)

MRS LOUDON, the wife of landscape gardener and writer John Claudius Loudon, was born Jane Webb and was orphaned at 17, whereupon she took up writing for a living. She married Loudon at the age of 23, when he was 47. She described in her book *Gardening for Ladies* (1840) how difficult it was for amateurs to learn gardening from professionals. She acted as a secretary and assistant to her husband, and although she started the *Ladies' Magazine of Gardening* in 1842, she abandoned it because of the extra work when Loudon became ill. After his death, she finished and updated his books, cared for their garden in Bayswater and brought up their daughter, Agnes. She emphasised the capabilities of women in gardening, stressing the rewards to be had for a little extra effort, and from her instructions it is clear that she was a practical gardener, not just a supervisor.

digging that can be required in a small garden, the soil of which, if it has been long in cultivation, can never be very hard or difficult to penetrate, and she will not only have the satisfaction of seeing the garden created, as it were, by the labour of her own hands, but she will find her health and spirits wonderfully improved by the exercise, and by the reviving smell of the fresh earth.'[10] Jane Loudon started the *Ladies' Magazine of Gardening* in 1842, but because of her husband's ill health she had to abandon it after a year. It covered the history of flowers and descriptions of gardens, and included letters from other ladies. She clearly felt it was important to concentrate on what women could do, rather than what they could not.

Another practical woman gardener of the same era was the anonymous author of *A Handbook on Town Gardening by a Lady*, published in 1847. It was presumably anonymous because the 'lady' did not feel it suitable to put her name to something sold for profit. She also wrote about the practical aspects of gardening, although she expected to have a labourer to do the heaviest work, such as digging large holes, but she sounds as if she would certainly have been outside, directing operations. A further woman writer who *was* prepared to put her name to a book in the mid-century was Elizabeth Watts, who published *Modern Practical Gardening* in the 1860s.[11] One of the best reasons to look at the work of women gardening writers, particularly those in the early part of the century, is that they give us an insight into the problems of all amateurs, both male and female, in having very little information to go on and not being

listened to. Almost all the male writers at the time were professional gardeners, botanists, florists or nurserymen, and they assumed that their readership was composed almost entirely of other professionals.

When the *Gardeners' Chronicle* started to include articles for amateurs in the 1850s, one was entitled 'A Word for the Ladies':

> The *Gardeners' Chronicle* is indeed, to a great extent, a gentleman's paper, yet there is much information scattered up and down its pages adapted for the gentler sex. If, when the paper is laid on the table, the ladies who love gardening will favour us with their attention, we shall hope to assist them in their pleasing employment . . . Ladies are great gardeners on a small scale, and a vast majority of the homes which are made more cheerful and elegant by flowers owe their charm to their hands. They generally love flowers for their own sake, and their attachment is less mingled than that of men with considerations of interest, such as beating their neighbours in their feats of horticultural skill, or adding a respectable adjunct to their domain. A woman looks upon a flower as she does upon a child, with an affection abstracted from external considerations of what trouble it will occasion, or what it will cost to keep. And as her principles are more pure in the department of gardening and its ends, so her pleasures are more simple

The whole family made use of the garden and helped maintain it. This picture shows a rustic table and summerhouse and the shrub *Aucuba japonica*, which was particularly suited to town conditions. (*Museum of Garden History*) and deep . . . The wife, on a fine June morning, is watering and transplanting, and anxiously training up to perfection some floral beauties, and a little help in stooping or carrying mould would then be a great boon. But the husband looks listlessly on and does nothing – or rather, as is too often the case, he grumbles at the time and labour bestowed; and in his careless perambulation sets his foot on the choicest pet of the neatly kept border. But, 'Sigh no more ladies, sigh no more,' for you have resources in yourselves in this department which will easily make you independent of all but labours of love, and contented to be without aid grudgingly bestowed.[12]

By the end of the century, as the position of head gardener in a large establishment was gradually being undermined by amateurs taking over the design of gardens and the matters of taste, so women were able to assume a much stronger position. In the last decade of the century it became quite common to see gardening books by women: Mrs Earle, Miss Willmott and Miss Jekyll became household names,[13] at least in upper middle-class households, and all dispensed with old-fashioned head gardeners as decision makers.

The class system in the nineteenth century was far more rigid than it is today. Now people feel free to classify themselves however they want to. A person's way of life generally depends on how much money they have and how they wish to live. In Victorian times, however, whatever people felt privately, they outwardly kept to a class which represented not the amount of money they had, but the occupation of the head of the family. Servants wore much simpler, drabber clothes than their employers, and many people's occupations could be determined by what they wore. Similarly, before the 1850s what someone grew in their garden was largely defined by the class in which they lived, and it was not thought desirable to try anything different. Joseph Paxton (1803–65) wrote in the *Horticultural Register* in 1831 about his idea for communal town gardens to be set up by subscription. There were to be fifty gardens of a quarter of an acre each, but they were to be divided into three or more different areas for different classes of society.

The traditional place for gardening for working people was the allotment. But allotments cannot be taken at face value. Their history is closely connected with the development of poor relief and the changes in farming that brought about enclosed land. Allotments were usually let on condition that the allottees observed rules concerned with church attendance, sobriety and not working on Sundays. Organising such schemes was often a useful occupation for ladies who had plenty of leisure time, or clergymen who wanted to set a good example. Publications specifically for allotment-holders

Cabbages were one of the most popular crops grown on allotments, as they lasted through the winter. (*Museum of Garden History*)

did not start until the 1880s, with the introduction of cheaper magazines such as *Amateur Gardening*. Before that, most of the information on allotment gardening was aimed at the people who organised allotment schemes and what they thought allotment-holders should be doing, not what the allottees necessarily wanted or needed to know.

Allotments as we know them today are usually on apparent wasteland, but often it is land that was originally common land, used by local people for centuries. Some are known as 'fuel land allotments' because rents or profits were used to provide fuel for the poor of the parish. Throughout the eighteenth century schemes were put forward to replace common land taken away from villagers by enclosure. Some schemes allowed land to be given by the parish to individuals, some to be worked communally, but all were based on the premise that the land was in lieu of poor relief. There were other types of scheme set up by private individuals, either for their own workers or for the public in a particular vicinity. Even though the food produced on allotments was an important part of the allotment-holder's diet, necessity was not the only reason for growing it.

Flora Thompson (1876–1947) said in *Lark Rise to Candleford* that only the men ever worked on the vegetable plots or allotments, but that 'the energy they brought to their gardening after a hard day's work in the fields was marvellous. They grudged no effort and seemed never to tire'.[14] Jeremy Burchardt, who has studied nineteenth-century allotments extensively,[15] believes that they gave people a source of hope in their otherwise dismal lives, and that the allottees valued both the attachment to the soil and the sense of community in working the land with other people.

Not all rented gardens were allotments: there were pleasure gardens on the outskirts of towns, often known as 'guinea gardens' from the annual rent paid for them,[16] which were usually let to the families of middle-class tradesmen. They probably fell into disuse when the families stopped living above the shop and bought houses in the new suburbs. They were usually divided by hedges and most had elaborate summerhouses where meals could be cooked and where weekends could be spent. Fruit and vegetables were sometimes grown, but the main purpose of a guinea garden was relaxation away from the town.

Science and technology were instrumental in creating the industrial revolution and also contributed to inventions that changed the face of gardening in the nineteenth century, but the garden itself was a high-maintenance, labour-intensive place compared to what we are used to today. Imagine no plastic, nylon or other man-made fibres. Pots were all terracotta: much heavier than modern ones and of course breakable. Seed boxes would be wooden and susceptible to rotting. Where we use plastic netting and fleece today, the Victorians would use cotton thread and different grades of hessian, the finest known as tiffany. Glasshouses would be made of deal, or pine, which meant regular painting, rather than easily maintained hardwood or aluminium. Watering would be one of the biggest chores. Without running water and convenient garden taps, ingenuity came into play to cut down on the time and energy needed to transport water around large gardens in summer. Similarly, with no electricity for heating, propagating plants out of season and protecting from frost meant that every Victorian gardener had to learn the secrets of insulation and to make full use of warmth from the sun. Candles and oil lamps were both used for bringing on seedlings, and the

In economical burning the stuff is made ready first, and a good fire being started, the heap is made up with a covering of turf or damp weedy stuff to shut in the smoke and cause a slow combustion in the way that charcoal is made. The result is a valuable bulk of burnt earth, potash, and charcoal, the finer parts of which are invaluable for dusting seed rows in spring as the young plant is sprouting.

Amateur Gardening, 7 November 1885, p. 326

professional gardeners jealously guarded the secrets of the hotbed, learnt over years of experience. Gardeners had to learn much more about gardening than they do today, with no self-service garden centres with well-labelled plants, ready potted up and just the right size for a small garden; an amateur would have to know what to ask for and the quantities needed. Composts and fertilisers did not come ready mixed and weighed in clean plastic bags; they had to be procured as raw ingredients, carted, stored and put together when needed, without any instructions. For an amateur with no handy reference guide, no easily approachable supplier of appropriate plants, and a garden where a thick layer of soot covered every surface and plant, there were enough problems in gardening to put most people off before they even started.

By the end of the century, however, when the plight of the amateur was recognised and the retailers discovered they had a ready market, gardening brought people together. National societies were formed for those interested in growing particular plants, which meant that professionals and amateurs of all social classes could meet and compete together. It was no longer unacceptable for a working person to grow exotic plants or strawberries or grapes, if he could afford them and had the time to care for them. Conversely, the wealthy were taking pride in their herbaceous borders consisting of plants that had hitherto been the mainstay of cottage gardens. Small conservatories appeared on the back of many houses in the suburbs. Greenhouses and lawnmowers and other gardening equipment was inexpensive and commonplace.

In 1888 *Amateur Gardening* gave its view on the position of gardening:

> A villa garden, as a rule, contains just enough space to be within the means of the owner or occupier to keep in order, and it happens more often than not that he does so even to a lavish extent. In doing so he is only acting in perfect harmony with the natural order of things, and everyone who has the means should certainly strive to have not only his house but his garden beautiful also. As well make a lady's dress without its lace or other trimmings, or a bonnet without its exterior adjuncts and call it finished, as to consider a home complete in the absence of a neatly laid out garden.[17]

Gardening magazines of the 1890s even became boring in their uniformity: everyone was interested in the same plants and were all going to the same shows at the Crystal Palace. Gardening had something for everyone and seemed immune to criticism as a social activity. It was healthy, educational, productive and decorative. It provided an outlet for the desire for ostentatious wealth and novelty. With a garden one could have something different and something new every year, or indeed several times a year, or one could perpetuate traditions and re-create the gardens of one's childhood. In the nineteenth century gardening truly became available to all.

CHAPTER TWO

'Every Man his own Gardener'

As early as 1767 a book came out called *Every Man his own Gardener*, sounding as if it would be a guide to gardening for amateurs. Its purpose was 'To convey a practical knowledge of gardening, to gentlemen and young professors, who delight in that useful and agreeable study'.[1] The 'young professors' were probably people training to be gardeners, who at the time were often described as 'professed gardeners', but who were the 'gentlemen'? The frontispiece shows two gardeners in breeches, buckled shoes and aprons, digging and hoeing, while a lady and gentleman pass them by on the way to a glasshouse. The sections of the book include The Kitchen Garden, The Nursery, and The Hot-House, and it becomes increasingly obvious that no 'gentleman' reading it would have any intention of going outside with a spade to do any work himself. Why then write such a book for 'gentlemen'? In the Age of Enlightenment many gentlemen were interested in collecting the rare plants coming into the country, but by the conventions of the day they were unlikely to have done any practical work in looking after them themselves.

In the first half of the nineteenth century, the word 'gardener' did not simply mean someone who enjoyed gardening; it invariably meant a professional gardener, properly trained. He might also be termed 'a practical gardener', to distinguish him from a botanist or an amateur. Anyone other than a professional would be described as simply 'an amateur' or be given a specific name in the context of gardening, such as florist,[2] botanist, or cottager. 'Amateur', however, is often used in the 1840s to mean a florist, to distinguish an amateur florist from a professional one, but until the 1850s the description 'amateur gardener' rarely occurred. If the meaning of 'gardener' is not understood, much of what is written in gardening literature of the time may be misconstrued. The following appeared in a review of James Shirley Hibberd's book *The Town Garden* in the *Gardeners' Chronicle* in 1855: 'We cannot, however, say much in favour of [the book], which does not seem to have been written by a gardener, if we are to judge from the plants recommended for cultivation, and from sundry little symptoms which the practised eye has no difficulty in detecting. Gardeners do not talk of "Asderas of suffocated greens" or "Tantalian lakes" or "Stagyrian retreats", whatever those phrases may mean.'[3] Shirley Hibberd (1825–90) was certainly a gardener in the modern sense, but the magazine was deriding him as not being qualified to write about gardening.

There was a traditional rivalry between gardeners and nurserymen, probably because one of the gardener's perks was to sell plants that were surplus to requirements, thus cutting out the nurseryman. But this was not always allowed. A report appeared in the *Gardeners' Chronicle* in 1857 of a gardener who was fined £20 for selling plants to the value of eight shillings, or could alternatively serve two months in prison.[4] It was said to be common for gardeners to sell produce to Covent Garden fruit and vegetable market in London during the winter months.

The photographs of organised, hierarchical garden staffs with a head gardener, under-gardeners and apprentices, ranged in lines in front of impressive hothouses, give a misleading impression of what life as a gardener was like. The majority of people with more modest establishments had to make do with only one or two gardeners, or maybe no one qualified as a gardener at all. They were more likely to have used whatever servants were available or who could be spared from their other duties, and training might not be on a formal basis. Edward Beck (1804–61), a nurseryman and florist, found a solution

EDWARD BECK (1804–61)

EDWARD BECK lived at Worton Cottage, Isleworth, Middlesex. He was a Quaker, had been a merchant seaman, and later set up business as a slate merchant and specialised in growing pelargoniums. He was one of the founding editors, and first proprietor, of the *Florist* in 1848. He wrote *Treatise on the Cultivation of Pelargoniums* (1847) and 'A Packet of Seeds saved by an old Gardener' to improve conditions for gardeners. He won a £7 prize from the Horticultural Society for putting out the best seedling pelargonium and donated it back on condition that others put up the same amount next year. His son Walter carried on the nursery after his death. The *Floral Magazine* said of Edward Beck, 'His memory will be long cherished as an upright, intelligent and enthusiastic grower'.

Edward Beck (1804–61). (Engraving from *The Garden*, 2 October 1886) (*Royal Horticultural Society, Lindley Library*)

for two unsatisfactory employees: 'His head gardener did not give satisfaction, not for want of honest desire to please, but his heart was not in his work, and therefore that work did not prosper as it ought. The master did not want to dismiss the man, but things must be altered. He had seen in his groom an interest in garden matters, little things that would have escaped the notice of a more ordinary observer; and to their own surprise the men were retained, their offices exchanged.'[5] Mr Beck was an expert on flowers and could train the man to run the glasshouses. Many people who were pure amateurs might have to learn the skills themselves first in order to teach their servants how to become gardeners. It seems that this is exactly what happened when middle-class people moved into suburban houses with medium-sized gardens: big enough to need help, but not big enough to employ a full garden staff.

By the 1830s suburban housing was increasing significantly. Loudon thought there was enough demand for a handbook of gardening for those living in the suburbs. He lived in one himself: Bayswater, now very much part of west London. His massive undertaking was eventually produced in two volumes out of a projected three, as he died before the third was written. *The Suburban Gardener and Villa Companion* dealt with the design and layout of houses and gardens; and *The Suburban Horticulturalist* described cultivation of fruit and vegetables.[6] The third volume would have covered ornamental plants. But who did Loudon mean when he referred to the suburban gardener, and how did he differ from any other gardener? In *The Suburban Horticulturalist*, Loudon describes his readership as being 'the retired citizen, the clergyman, the farmer, the mechanic, the labourer, the colonist, or the emigrant'. He went on to say:

> The possessor of a garden may desire to know the science and the art of cultivation for several reasons. He may wish to know whether it is properly cultivated by his gardener; he may wish to direct its culture himself; he may desire to know its capabilities of improvement or of change; he may wish to understand the principles on which the different operations of culture are performed, as a source of mental interest; or he may wish to be able to perform the operations himself as a source of recreation and health.[7]

Note that actually working in the garden himself comes last in the list, almost as an afterthought. Loudon's villa gardens are described as ranging from ten acres or more, perhaps including a park or farm, down to houses in streets or rows with a garden of one perch to one acre.[8] He is writing for a broad spectrum of people who want to learn

> A wall is an ugly thing in a flower garden, although a good protector. To hide its unseemliness, it may be covered with ornamental creepers, or with fruit trees, which none can think an eyesore. A wall of turf may be made lasting under proper treatment. Sow it well with furze seed, when it grows, clip it, and keep the whole surface regularly clipped, and in time it will be like a good-looking green wall.
>
> Elizabeth Watts, *Modern Practical Gardening*, p. 193

about gardening, regardless of the size of their garden; in other words, someone we would now call an amateur gardener.

Loudon tailored his gardens to suit his readers. A suburban villa with a one-acre garden could be managed by its occupier, a person of leisure 'attached' to gardening, with the help of 'a couple of labourers'.[9] For a terraced house in a street of similar houses, he suggests a garden consisting mainly of trees and shrubs: 'This garden would be very suitable for an occupier who had no time to spare for its culture, and who did not wish for flowers. It would not suit a lady who was fond of gardening: but for one who was not, or had no time to attend to it, and who had several children, this garden would be very suitable, because it would afford the children abundance of room to play in without doing injury.'[10] A single detached house and grounds, occupying about an acre and three-quarters, with a kitchen garden and greenhouse, 'might be cultivated by the master, with the assistance of a labourer and a mowing machine; or by a head gardener, with a labourer, or the occasional assistance of a house servant'.[11]

From the last extract, one can see the difficulty of having a small establishment and needing a good gardener: a properly trained one will be unwilling to work by himself and not want to do the routine, boring or heavy work. This was further illustrated by a correspondent to the *Gardeners' Chronicle* in April 1858: 'Gardeners for moderate people are scarcely to be found . . . it is almost impossible to find in Scotland or England a gardener who will manage a small place efficiently and economically . . . reliance must be placed on jobbing gardeners, and we must be satisfied with such productions, ornamental or useful, as they can give us.'[12]

This brings us to the final category of professional gardener: the jobbing gardener, a man to be avoided at all costs. Although he was the last resort, he was the one most commonly employed by the

This would be the total workforce of a typical amateur's garden, and many professionals started their working lives as boys not much older than this one. (Photograph taken in Walsall about 1880) (*Museum of Garden History*)

REVD NATHANIEL PATERSON
(active 1830–40s)

NATHANIEL PATERSON was minister at Galashiels, Berwickshire, and later a leading member of the Scottish Free Kirk. He wrote *The Manse Garden*, one of the first gardening books written for amateurs. He wrote it because he knew there were other people in his situation, finding themselves in charge of a garden with no experience and not enough money to employ good gardeners. He also recognised that being so far north in the British Isles meant that many instructions for gardening did not apply. So he went about his work teaching himself and training up a garden boy because he could not afford a professional gardener. His writing is both informative and humorous, showing the realities faced by amateurs who had no way of obtaining advice and learned through trial and error.

middle classes. Shirley Hibberd said that the jobbing gardener 'fiddles away his employer's time and his own earnings in the low enjoyment of beer':[13] 'Periodical digging, "as a matter of course", such as the jobbing gardeners designate "turning in", has for its sole object the destruction of plants; but that object is disguised by describing the operation as "making things tidy". When you are tired of herbaceous plants, let the jobbing gardener keep the border tidy, and you will soon be rid of the obnoxious lilies, phloxes, ranunculuses, anemones, hollyhocks, paeonies, and pansies, without the painful labour of pulling them up and burning them.'[14]

Nathaniel Paterson, the clergyman author of *The Manse Garden*, solved his problem of help in the garden by recommending training up a boy:

Let the lessons be one at a time, and amazingly simple. As to cleaning a piece of ground previous to digging, teach so much of the botany of three or four of the worst weeds as that each may be known in a crowd, or at any distance. Let it be a rule that these are to be taken up as carefully as a crop of beet, and laid aside, that it may be seen how little injury they have suffered in the act of uprooting. The ground being thus cleared, let it be understood that digging means lifting earth to the depth of fifteen inches, and laying it upside down, the common substitute for which is a mere disordering of the same surface that was uppermost before; hence the wetness and coldness of soil, the late sowing and little reaping, together with the waste of manure, which occur in the gardens of the peasantry, a loss sustained through life for the want of a single lesson.[15]

The problems of town gardeners originated in the nature of towns themselves. Town gardens tend to be small and their enclosed character often makes it more difficult to give plants enough light. Pollution was caused by soot, which was sticky, greasy and poisonous. It fell in all weathers. Even in summer, coal was used for cooking, in factories and on the railways. Although the Smoke Prevention Acts were supposed to lessen the problem, they had little real effect, and 'pea-souper' fogs were known until the 1950s. Nurserymen and market gardeners moved out in the 1850s and towns and cities had little interest for any type of professional gardener. Shirley Hibberd described the typical appearance of urban gardens:

> In the musty courts and alleys, wall-flowers, stocks, and musk-plants are purchased every spring, and set to flourish in broken teapots, saucepans, flower-pots – damned forever by green or brown paint – or rotten boxes filled with stuff called mould, but which looks like the dust of a perished mummy. These go black in the face in four days

Shirley Hibberd in his Stoke Newington garden in the 1860s. (*The Fern Garden*, p. 35) (*Author's collection*) from the date of planting, and die three days after that from sheer suffocation, gasping up to the last moment for light and air. Geraniums pass a torpid life on window-sills and in dark parlours, where none but the housekeeper can aver they are geraniums – such naked, smoke-dried sticks they do appear . . . Thousands of beautiful plants are every spring and summer bought from the nurseries round London, and sold in the city to undergo the slow death of suffocation – dying literally from asphyxia, from an absorption of soot in the place of air – their demise being accelerated by copious supplies of water at improper times, or the withholding altogether of the refreshing element. The wonder is, not that such plants perish miserably, but that they last so long, when plunged without hope of relief, into such a 'Black Hole of Calcutta'.[16]

But the problem for town gardeners was not just the pollution itself; it was the problem of obtaining any advice on how to deal with it. Because the professionals deserted the cities and refused even to contemplate the problems, an amateur had to find out for himself how to handle the dirt and pollution and what plants might be able to cope with it. Gradually, an inextricable link was forged between amateur gardeners and town gardeners. It was when town gardeners began to need information about gardening that amateur gardening began to be noticed.

Professional gardeners tended not to be very innovative. They had trained in a world where everything was done properly. All the glasshouses, potting sheds, frames and tools they might need were available. They did not recognise the little patches of shaded, polluted ground as 'gardens' at all, so why should they bother to write about them or give their owners advice? They did not exist. To the professional of the nineteenth century, a garden was a pre-planned, designed tract of land with trees, grass, flowers and shrubs, and ideally a separate kitchen garden, all of which would be looked after by one or more trained men acting as members of a team. Only the head gardener would take some part in planning or designing the garden. The amateur, on the other hand, is his own designer, head gardener and labourer. He can do what he likes with his patch of land and need not follow rigid rules about dividing the space into different departments. To an amateur, therefore, a 'garden' is an experiment and a fantasy. It may never look as perfect or be as productive as a professional's garden, and it may not even ever be finished, but it will represent more of the individual spirit of the garden's owner than a professionally designed garden ever can. The amateur can even be a gardener without a garden. The florists who grew all their plants in pots would have considered themselves gardeners, and it seems that many of them were in fact professional gardeners. The small patch of ground outside a cottage or a courtyard outside a town house can both be gardens in the sense of places to grow things, although the plants may principally be grown in containers, because the people doing the growing and indulging in horticulture are said to be 'gardening'.

So the amateurs had to teach themselves. Books written by the professionals usually posed more problems than they solved. It was like asking someone the way and being told that they should not have started from there in the first place. John Loudon's wife, Jane, explained how she came to be writing for amateurs:

> When I married Mr Loudon, it is scarcely possible to imagine any person more completely ignorant than I was, of every thing relating to plants and gardening; and, as may be easily imagined, I found every one about me so well acquainted with the subject, that I was soon heartily ashamed of my ignorance. My husband, of course, was quite as anxious to teach me as I was to learn, and it is the result of his instructions, that I now (after ten years experience of their efficacy) wish to make public for the benefit of others. I do this, because I think books intended for professional gardeners, are seldom suitable for the wants of amateurs. It is so very difficult for a person who has been acquainted with a subject all his life, to imagine the state of ignorance in which a person is who knows nothing of it, that adepts often find it impossible to communicate the knowledge they possess. Thus, though it may at first sight appear presumptuous in me to attempt to teach an art of which for three fourths of my life I was perfectly ignorant, it is in fact that very circumstance which is one of my chief qualifications for the task.[17]

The author of *Handbook of Town Gardening by a Lady* found herself in a similar situation and explains how she managed most of the operations in the garden with the minimum of assistance:

> It is not intended for the professional florist, but simply for those who, forced by circumstances to live in towns, wish to enjoy some of those pleasures which the country so abundantly affords. . . . The results have been obtained without the assistance of a professed gardener, and any lady can manage a small town garden with the aid of a common labouring man, such as a helper in a stable. This help would be required in digging large holes, sifting and mixing earth, clipping grass and hedges, raking and rolling gravel, and similar fatiguing operations, for which a lady has not sufficient strength, but everything besides may be, and has been, easily done alone; and there is great pleasure in feeling, when we have been successful, that it is the work of our own hands.[18]

JAMES SHIRLEY HIBBERD (1825–90)

SHIRLEY HIBBERD was born in Stepney, east London, and worked as a journalist, specialising in science and natural history. As an amateur gardener, he recognised a need for books for town gardeners and wrote *The Town Garden* (1855) from his own experience. This was quickly followed by *Rustic Adornments for Homes of Taste* (1856) and over a dozen other books on gardening and natural history. He started the *Floral World*, took over the *Gardener's Magazine*, making it the most popular weekly of its time, and started *Amateur Gardening*. He tried out everything he wrote about in his own garden, worked tirelessly as a public speaker, edited a scientific journal, and wrote for several other popular magazines. When his health failed, he concentrated on reviving the RHS garden at Chiswick and organising international conferences. His sudden death was said to have been from exhaustion.

The *Handbook* was used by Shirley Hibberd when he began his garden in Pentonville, almost in the shadow of King's Cross station. He found the professionals' advice difficult to follow:

> Works on gardening are so full of complicated instructions, and purely professional views of things, that plain people are usually frightened at their perusal, and fling them aside under the pressure of fearful visions of inevitable expense, painfully acquired skill, and innumerable impossibilities, which seem woven up with a pursuit at once simple, profitable and delightful . . . It is generally thought that a city garden is an impossibility, that vegetation cannot be reconciled to the close air, the darkness, and the smoke of towns; and that all attempts to mingle the rural with the urban must . . . turn out failures. There can be no greater mistake than this; and though city gardening has its disadvantages and difficulties, the man determined to succeed, may produce not only green stuff but flowers, in a north aspect, and under the very shadow of a gasometer. The problem is how to grow flowers in a soil of cinders, and an atmosphere of smoke; and flowers which, of all things, revel in sunshine, and demand their daily food.[19]

Hibberd's book and William Paul's *Hand-book of Villa Gardening*,[20] both published in 1855, led to a discussion on town gardening in the *Gardeners' Chronicle*. Paul (1822–1905) was a nurseryman from Hertfordshire and the *Chronicle* approved of him more than Hibberd, as he was a professional. Like other professionals, he implied that an amateur would not be able to manage without help. He advised, 'You will, of course, require a gardener, either occasionally or constantly' and 'You would hardly think, however, of planning or re-modelling a garden without first seeking professional advice'. More perceptively, he referred to the increased interest in gardening: 'A few years since, gardening was the recreation of the few – the opulent, the scholar, the man of leisure . . . In recent times, the art has undergone an entire change, and what was of old the pursuit of the few, has, in varied forms, become the recreation and delight of the many.'[21]

The comments on town gardening led several readers to write in about their personal experiences. *The Florist* followed in May 1855 with an article by John Edwards (d. 1862), a florist from Holloway in north London, relating his success in growing florists' flowers for many years. In August 1857 *The Florist* began to publish a series of articles called 'Chronicles of a Small Garden' by a country clergyman known as 'D of Deal'. He explained that he grew everything in his small garden by himself, with the assistance of a pensioner, who did the weeding 'for a trifle', and a gardener two hours a week who did the 'nice jobs' such as budding and planting out. He commented that he would not need this help if he had leisure of another three hours a week. Deal (a small town on the Kent coast) would not have had the pollution problems of London, but the articles show how ordinary people with small gardens were prepared to learn the skills and do the work in gardens themselves if they had to.

By 1858 the *Gardeners' Chronicle* had started to publish articles which it said were specifically for amateurs: 'Although a great deal of

JOHN EDWARDS (d. 1862)

JOHN EDWARDS lived at Wace Cottage, Holloway, north London, from 1847. He was a joint founder of both the *Florist* and *Gossip of the Garden*. He started the National Floricultural Society in 1851 to further the cultivation of florists' flowers, and was president of the Stoke Newington Chrysanthemum Society from 1851 to 1860, when he sparked off an argument with the treasurer, causing half the members to set up a rival society. Edwards sold his flower collection when his garden was built over, but he continued to participate in horticultural societies, particularly as a judge of competitions. He was an early pioneer of town gardening, bringing out the *National Garden Almanack* in 1853 as a guide to reliable suppliers, and writing 'Florists' Flowers in London' in the *Florist* in May 1855.

information adapted for the large class of persons who cultivate their own gardens is scattered over our pages, it is thought advisable to furnish some papers more directly aiming at their instruction; and we shall endeavour so to present the results of our own long and extensive experience as to increase their knowledge and guide their practice.'[22] In other words, it was saying that it was all very well for amateurs to start publishing their own experiences, but they were not really qualified to do so, and there also seemed to be some confusion about who those amateurs were. One correspondent thought the articles were not aimed at the right sort of amateurs: 'Let us not, however, overlook the real amateur, who with an occasional gardener is mainly indebted to his own energy and skill for the show he annually makes in his little garden.'[23] The *Chronicle* of course wanted to include as many potential readers as possible, so it published its own definition of an amateur gardener to try to keep everyone happy: 'An amateur gardener with us is one who pursues the art for the love of it, according to the etymology of the term . . . an amateur may be a rich man . . . he may have greenhouses and frames, and keep a servant to assist him and be able to buy expensive plants. Like ourselves, he loves gardening for its own sake, and would rather attend to the cultivation of his domain, whether small or large, himself, than entrust it to others.'[24]

Not all 'small or amateur' gardeners were in towns, of course, and later in the century the country amateurs began to be heard. The modern myth that the cottage garden was full of herbaceous perennials, roses and fruit trees seems to have been created as a reaction to formal gardens relying on lawns, hedges and bedding plants. The cottage garden seemed a haven of prettiness and scent in comparison. Of course cottagers did grow vegetables and fruit in their gardens, and flowers were put in where there were gaps, but it is as doubtful that the true cottage garden was full of roses and flowers as that every cottage was idyllically thatched and eaved. It is far more likely that the true cottage garden was mainly utilitarian and not particularly attractive overall. The myth seems to rely largely on the writing of Gertrude Jekyll and William Robinson (1838–1935) in the late nineteenth century and was strengthened by sentimental Victorian paintings. Jekyll and Robinson themselves appeared in print in the later part of the nineteenth century and did use many 'cottage garden flowers' in their planting schemes. However, Jekyll's vast herbaceous borders and Robinson's 'wild gardens' cannot in reality be compared to real gardens of cottagers, partly because they are much too large, but mainly because they are far too contrived and specialised. It was not the cottage gardens themselves that Jekyll and Robinson so admired, but the flowers grown by the cottagers, which were often only slightly removed from the wild flowers growing in the hedgerows and fields. Nineteenth-century cottage gardens were mainly vegetable plots and animal pens with a few flowers edging the beaten earth or cinder paths, more like modern-day allotments. The picturesque cottage of the nineteenth century was likely to be dark and cramped and in poor repair. The scent of roses and honeysuckle would barely disguise the smells of the privy and dung heap.

The gardening skills of cottagers were probably handed down from parent to child and may not have been very great. John Loudon used many pages of his *Gardener's Magazine* trying to promote skills among cottagers, giving lists of books he thought they would find useful.[25] He tried to persuade landowners to provide new, better-designed cottages for their workers,[26] and seems to have contributed to the myth by publishing drawings of fanciful cottages which were probably meant to appeal more to the estate owner or his wife, who wanted attractive cottages on their land, rather than the workers themselves, who simply wanted a dry, clean, warm place to live in. In 1830 Loudon published the results of an essay competition on cottage husbandry and architecture.[27] The winner, who was anonymous, showed how a family could produce not only food, but also beer, firewood, medicine (including opium substitute) and tobacco.[28] The house included a bee-house, dog-kennel and pigeon-loft.

Amateur Gardening gave an idealised view of the cottage garden in 1888. It published a picture of a thatched cottage overgrown with creepers and a garden full of flowers:

> Gardening has always received a large amount of attention at the hands of cottagers, especially in country districts, and hence they are entitled to be placed in the front rank of skilful amateur horticulturalists. They have every advantage to enable them to attain success culturally in the shape of a large amount of land at a low rental with light taxes. They have, moreover, what their suburban brethren have not, and that is, the pure air in which not only man but plants love to revel. Under such congenial conditions as these, it is no wonder that many a cottager can exhibit produce from his garden, noteworthy for its quality and quantity.[29]

Gardening Illustrated also praised the skill of cottage gardeners when it published a reader's illustration: 'In addition to their picturesqueness we have often noted in cottage gardens an excellence of culture that would put to shame the gardening in many far more pretentious places, being a striking proof that a little garden well

managed is a source of far greater pleasure and profit to the owner and looker-on, too, than a large and often badly-managed one.'[30]

A Hampshire cottage garden from *Gardening Illustrated*, 31 December 1892. (*Museum of Garden History*)

Not all country gardeners were labourers or cottagers. Some of the best examples of middle-class country gardeners were clergymen, who play a similar role to women in gardening history. Both often found themselves in possession of a garden through outside circumstances and may have had a reasonable amount of leisure time during the day to pursue their interest. Although most of them probably employed some paid help, they may not have had enough money to employ a well-qualified staff, and would therefore have had to take on the role of head gardener themselves. They were also in the position of having to be seen to set a good example. The clergy's role in the parish extended to encouraging cottagers and allotment-holders in gardening, and they played a conspicuous part in local flower shows, helping with the judging and presenting the prizes. The booklets, 'Manuals for the Many', published by the *Cottage Gardener*, were sold at a discount to 'clergymen and gentlemen who wished to distribute them to their parishioners'.[31] Like royalty patronising national societies, the clergy would have helped to bolster the importance of flower shows as local events. Suttons Seeds supplied seeds at a discount price to clergymen and others who wished to encourage cottagers in the cultivation of their gardens. From the middle of the nineteenth century several clergymen began

THE REVD HENRY HONYWOOD D'OMBRAIN (1818–1905)

THE REVD H.H. D'OMBRAIN studied at Trinity College, Dublin, where he started the Natural History Society of Ireland, and then became vicar of Deal, in Kent, where he grew auriculas and gladioli. His earliest articles, 'Chronicles of a Small Garden', appeared in the *Florist* from 1857 under the pseudonym 'D of Deal', and he also wrote as 'Wild Rose' in the *Gardeners' Chronicle*. Later he was vicar of Westwell, Kent, and from 1862 he edited the *Floral Magazine* with the botanist Thomas Moore. D'Ombrain was one of the early promoters of town gardening and described tending his garden himself with only a little part-time help. He was a founder member with Dean Hole of the National Rose Society, and its first secretary, as well as secretary of the Horticultural Club. He wrote *The Gladiolus: Its History, Cultivation and Exhibition*, and was one of the first recipients of the RHS Victoria Medal of Honour.

The Revd Henry Honywood D'Ombrain (1818–1905), who also wrote as 'D of Deal'. (Carte de Visite *from the Royal Horticultural Society, Lindley Library*)

to write for gardening magazines. 'D of Deal' was a pseudonym used by the Revd Henry Honywood D'Ombrain (1818–1905), but Samuel Reynolds Hole (1819–1904), Dean of Rochester, was happy to write under his own name. The Revd William Wilks (1843–1923) made his public contribution to gardening by acting as secretary of the Royal Horticultural Society for twenty-five years while privately breeding new plants in his own garden. Gardening was used by the clergy to persuade people to use their leisure time productively, but clergymen also represented the view of the amateur in gardening, and because of their gender, and the likelihood that they were more highly educated than women, they would have had more success in publicising the difficulties of amateurs and in securing the attention of publishers and professional gardeners.

PART TWO

Learning to Garden

CHAPTER THREE

The Quest for Information

In the early part of the nineteenth century, information for gardeners came in two forms: practical gardening manuals and botanical magazines. The manuals were written by professional gardeners, such as John Abercrombie (1726–1806), whose *Every Man his own Gardener* reached the twenty-third edition by 1857.[1] A more practical book of the same era was William Cobbett's *The English Gardener* (1829), which claimed to be a complete guide to 'what is to be done relative to every plant and tree known in the gardens': 'The far greater part of persons who possess gardens, and who occasionally partake in the management of them, really know very little about the matter. They possess no principles relating to the art: they do things pretty well, because they have seen them done before; but for want of proceeding upon principle, that is to say, for the want of knowing the reasons for doing the several things that are done in the garden, they are always in a state of uncertainty: they know nothing of the causes, and, therefore, are always rather guessing at, than relying upon the effects.'[2]

The overwhelming feeling of the manuals was that they were attempts to explain the 'secrets' of gardening to the upper and middle classes, who might be interested in the subject for intellectual stimulation. The professionals regarded amateurs as people who enjoyed looking at gardens and collecting plants, and had plenty of space and money to indulge the passion, but relied on trained professionals to do the practical work. The idea of amateurs doing the work themselves was not even contemplated.

Practical manuals did not provide topical information on the new plants flooding the country. The techniques of growing and propagating many of them were unknown to British gardeners, who were learning as they went along. The periodical botanical magazine was created to publish news of these plants as and when it became available. William Curtis (1746–99) started his *Botanical Magazine* in 1787. He was 'demonstrator' at the Chelsea Physic Garden in London and the illustrations were drawn from life. The magazine was

Now and then I see signs of a mouse, but a good garden cat and a few traps get rid of the little plagues. Once, however, the mice, or rather small field voles, entirely destroyed a number of young apple trees, eating all the roots away, but not touching any part overground. For some time they refused all baits, but at last I tried the Brazil nut, and that was irresistible.

Canon Ellacombe, *In a Gloucestershire Garden*, p. 34

really a 'part-work' and continued until 1983.[3] The other botanical magazines had mixed fortunes, but proliferated mainly in the 1820s and 1830s. One of the last to start, in 1834, was *Paxton's Magazine of Botany*, produced by Joseph Paxton, who at the time was gardener to the Duke of Devonshire. The magazines were expensive luxuries and only of interest to those wealthy enough to grow the new plants.

The first publication to call itself a magazine for gardeners, rather than botanists, was Loudon's *Gardener's Magazine*, started in January 1826. This was not the ancestor of all the later gardening magazines simply because it has the same or a similar name. It was started as a way of disseminating news and education for professional gardeners, and its character was more like a collection of papers by learned writers than a commercial newspaper produced for profit. It began as a quarterly publication of book size costing five shillings.[4] It had a few line illustrations but no colour. Loudon described himself as the 'conductor' and said the magazine would put gardeners in distant parts of the country on an even footing with those about the metropolis.[5] He wanted to promote gardening as an art of design and taste, and education of gardeners was expressed as his most important aim. Each issue concentrated on different topics as Loudon became interested in them. Thus, after discussing living conditions and education of gardeners, he started his campaign to improve the homes of agricultural labourers. His final campaign was to improve the design of cemeteries. Loudon often comments that many gardeners could not read, and its cost would put the magazine out of the reach of any but head gardeners, so it must be supposed that it was more likely to be the garden owners who bought it and then passed down the information to those they employed. Loudon's reports of his own visits to gardens show that gardening was still very much divided between social classes: he expected fruit to be grown only by trained professionals, cottagers had to be instructed in how to grow food by the more educated classes, and florists were expected to grow only florists' flowers.

Loudon was an extraordinary man and his work has had a lasting impact on gardening, but he cannot be regarded as the founder of gardening periodicals in the true sense. His magazine was unique, almost purely the whim of its creator, and not driven by the demands of its readers, whoever they might have been. It ceased on his death in 1843, and was already being eclipsed by the work of more far-seeing men such as Joseph Paxton, Joseph Harrison (d. 1855) and George Glenny (1793–1874).

Before his botanical magazine, Paxton had started a paper in 1831 with Joseph Harrison, a professional gardener from Sheffield, Yorkshire. The monthly *Horticultural Register* was intended to be a cheap alternative to botanical magazines and Loudon's *Gardener's Magazine*: 'It is evident, that a taste for Horticulture, in all its branches . . . has, within the last twenty years, very rapidly increased, and a corresponding improvement has consequently attended it: for at no period of time has it reached so high a state of perfection as at present.'[6] However, the editors went on to say that although 'practical' (by which they meant professional) gardeners had been able to publish their experiences in the existing publications, because they were so expensive the information 'was thus out of reach of many persons in the humbler classes of society and necessarily became very limited in its circulation'. This adds weight to the theory that Loudon's magazine was read mainly by head gardeners and employers, rather than suburban amateurs, and certainly not untrained working people. But it also shows that there was a growing demand for information among all classes of society and that these two editors, although they were professionally trained, were aware of what amateurs wanted.

In the second issue of the *Horticultural Register* a letter from 'A.J.' of Nottingham was published asking whether the magazine would be giving general directions for what should be done in a small garden each month and instructions for laying out a small tradesman's garden:

I expect to see [the *Horticultural Register*] the monthly companion of our artizans, and to hear its pages read over carefully, and its contents examined in most of the little summerhouses on Mapperly-hills, or the sides of our ancient forests. For we are here Horticulturalists and Floriculturalists to a great extent: and our Frame-work-knitters and Twist-hands, when they have completed the labours of the day, adjourn to their hundred yards of land on the outside of the town to superintend the blowing of an auricula or a tulip, to mark the first folding of the

leaves of a cabbage, or the gradual growth of a favourite cucumber: each
vying with its neighbour in producing the best or largest specimen.[7]

This sounds almost too good to be true: the artisans with their
'guinea gardens' and the florists with their auriculas and tulips. But
even if it were not written by a genuine correspondent, it created a
picture of the people whom the editors wanted to attract as readers.
The information, including notices and reports of local florists'
society meetings, was for the florists themselves, not upper-class
people trying to persuade working people into gardening.

According to Jane Loudon in the account of her husband's life,[8]
Loudon first saw the *Horticultural Register* when visiting the north of
England after laying out Birmingham botanical garden. The sales of
his magazine then decreased and never recovered. Paxton took on some
of the same topics as Loudon, providing space for correspondence on
building labourers' cottages and even publishing the views of 'a
bricklayers' labourer' and he took delight in his rivalry with Loudon.

In 1833 Harrison left the *Horticultural Register* and it gradually veered
towards natural history and rural affairs. He launched a much more
successful paper, the *Floricultural Cabinet and Florist's Magazine*, which
aimed to provide something affordable for everyone interested in flowers,
of whatever type: 'Although there are existing publications in whose
pages the culture of flowering plants is admitted, yet they are too general
a character for great numbers of Floriculturalists . . . to such persons the
purchasing of the works referred to, much unnecessary expence had to be
incurred.'[9] The first issue included articles written by both florists and
gentlemen's gardeners. It also reviewed all the current botanical
magazines. By November of its first year it claimed it had sold fifty
thousand copies in the first nine months.[9] It ran until 1859 and seemed
to appeal to both professional gardeners and amateurs. It must have been
cheap enough for working people to buy and it provided the information
they wanted on flowers they could afford to grow.

If Loudon and Paxton exhibited animosity towards each other, it
was nothing compared to the libellous comments of George Glenny,
described by his biographer as a 'horticultural hornet'.[10] Glenny was
a watchmaker from Clerkenwell, east London. He made money
partly through a lucrative marriage and also through selling
insurance. He took up growing florists' flowers as a hobby, while
launching himself into magazine publishing. In 1831 he started the
Royal Lady's Magazine and began to feature articles on florists'
flowers, perhaps at first to fill up space. In 1832 he set up the
Metropolitan Society of Florists and Amateurs 'to promote the
science of Floriculture' by holding competitions. The society was
aimed directly at promoting florists' flowers in fashionable circles, in

GEORGE GLENNY (1793–1874)

GEORGE GLENNY was a watchmaker and amateur florist from Clerkenwell, London. As proprietor of the *Royal Lady's Magazine* in 1831, he started to publish articles on florists' flowers. In 1832 he set up the Metropolitan Society of Florists and Amateurs in direct opposition to the Horticultural Society, and his magazine became the *Horticultural Journal*. He began to expound his views on all matters and people horticultural. Eventually the Horticultural Society banned him from their shows and Glenny's career as a journalist started on a constant cycle of short-lived success and financial ruin. He started the first weekly horticultural paper, the *Gardener's Gazette*, which he was then forced to sell, but later revived and then lost again. In 1852 he claimed that he was writing for 65,000 readers, and in 1872 he claimed half a million. He produced the *Florist's Journal* as successor to the *Horticultural Journal*, comparing it to others, which were 'mere gatherings of scraps'. He ended his long career as the first gardening columnist in a newspaper, *Lloyd's Weekly London Newspaper*.

George Glenny (1793–1874). (Engraving from *The Gardener's Magazine*, 23 May 1874) (*Royal Horticultural Society, Lindley Library*)

opposition to the Horticultural Society, which was reluctant to feature the flowers in its shows. In 1833 the *Royal Lady's Magazine* became the *Horticultural Journal and Florists' Register*, stating: 'Our object, therefore, is merely to supply that information which no other work supplies, and which there are still many persons who think degrading. Be it so until we show the contrary. We shall go on in our humble way till we can prove that florists' flowers belong to the highest instead of the lowest grade of floriculture; and that tailors, tinkers, and weavers, who knew them and grew them a century ago, though not one in a hundred could read or write, were better judges than botanists of what constituted a good thing.'[11]

Glenny tolerated no one else's opinion. He described Loudon's *Gardener's Magazine* as having 'every appearance of decay'. Of the *Horticultural Register* he said, 'it contains the usual quantity of what every practical man already knows; and rather more than usual of readable, though not very interesting original matter'. Of the *Floricultural Cabinet*, he said, 'the original communications are, as

I honour Dr Lindley, but I do not envy, because, strange as it may seem, he is very rarely an enthusiastic gardener; I never remember to have seen a scientific botanist and a successful practical florist under the same hat. Wherefore I am content, when I put my on my own, to confess meekly that it covers a skull void and empty of scientific treasures, but the property, I trust, of a true gardener.

S. Reynolds Hole, *A Book about Roses*, p. 100

they always are, the mere overflowings of imbecility and folly'.[12] In 1837 he started the *Gardener's Gazette*, which as a weekly paper for gardeners was something totally new. However, Glenny was incapable of being objective and its pages were dominated by quarrels, particularly with the botanist John Lindley (1799–1865), the Horticultural Society's assistant secretary and the person responsible for organising its shows. In 1839 Glenny was banned from them. By the end of that year his personal finances collapsed. He sold the paper but continued as editor at £500 per year. However, he quarrelled with the new owners and resigned in 1840, whereupon Loudon, by then also in financial difficulties,[13] was persuaded to take on the editorship (at £300 per year).

The first weekly paper to attain a consistent, reliable readership was the *Gardeners' Chronicle*, which was started in January 1841. It was not a speculative commercial venture out to attract a readership which it believed was there; it was a calculated attempt to silence Glenny once and for all, and had the support of the Horticultural Society, which wanted to establish itself as the face of British gardening. The paper was started by Joseph Paxton and the botanist John Lindley, with the backing of established publishers Charles Wentworth Dilke and William Bradbury (publisher of *Punch*, *The Daily News* and *The Field*). The prospectus stated that it was intended to provide: 'a weekly record of everything that bears upon horticulture or garden botany . . . thus the gardener, the forester, the rural architect, the drainer, the road-maker, and the cottager, will all have the improvements in their respective pursuits recorded.'[14]

In relation to florists it was declared that not only would they be kept fully acquainted with new varieties and the best modes of cultivation, but the editors would take care that the opinions given were the results of honest examination by 'competent judges unbiased by any personal interest'. This obviously referred to Glenny, but in case it was lost on anyone the first editorial stated that the paper would avoid wrangling and abuse in connection with florists' flowers. Loudon was not left out either: to complete their aims, the editors declared that the paper was interested in the improvement of the condition and education of gardeners.

The *Chronicle* further exhibited its credentials by providing a list of intended contributors, which included four professors, twenty-two head gardeners of estates, eight from botanic gardens, and eight from parks. Amateurs, nurserymen, gardeners and all other persons interested in horticultural pursuits were invited to favour the editor as early as possible with their comments. The first two pages contained advertisements for nurseries, plants, seeds, heating apparatus and situations wanted; the last two, advertisements for gardening books and journals. The main part of the paper included features on trees, new plants, recent displays at nurseries, correspondence, proceedings of societies, reviews and a calendar of work in the garden for the week. It was aimed at the gentry and upper classes who wanted to improve their gardens, but also at professional gardeners and nurserymen, who were the intended readers of Loudon's *Gardener's Magazine*. By 1844 a separate part of the paper was designated the *Agricultural Gazette* and much of the general news was dropped. Although amateurs had been urged to correspond, most articles were still written solely by head gardeners, nurserymen and academics. Reports were given of meetings of learned societies, but there were none of local flower shows or florists' societies, although the advertisements for flowers were almost exclusively for florists' flowers, because many nurserymen would have a good trade in selling florists' flowers to amateur florists.

For six years battle ensued between the *Chronicle* and several successive versions of Glenny's *Gazette*. Robert Marnock (1800–89), curator of the Royal Botanic Society's garden, created a triangular scenario when he introduced the *United Gardeners' and Land Stewards' Journal* in 1845. The fortunes of the two newer papers waxed and waned while the *Chronicle* looked on, claiming six and a half thousand readers. Glenny also produced the *Florist's Journal* as successor to the *Horticultural Journal* and worked on other papers, such as the *Country Gentleman*.

By the late 1840s florists decided that if they wanted a publication suitable for their own interests, they would have to start one themselves. In 1847 the *Midland Florist and Suburban Horticulturalist* was begun by a Nottingham nurseryman, John Frederick Wood: 'The teeming bosom of the earth produces in illimitable supply its abundant treasures of flowers, fruits, and vegetables, for the happiness and enjoyment of *all*, who by skill, assiduity, and attention, are desirous to procure them. It is for the information of these that the present periodical is established, – to convey in a popular and easily understood manner, to our readers, intelligence of what is passing in the world of fruit and flowers, and to fill up a vacancy in the garden literature of the day, at a price which will be within the means of all who love a garden.'[15]

The paper concentrated on florists' flowers and competitions, but also featured fruit and general horticulture. In 1851 it started a series called 'The Cottage Allotment', covering fruit trees, edging plants and vegetables. By 1857 it was edited by Alfred G. Sutton (1818–97), the son of the founder of Suttons Seeds and himself a partner in the firm. It was obviously losing readers and attempted to re-launch itself: 'If our readers will gain us a thousand additional subscribers, we can promise them, in return, twelve additional pages every month.'[16] It even took on Glenny as a writer, and was amalgamated with the *Gardener's Gazette* in 1863.

In 1848 *The Florist* was started. Edward Beck, the pelargonium grower, brought together a group of influential florists: Henry Groom (a nurseryman at Walworth and Clapham in south London), John Edwards, the florist from Holloway, Charles Fox (1794–1849) (an illustrator who had worked on the *Floricultural Cabinet* and the *Gardeners' Chronicle*), Charles Turner (1818–85) (a florist– nurseryman), and Thomas Rivers (1798–1877) (a nurseryman from Sawbridgeworth, Hertfordshire, specialising in fruit and roses). The paper's objects were: to be a medium of communication between lovers of floriculture and a book of reference with accurate descriptions; to exhibit improvements in flowers, effected by skill and cultivation; to call attention to plants which had been neglected through want of novelty, to the disadvantage of gardens; and to contain occasional articles on all subjects connected with floriculture, from the cultivation of plants in cottagers' gardens, windows or cucumber frames, to the various objects and arrangements required by the more wealthy.[17] The first issue contained a piece by 'a working man', Peter Mackenzie, on the love of floriculture among his colleagues, who commented: 'Although Providence has placed them in the humble sphere of life, it does not follow as a matter of course that they should be low-minded.'

A point was being made by the florists that they considered themselves worthy of the notice of the establishment and were no longer willing to be considered second-class citizens at flower shows. It echoed what Glenny had been saying for years, but it was said more rationally. The theme continued in 1848 when a complaint was published from three (anonymous) florists who said they had asked to

CHARLES TURNER (1818–85)

CHARLES TURNER was born at Wilton, near Salisbury, and began a life of floriculture growing pinks, winning his first prize at the age of fourteen. He trained as a nurseryman and set up his own business near Slough, eventually taking over the Royal Nursery there. From 1832 to 1848 he won 498 prizes and then stopped counting. He eventually grew all the traditional florists' flowers for exhibition and competition, as well as azaleas and roses. He took over Shirley Hibberd's collection of ivies and propagated them for sale, and he commercialised the Cox's Orange Pippin apple. Turner was a member of the Floral Committee of the Royal Horticultural Society, and an active member and judge of many other floral societies and a supporter of the International Potato Exhibition. He represented florists at the memorial dinner for the actor Charles Kean in the 1860s, to which a representative of every trade or profession was invited.

Charles Turner (1818–85). (Engraving from *Gardening World*, 16 May 1885, p. 585) (*Museum of Garden History*)

compete in the Horticultural Society's show at Chiswick in 1847 but their plants had not been given a stand and the vice-secretary seemed to have been indifferent to florists' flowers. They had not had the same experience at the Botanical Society's show. In 1852 Robert Hogg (1818–97) took over as editor. He was a Scottish nurseryman who had been educated at Edinburgh University, so florists could no longer be considered as uneducated working men. Hogg's speciality was fruit growing, and in 1851 the paper renamed itself the *Florist, Fruitist and Garden Miscellany*, to become the *Florist and Pomologist* in 1862.

The real challenge to the *Gardeners' Chronicle* came in October 1848, when the weekly *Cottage Gardener* was launched. Sub-titled the 'Amateur and Cottager's Guide to Out-Door Gardening and Spade Cultivation', it was started with the idea of advising the middle and working classes of the operations to be attended to in a small garden. It was 'conducted' by George W. Johnson (1802–86), a barrister, who had come to gardening through an interest in fertilisers. His aim was to divert interest from the exotics and botanical curiosities so loved by the *Chronicle*: 'Where is there a periodical that devotes attention and space to promote its advancement [outdoor gardening], even equally

GEORGE WILLIAM JOHNSON (1802–86)

GEORGE W. JOHNSON was one of the first journalists to attempt to provide a paper for amateurs. He started the *Cottage Gardener* to try to get away from the emphasis on botany and exotic plants in the *Gardeners' Chronicle* and to publicise 'spade cultivation'. But it seemed that the world would not be ready for a totally amateur paper for another ten years. Johnson's father had owned a salt works in Essex, and both George and his brother Cuthbert experimented with the use of salt as a fertiliser. Cuthbert went on to concentrate on agriculture, but George qualified as a barrister and worked in India for some years. On his return to England, he practised law and wrote *The History of English Gardening* and *Principles of Practical Gardening*, as well as dictionaries and almanacs of gardening. Soon garden journalism became a career. He edited the *Cottage Gardener*, at first alone and then jointly with Robert Hogg, and like Hogg he had a life-long interest in fruit growing.

George W. Johnson (1802–86). (Engraving from *Journal of Horticulture*, 7 July 1881, p. 13) (*Royal Horticultural Society, Lindley Library*)

with that of the other departments of horticulture, which, from their costliness, are only within the reach of a comparatively few?'[18] Concentrating on outdoor gardening and spade cultivation therefore meant pursuing the cultivation of hardy plants and food crops, 'which all have the means of pursuing . . . Utility is our prime object . . . we shall especially trim our lamp for the amateur of moderate income and the cottager'. It was the first time that the amateur (as opposed to the florist) was put at the top of a list of prospective readers.

The features in the first issue of the *Cottage Gardener* included fruit, flower and kitchen gardening for the week, information on cheap manures (including filtered house sewage), raspberries, potato planting in Ireland and the first part of a series on Cottage and Allotment Gardens written by George Johnson himself. The price seems to have been threepence, which could be managed because there was no general news and therefore no tax. However, was this low enough to appeal to the cottager or allotment-holder, and were they likely to read it anyway? Was it again aimed more at the benefactor or philanthropist who wanted to encourage gardening among the working classes? The writers given as responsible for each section were, again, all head gardeners or nurserymen. The paper was quick to publish readers' letters, often under pseudonyms, such as 'a working man but an anxious amateur'.[19]

For all his good intentions, Johnson's thinking was probably ahead of its time. In January 1855 the paper had adapted its name to the *Cottage Gardener and Country Gentleman's Companion* and was incorporating sub-papers called the *Poultry Chronicle* and *Beekeeper's Chronicle*. With its agricultural content it appeared most likely to appeal to the same readership as the *Gardeners' Chronicle*. By 1855 the *Cottage Gardener* included sections called 'The Fruit and Forcing Garden' and 'Stove and Florists' Flowers', which showed that the readers were happy with their exotics and content to leave 'spade cultivation' to their paid gardeners. However, Johnson persisted in helping the cottagers and allotment-holders by producing cheap booklets called 'Manuals for the Many'. They cost fourpence, with a discount for clergymen and others who required a number of copies for distribution. The prevailing attitude therefore was not very different from that of Loudon and Paxton twenty years earlier, giving advice to the middle classes as to how to treat their labourers and parishioners.

Although the content of the *Cottage Gardener* became similar to that of the *Gardeners' Chronicle*, the style was more conversational and practical. This is nowhere more evident than in the Queries and Answers part of the paper, which the *Cottage Gardener* gradually expanded to fill the whole middle section, many letters from readers being over a column long. All popular papers had readers' columns: what better way to sell a paper than for the readers to hope their letters had been published or their questions answered? It was the Victorian equivalent to the radio phone-in.

In January 1850 an attempt was made to establish a cheaper weekly paper, with the launch of the *Gardeners' Hive*, described as 'a weekly miscellany of Floriculture, Horticulture, and general gardening literature' and edited by J. Neville. Its first editorial stated that seventy thousand gardeners were employed in England, and, added to that figure, the amateurs of 'high and low degree' made about a hundred thousand gardeners, of whom many were unable or disinclined to purchase expensive works on gardening. What was wanted, it said, was a cheap paper dealing only with floriculture and horticulture (presumably, then, not farming). Although the monthly papers were praised, because of their embellishment (meaning illustrations) they were said to often cost up to three shillings and sixpence (the *Hive* cost only twopence). A favourable review was given of what they called 'Beck's *Florist*', describing it as 'eclipsing every work on Floriculture in the "getting up" and highly worthy of the four thousand monthly subscribers aimed at by its superintendent'. Beck had to be flattered because on a separate page was his advertisement for pelargoniums and slate ornaments.

Another provincial paper, the *Birmingham and Midland Gardeners' Magazine*, was published in 1852 and 1853, edited by C.J. Perry and J. Cole, professional gardeners from the Birmingham area. It was started for northern gardeners because many flowers which flourished in the south were found disappointing in a colder climate. The editors stated: 'During the last few years thousands of villa residences have sprung into existence in the vicinity of manufacturing towns; and the proprietors of such abodes would gladly avail themselves of the knowledge which would enable them to cultivate and decorate their small surrounding domains in the manner that would contribute most largely to their pleasure and personal gratification. On this account, we purpose devoting a portion of each number to "The Villa Garden".'[20]

Something slightly different appeared in March 1856: *Gossip of the Garden*, 'a Handbook for the Florist and Suburban Horticulturalist', started by E.S. Dodwell (1819–93), a carnation and pink grower, and John Edwards, the florist from Holloway. It was intended to be a work of reference for florists and provide easily understood directions on the culture of fruit, flowers, plants and vegetables. The editors invited 'liberal correspondence' and aimed to promote public exhibitions. They also included 'The Ladies' Page', and addressed such issues as 'Floriculture versus Fraud', which dealt with the 'dressing of

EPHRAIM SYMS DODWELL (1819–93)

E.S. DODWELL was a retired cigar merchant from Derby, who specialised in pinks and carnations. He was secretary of the Midland Horticultural Society and supported the National Carnation and Picotee Society, which presented him with a testimonial of sixty-five sovereigns in 1854. In 1851, at the Great All England Tulip Show in Derby, where northern growers were taking all the prizes, he suggested setting up societies in every town and village throughout Britain. He was one of the founder editors of *Gossip of the Garden* in 1856, one of the aims of which was to bring together florists to share information and set unified standards nationally. On moving to Oxford in 1881, he founded the Carnation and Picotee Union to promote communication between members in the north and in the south. His main interest was in raising yellow carnations.

chrysanthemums'. Perhaps they felt that *The Florist* had become too professionally oriented and had veered away from the amateur florist. They were sincere in their aim to provide practical directions: their calendar of operations for the month was seven to nine pages, which was far longer than the notes that appeared in all the other papers. They also listed all the shows for the coming month and offered discount prices to nurserymen, stating that although the first edition had been reprinted, doubling its original circulation of a thousand, it would only be able to continue with a circulation of five thousand.

Gossip of the Garden was never a serious rival to the bigger papers, but it added an alternative. As the 1850s drew to a close the amateur was now being considered in his own right, and amateur did not just mean a florist, but a practical gardener who wanted practical information. In 1858 a paper was at last launched primarily for amateurs; it came about after the success of Shirley Hibberd's book, *Rustic Adornments for Homes of Taste* of 1856.

Hibberd was born in east London in 1825. He was a journalist and public lecturer with an amateur interest in gardening. His constant contact with the public gave him valuable knowledge as to what people wanted and he worked out solutions to amateurs' problems through his own experience. He also believed that physical work in the garden gave a person pride, regardless of his status in society, an idea that went much further than the remarks in the *Gardeners' Chronicle* in 1858. The *Chronicle* simply said that an amateur was someone who loved gardening for its own sake; Hibberd was saying that gardening made you a better person.

In *Rustic Adornments for Homes of Taste* Hibberd guided readers through the practicalities of gardening, such as preparation of the soil, choosing plants and cheap equipment,[21] and he also made them believe that acquiring and keeping a garden would enhance their lives and put them in good standing in society. Its success encouraged the publishers, Groombridge and Sons, to start a serial version, a monthly magazine called *The Floral World and Garden Guide* 'for amateurs with moderate means and ambitions to excel in the various practices of horticulture', but the professional gardener was also 'to be welcomed warmly'. In April 1858 Hibberd offered free seeds from his own garden to readers sending in a stamped addressed envelope. The offer was so popular that in May he had to reduce the number of seeds sent from six to three or four. By October he instigated a seed exchange scheme. Later he captioned a page of the magazine 'Fingerpost', which 'pointed' to the best products and plants available for readers' purposes. The fact that the *Floral World* was a monthly may also have helped; it was not a direct competitor to the *Gardeners' Chronicle* or the *Cottage Gardener*, but could be bought in addition to a weekly.

The *Gardeners' Chronicle* could not ignore the success of the *Floral World* and the needs of amateurs. In March 1858 it announced its intention to 'furnish some papers more directly aiming at [the] instruction [of amateurs]'. This was really missing the point and did not go nearly far enough. The amateurs did not want information adapted for them by professionals who thought they knew what the amateurs wanted; they wanted it written specifically for their own needs. The professionals found this difficult because they had been trained for gardening in different circumstances from the amateurs. Their articles appeared sporadically under the sub-heading 'Amateur Gardening' and included pieces on annuals, bedding plants, the dahlia, the chrysanthemum, wall fruit, the auricula, 'a word for the ladies', strawberries, and potting up plants.

Between 1858 and 1861 all the gardening papers redefined themselves. Robert Hogg continued to run *The Florist*, but also joined George Johnson at the *Cottage Gardener* in 1858. In 1861 the *Cottage Gardener* renamed itself the *Journal of Horticulture*, no doubt calculated to give it a more serious air and widen its appeal.

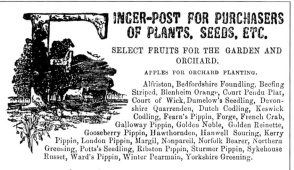

'Finger-Post for Purchasers' from *Floral World*, November 1872, p. 34. It helped to 'point' amateurs in the right direction for the best products to buy. (*Hackney Archives*)

In January 1861 *The Florist* published an introductory note, called 'Envoi' by 'D of Deal', who had now become a prominent contributor and perhaps editor. As the Revd Henry Honywood D'Ombrain he joined Thomas Moore (1821–87), a botanist, as joint editor of the *Floral Magazine* in 1862. This was almost a throwback to the botanical magazines, featuring new plants with descriptive papers and coloured illustrations, which of course were now much cheaper to produce.

In 1855 Joseph Harrison died and in 1860 his sons replaced the *Floricultural Cabinet* with the *Gardener's Weekly Magazine*, a small-sized newspaper costing only a penny ha'penny. This was emphasised in the 'introductory address':

The present are . . . not ordinary times. We have outlived the days of stage-coaches, and have been for some years reaping the benefits of a more rapid and perfect means of communication, interchange of sentiment and thought. In short, we live in the days of <u>cheap literature</u>, which is the 'order of the day'. The benefits attending on this state of things are numerous and unquestionable; to the gardener especially, whose operations are so much dependent on the state of the weather and season, it is a matter of importance to have the assistance of a weekly monitor, and an advantage to be made speedily aware of all matters of interest that transpire in connection with its pursuits, as well as to be able to communicate quickly, and at the lowest possible cost, with his professional brethren and amateurs throughout the length and breadth of the kingdom.[22]

It went on to urge each reader to find another subscriber to double the readership and make it possible to increase the size of the paper. It seemed as if the title was being kept alive pending the arrival of a good editor to breathe some life into it, and in 1861 the ideal editor was found in Shirley Hibberd. In 1865 the paper was relaunched in a larger format as the *Gardener's Magazine*. It was a real rival to the *Gardeners' Chronicle* and the *Journal of Horticulture*. At twopence a week it undercut the *Journal* by a penny (the *Chronicle* was still sixpence). Unlike the others, the *Gardener's Magazine* did not have an agricultural sub-paper. It was therefore calculated to pick up readers from both papers who were amateurs and not interested in farming or smallholdings, and had previously bought the other papers only because there was no alternative.

In 1865 Lindley and Paxton both died. The *Chronicle*'s new editor was Maxwell T. Masters (1833–1907), a botanist and expert in vegetable teratology, or monstrosity in plants. There followed a golden age of horticultural publishing, in which the three great weekly papers existed side by side with the monthly *Florist* and *Floral World*, as well as two new papers, *The Gardener* and the *Villa Gardener*. All this was shattered, however, in 1871, when William Robinson, a professional gardener turned journalist, burst on to the publishing scene with *The Garden*. S. Reynolds Hole described where the idea originated: 'I sat with my friend, William Robinson, under a tree in the Regent's Park, and suggested *The Garden* as a title for the newspaper which he proposed to publish, and which has been so powerful in its advocacy of pure horticulture of the natural, or English, school, free from rigid formalities, meretricious ornaments, gypsum, powdered bricks, cockle-shells, and bottle-ends.'[23]

Robinson was born in Ireland in 1838 to a poor Protestant family. He trained as a gardener from an early age, after his father had deserted the family. He worked under Robert Marnock at the Royal Botanic Society's garden in Regent's Park, London, where he was responsible for the herbaceous section, and became an expert in native

The Goethe plant was bruised and broken off last autumn by the cat, then half drowned for some weeks in water, where it was neglected till within an inch of its little life, since which time it has once or twice been nearly baked to death on the stove; and now, though thick and white with dust, it is struggling out a firm little leaf, and has the crisp sturdy bearing of a plant that means to thrive.

Floral World, April 1874, p. 112

British flowers. He toured Britain, and later Europe, visiting botanic gardens and nurseries, writing articles for both the *Gardeners' Chronicle* and Hibberd's *Floral World*. France and the Alps provided inspiration for his book *Alpine Flowers for English Gardens*. This was quickly followed by the more revolutionary *The Wild Garden* (published in 1870), which started his reputation for changing the course of British gardening. His ideas were developed later in *The English Flower Garden* (1882), but in the earlier book he started to persuade people to turn away from the formal style of gardening with bedding plants to using permanent, hardy plants in informal, naturalistic designs.

The Garden succeeded from the start, as Robinson had done his homework. He used well-known contributors, taking them away from other publications. Some of the material, however, was not actually new. Reynolds Hole's serial story of a horticultural society, *The Six of Spades*, had appeared in *The Florist* in 1860. The colour plates of H. Noel Humphreys (1810–79) were originally drawn for Jane Loudon's *British Wild Flowers*. It was not the content of *The Garden* which was so revolutionary, but its appearance. The two-column newspaper format was usual for the weeklies, but Robinson produced something more attractive and ornate. The layout of the other weeklies was often poor and haphazard. Articles were broken up over several pages and illustrations did not always appear on the same page as the accompanying text. Robinson produced a more polished magazine and divided it into separate sections with decorative headings. The bound volumes were inscribed with gold lettering in Arts and Crafts style, with a facsimile of Robinson's signature on the spine. Right from the start, he gave the magazine his personal stamp. He was the first to introduce colour plates into a weekly magazine.

The Garden quickly upset the balance of the established papers. In January 1872 Hibberd referred to it as 'that pretentious periodical' and claimed Robinson had copied his list of kitchen garden vegetables: 'The very first line, which declares that there is "but one sort of asparagus", our own readers will be familiar with; and those who are interested in tracing coincidences may be amused with what follows.'[24]

Allegations of plagiarism and Robinson's lack of knowledge in growing vegetables were to be recurring themes in the years that followed, but the influence of Robinson's paper was enormous. All the weeklies changed their format, dividing the papers into sections with decorative headings. By 1875 there were more gardening papers than there had been for forty years, but now they were mass-produced, cheap papers, full of information and news and available to everyone. They could be bought at bookstalls in railway stations without a subscription, so readers could pick and choose which one they wanted any week or month.

In 1879 Robinson introduced a new paper, *Gardening Illustrated*, which broke new ground in being the first gardening paper to cost one penny. At last, it seemed, gardening literature really was available to all gardeners. It was aimed at 'the smaller class of gardens', including town, villa, cottage and window gardening. With pictures of rustic summerhouses and indoor aquariums it was uncannily reminiscent of *Rustic Adornments for Homes of Taste* (which had been reissued in 1870 to latch on to the popularity of *rus in urbe*). Not content with his rising stardom, Robinson set out to goad all the other editors into submission. He reprinted an article from the *Journal of Horticulture*, sued Hogg for libel when he complained, but lost and was ordered to pay costs. Then he conducted a long-running feud with Hibberd, starting over an asparagus competition, continuing with circulation figures and ending with mutual racist remarks, which Hibberd won in style. But he could not be ignored. Although he is often credited with creating a new style in gardening, Robinson's most important contribution to horticulture was his publishing empire. He started the cheapest papers and yet he also brought into publishing a new class of writers. Reverend gentlemen such as Canon Ellacombe (1822–1916) and Henry Harpur-Crewe (1830–83), gentry such as H.J. Elwes (1846–1922) and women, the best known of whom was Gertrude Jekyll, all appeared in his pages. They no longer needed to write under pseudonyms, as it became acceptable to be paid as journalists, and these wealthy upper middle-class amateurs began to usurp the place of the head gardener in designing and planting their gardens.

Between 1880 and 1884 horticultural publishing reflected Robinson's impact. It was no longer financially worthwhile to produce monthly magazines and by 1884 even the mighty *Florist* had disappeared. Their place had been taken by much cheaper books

REVD HENRY T. ELLACOMBE (1790–1885) and
REVD HENRY NICHOLSON ELLACOMBE (1822–1916)

HENRY T. ELLACOMBE trained as an engineer before taking holy orders, and was vicar of Bitton, between Bath and Bristol, from 1835 to 1850. He wrote for *The Garden*, describing his half-acre plot containing hardy plants, trees, shrubs and roses, which never succumbed to the bedding craze. His son, HENRY NICHOLSON ELLACOMBE, who became Canon Ellacombe, lived at Bitton for sixty-eight years and took over from his father as vicar. He was an amateur botanist, and twenty plates in the *Botanical Magazine* were drawn from his plants. He looked at all plants for their own worth, even admitting that he liked to grow some weeds as long as they were not too invasive. He wrote *Plant Lore and Garden Craft of Shakespeare* (1878), *In a Gloucestershire Garden* (1895) and *In My Vicarage and Elsewhere* (1902). He also encouraged education in the parish and helped to restore the church.

written with amateurs in mind. The weekly periodicals still served their purpose in supplying topical news and advertisements, but now came down in price as they were regarded as throw-away newspapers. In 1884 two new weekly papers, the *Gardening World* and *Amateur Gardening*, appeared, each costing a penny. The *Gardening World*, or the *Gardening World Illustrated*, as it proclaimed itself, despite containing only four illustrations in fourteen pages, said it was 'exclusively devoted to all branches of practical gardening'. Its first editorial answered the question, 'why another paper for gardeners?' by asking, who could doubt that in the United Kingdom there were 'fully a million persons deeply imbued with a love for gardening?'

The other new paper, *Amateur Gardening* ('For Town and Country, For the Home Garden, Villa Farm, Poultry Yard, Bee Shed and Housekeeper's Room'), was launched by Collingridges, the publishers of the *Gardener's Magazine* (now called the *Gardeners' Magazine*), under the tried and tested editorship of Shirley Hibberd. It contained the usual mix of items Hibberd had been writing about for years and, despite its universal designation, was aimed at the small gardener who did all his own work. Interestingly, it included the sub-papers originally featured in the *Cottage Gardener*. The editorials were heavily weighted towards improving the environment, with pieces on the treatment of sewage, a 'green belt' around London and the promotion of the use of gas for cooking to avoid soot pollution. By 1885 it was offering a prize of five pounds in an essay competition.[25] On 4 April

1885 prizes were offered simply for sending in coupons from four issues of the magazine. The top prizes were a greenhouse, cold frame and lawnmower, and there were a hundred small prizes. The paper seemed shameless in sparing no expense to increase its readership.

Such popularity with amateurs led to the *Garden and Horticultural Sales and Wants Advertiser*, starting in March 1888 in Manchester. It contained notices of plants, equipment, hay, rabbits and similar items for sale, as well as advertisements for gardeners wanting situations. It attracted readers by offering prizes for articles or essays on gardening. It stated that it was started chiefly 'as a hobby' for gardeners in the north. The readers' questions were in a Notes and Queries format, the questions asked one week being answered by readers the following week. Sometimes discussions continued for several weeks. Over a hundred pounds a year was reputedly given away as prize money for essays on horticulture.

William Robinson continued to produce one new paper after another. His cheapest was *Cottage Gardening*, started in 1892, which was only a halfpenny. It lasted for six years. By 1895 there were eight weekly papers; but all were drearily similar. The *Gardeners' Chronicle* had reduced in price to threepence, and half its thirty-two pages were advertisements. The *Journal of Horticulture* remained conducted by Robert Hogg, Johnson having died in 1886. D of Deal had joined the team and there were plenty of news items (Notes and Gleanings) as well as articles on flowers and fruit. The *Gardeners' Magazine* had lost Shirley Hibberd on his death in 1890, and was now edited by George Gordon (1841–1914). It had a plainer appearance and about ten pages of text, and still cost twopence. A colour plate was sometimes offered, as well as the Christmas supplement. Robinson's *The Garden* gave away a colour plate each week and continued its sectional format. Of all the papers, it had changed the least.

By the 1890s the papers seemed to have lost their individuality: they all focused on the same topics, such as orchids and exotic fruit. They all wanted to appeal to beekeepers and botanists as well as practical gardeners. In trying to keep their prices down so as not to lose readers, they seemed to have cut corners and produced something so basic that there was no originality. Perhaps it was inevitable that the balance would eventually tip the other way. Cheap papers were all well and good for those who needed them, but by the end of the century printing processes and photography had improved so much that they had to be used for something as visual as gardening. The more expensive magazines were now using photogravure instead of engravings to provide more realistic illustrations, and it was not long before a new paper was started which used modern techniques to their best advantage.

Country Life began in 1897. It was a weekly costing sixpence, founded by Edward Hudson (1854–1936). Its main attraction as far as gardening was concerned was to present the real gardens of the privileged classes to other people of similar standing. The taste of the owner was emphasised, not the skill of the head gardener. This was the beginning of armchair gardening, a peep through the keyhole. Loudon had marvelled at the talents of Louisa Lawrence, and criticised Paxton's garden at Chatsworth, but he had been unable to show it to his readers. Now they could see gardens as they really were, albeit in various shades of grey. It was not predominantly a gardening magazine but it was the forerunner of the 'glossy' gardening magazines which came later, such as *Homes and Gardens*. The first picture of a garden in *Country Life* was of Stoneleigh Abbey in February 1897. In the issue of 6 March 1897 the column 'In the Garden' began. As well as describing a mixed flower border, it offered to answer readers' questions in future issues.

Robinson's *Cottage Gardening* was incorporated into a new *Gardener* in 1899 (costing one penny), and the same year *Popular Gardening* was launched. They amalgamated in 1919 and were eventually taken over by *Amateur Gardening*. Of the three great weeklies that had started in the mid-nineteenth century, the *Journal of Horticulture* and the *Gardeners' Magazine* both lasted until the First World War, when gardening, like most of life, changed for ever. Many of the huge garden staffs who went off to the war never returned, and the market for papers for professionals disintegrated. The amateur became the principal buyer of gardening papers. The *Gardeners' Chronicle* outlived its rivals and remained the paper for the professionals, even absorbing Robinson's *Gardening Illustrated* in 1956. It was amalgamated with the *Horticultural Trade Journal* in 1969. The *Gardening World* carried on until 1909, by which time there were several other cheap papers, such as *Garden Life* (started in 1901 and costing one penny) and *Farm, Field and Fireside* (starting in 1906 and also one penny). Robinson gave up personally editing any of his papers in 1899 and sold them in 1919. *The Garden* gradually moved up market. Gertrude Jekyll was editor in 1900 to 1901, with Ernest T. Cook (1870–1915), who had worked under Shirley Hibberd on the *Gardeners' Magazine*. *The Garden* was amalgamated with *Homes and Gardens* in 1927.

Although George Glenny started his gardening column in *Lloyd's Weekly Newspaper* in 1852, papers generally do not seem to have featured them until the early twentieth century. *The Times* started one in 1907. In the first decade of the twenty-first century there are two magazines that survive from before 1900: *Amateur Gardening* and *Country Life*. They represent the two ends of the spectrum: practical guidelines on do-it-yourself gardening, and passive observation of the privileged at home.

CHAPTER FOUR

Nurserymen, Seedsmen and Florists

The amateur gardener in the nineteenth century bought his plants from a nursery, but there was no Victorian equivalent of a garden centre where everything was available under one roof and specially aimed at the needs of the amateur. Nurseries supplied only plants and trees, and often in a limited range. Seeds, if you did not keep your own or get them from a friend, came from a seedsman. As the century went on, however, and retailers started to deal with amateurs as major customers, they began to produce more elaborate catalogues and to sell a wider range of products, such as manures, fertilisers and pest control gadgets. Some nurserymen were florists, selling only florists' flowers, originally grown for competitions. Some began as amateurs and turned professional; others evolved from the opposite direction, being nurserymen who started to specialise in florists' flowers, which became increasingly diverse as the century went on.[1]

Nurserymen

Huge numbers of new plants became available in the course of the nineteenth century, and many new varieties of well-known plants were produced. A retail trade in plants developed to cater for the needs of a mass market, but at the beginning of the century the main customers for nurseries were the very wealthy, some of whom actually financed expeditions to collect plants from abroad.

The skills of gardeners developed as they learned to cultivate the new plants and keep them alive in the primitive conditions before glasshouses and their heating systems were fully developed. Professionally trained gardeners had learnt their trade in British gardens, growing vegetables, fruit, flowers and shrubs, many of which had been cultivated in Britain for centuries. They found new challenges in imported trees and exotic plants like orchids from South

When orchids were first introduced they were looked on with awe, their fleshy snake-like roots puzzled the old gardeners, and hundreds of them perished because they were considered to require supernatural skills. It is all changed now, and orchids are becoming household plants, because it is found that they are not so vastly different in their requirements from their brethren.

Amateur Gardening, 10 January 1885, p. 439

America and Asia, and even the less demanding tender or hardy plants from South Africa or North America. It is not surprising that Loudon, writing in 1826,[2] said that one of the aims of his *Gardener's Magazine* was to rejuvenate the ailing British orchards. Many of the best young gardeners had deserted the provinces for the exotic nurseries in London where they could learn to care for the new plants and then put themselves on the job market at a higher price.

Plant collecting increased in the early part of the nineteenth century partly because the improvements in glasshouses made it easier to maintain and breed the plants, but also because of the introduction of the Wardian case in the 1830s, which was like a miniature greenhouse used to transport plants on the decks of ships. Before these were used, living plants usually perished on the voyage home because of exposure to sea spray, wind and cold. The discovery of the principle behind the Wardian case is attributed to Dr Nathaniel Bagshaw Ward (1791–1868), who noticed how a green plant had grown by accident in an enclosed glass jar he had been using for hatching out a chrysalis. He realised that the plant could grow in its own sealed microclimate, and that this could be used in difficult conditions to protect the plant.[3] Ward was related by marriage to George Loddiges of the Loddiges nursery and together they experimented in bringing plants back from Australia.[4] The case consisted of a wooden box at the base, with a glazed roof above. Some of the originals can be seen in the Chelsea Physic Garden and in the Museum of Garden History in London.

Although it was hard to keep living plants alive on sea voyages, many plants were successfully imported if they could be brought over in a dormant state, such as a bulb, or as seeds. Then the challenge was to germinate and nurture the new plant, often perhaps without any knowledge of what it was. This was an age of great experimentation and excitement for anyone who was interested in botany or horticulture, and an enormous fund of knowledge and skill developed among gardeners who were growing the new plants. At first they were sold as rarities to the wealthy, but later, as the middle classes developed an interest in gardening as a hobby and the once-exotic plants became almost commonplace, a new retail market developed. In 1843 monkey puzzle trees were selling at £10 for a hundred, but the rare orchid *Vanda caerulea* cost £100 per plant. In 1854 a Wellingtonia seedling cost two guineas, or 12 guineas a dozen. Later in the century, however, no suburban garden was complete without its monkey puzzle on the lawn. As for orchids, by the 1880s they were the staple fare of many commercial nurseries in all the big towns. Veitch's Chelsea nursery, which became famous for its orchids, had opened in 1853. Another establishment with a reputation for orchids was the Victoria and Paradise Nurseries of Benjamin Samuel Williams (1824–90) in Holloway, north London.[5]

Although exotic plants were dramatic in their effect and became popular in conservatories and parlours, it was the colourful bedding plants that had most impact in gardens. The idea of planting out

B.S. WILLIAMS (1824–90)

BENJAMIN SAMUEL WILLIAMS was born in Hoddesden, Hertfordshire, the son of a gardener, and he started work under his father. He became a specialised orchid grower and passed on his skill to others in his articles in the *Gardeners' Chronicle*, 'Orchids for the Million', published as *The Orchid Grower's Manual* in 1852. It was one of the first guides to orchid growing, remaining in print until after his death, and encouraging many amateurs to try orchids for themselves. Williams' Victoria Nursery was at the foot of Highgate Hill and was expanded with the addition of the Paradise Nursery further down Holloway Road. By the 1880s he had fifty different glasshouses, including a conservatory full of palms and cycads, rhododendron, camellia and azalea houses, and specialised collections of ferns, orchids, carnations, heaths, and many subtropical foliage plants.

B.S. Williams (1824–90). (Engraving from *Gardening World*, 14 March 1885, p. 441) (*Museum of Garden History*)

colourful tender plants in formal beds, like all fashions in gardens, had started in the gardens of the wealthy, but when Joseph Paxton planted out the parterres and water gardens for the reconstruction of the Crystal Palace at Sydenham in 1856, he introduced the idea to the masses. It became the predominant style of planting in public parks and was soon imitated in small suburban gardens. As most people of modest means did not possess the skill or the facilities to raise the plants themselves, they bought them every summer from nurseries, which were constantly developing new varieties. Many of the colourful tender or half-hardy plants which became popular, such as penstemons, zinnias and petunias, originated in America, but were hybridised almost out of recognition by the end of the century to produce brightly coloured plants that were the right size for small gardens and could withstand the British climate.

In cities like London, full of pollution, it was not possible after the 1850s to keep nurseries going without a large expanse of glass to protect the plants. Glasshouses became cheaper to produce, and with the demand from a mass market, it paid to set up huge nurseries with a great stock of plants. In the 1880s William Bull of King's Road, Chelsea was advertising exotics, such as tree ferns up to 12 feet high, with prices 'available on application'.[6] More mundane were the hundred different varieties of fuchsia, and four hundred different chrysanthemums, as well as ten catalogue pages of pelargoniums. On a smaller scale, John Wood, of 'Woodville', Kirkstall, Leeds, was running a Hardy Plant Club in the 1880s, through which he supplied hardy perennials and 'Old-fashioned Garden Flowers' from his own garden.[7] Rose and shrub specialists also came in all sizes. Paul and Son of Cheshunt were one of the best known for shrubs, whereas William Paul, a son of the founder, set himself up as a rose specialist in nearby Waltham Cross. A less well-known rose grower was George Cooling, whose catalogue of 1884–5 advertised 'Niphetos, the finest white rose in cultivation, beautiful as a pot plant'. The dwarf size cost one shilling and sixpence and a standard, two shillings. He also supplied grape vines in three sizes or extra-strong canes for fifteen shillings.[8]

But if you did not live near a nursery, there were still plenty of plants available by mail order, advertised in the gardening papers. The *Gardeners' Chronicle* in 1856 advertised the following service: 'To Gentlemen engaged in planting, list of rare and hardy conifers, shrubs, etc. Communications by steamer and railway to all parts of England, Ireland and Scotland, as well as to the continent. All orders of £2 upwards delivered carriage free to London, Newcastle and Hull, as well as any railway station within 150 miles of the nurseries. Youell & Co., Royal Nursery, Great Yarmouth, Norfolk.'

As in all spheres of life, mass production could lead to a decline in standards. Small nurseries may not have had the experience or the skilled labour of the larger establishments, which could lead to disasters for the unwary, and of course the middle-class amateur would typically be unwary. Shirley Hibberd commented in 1859:

> In the suburbs of London there are numbers of small nurseries, where 'a little of everything' is to be had at a moment's notice – fruit trees, evergreens, roses, &c, &c. The way in which most of these are grown is such that they are utterly unfit to be removed when sold. They are planted in close rows, have as little attention as possible, and are never transplanted, because the cost of labour is considered a waste of money. The trees do pretty well, and a purchaser makes his selection according to their healthy appearance, not aware that many of them have been allowed to form tap-roots, and have never been moved from the day they were put out to make heads. When it comes to removal, the roots are cut in all round with the spade, the deep roots are loosened, and the tree is wrenched out. It never recovers the shock, and people think the soil, the air, or their own management is to blame.[9]

A feature of nurseries that we are not familiar with today was the willingness of the proprietor to buy good plants raised by amateurs, or to buy back plants once they had grown too large. Shirley Hibberd referred to the nursery stock in his fernery being worth more than it was on starting,[10] and the author of an article on palms in the *Floral World* referred to taking back a large palm tree and exchanging it for something smaller, after growing it for eight or ten years.[11] Mary Russell Mitford wrote to a friend in 1845 that she had sent her 'cast-off' seedling geraniums to a nurseryman, in exchange for pots and new plants.[12] She had had an unpleasant experience the year before

Sutton's Duke of Connaught. This remarkably handsome cucumber is the finest white-spined variety known. It is perfectly level, with a bright green skin, well covered with bloom, spine scarcely discernible, and the fruit very little ribbed. Its great recommendation is its wonderfully small handle, not more than an inch in length. This gives it a beauty of form not possessed of any other cucumber.

Suttons Seed Catalogue, 1881, p. 15

when some of her geraniums were advertised for sale after they had
been stolen by a local man she had employed. When he realised they
had been bought by Miss Mitford's neighbour, he had stolen them
again, so as not to be found out.[13]

Seedsmen

The seed trade was more closely allied to market gardening than to
the nursery trade, as seeds were grown on farms and harvested, dried
and cleaned before being sent to town or to local markets. However,
the seed companies needed an office in town where orders could be
taken, and a warehouse for storage and dispatch. In London the seed
merchants tended to be based near Covent Garden, where the old-
established fruit and vegetable market was. Suttons Seeds, which
claimed to be the first seed company to print catalogues with prices
in 1806, still had an office there in the 1970s.

Sutton & Sons' Royal Seed
Establishment, Reading, from
where seeds were dispatched
throughout the world.
(Engraving from *Sutton's
Amateur's Guide in Horticulture
for 1896*) (*Suttons Consumer
Products Ltd*)

One of the biggest nineteenth-century seed firms was Carter's. Its
offices were in High Holborn, London, and its warehouses gradually
expanded to occupy a large part of the area between High Holborn and
Lincoln's Inn Fields. The firm had been founded in about 1816 by James
Carter, whose father had been a warehouseman to another seed merchant

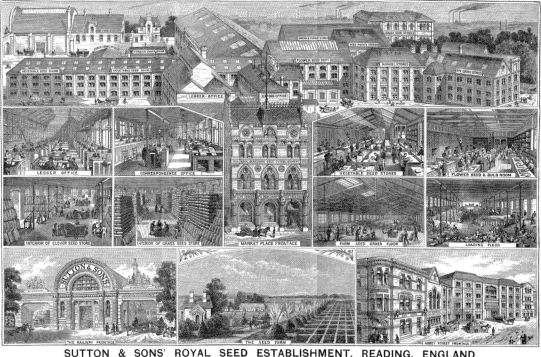

SUTTON & SONS' ROYAL SEED ESTABLISHMENT, READING, ENGLAND.
The buildings represented cover about six acres of ground, and do not include the extensive ranges of Glass employed in saving seeds of Begonia, Calceolaria, Cineraria, Cyclamen, Gloxinia, Primula, &c.

in Covent Garden. Carter's had established a good reputation by the 1840s. The *Gardener's Magazine* gave a detailed history and description of the seed firm in 1874 and 1876.[14] The seeds were mainly grown on three farms near Colchester, Essex, together comprising 600 acres, with other farmers providing further stock. The seeds were cleaned, weighed and packed in Holborn, and thence dispatched throughout the world. Ninety-six acres of land were used for cabbages, 70 for beans and a huge 814 for peas. The *Gardener's Magazine* described the warehouse:

> The sorters are placed beside great benches, on which the seed is poured out in quantities. At the edge of the bench is a small slit, and beneath the slit hangs a great bag. The sorter draws forward the seed and rolls through the slit into the bag every grain that is the proper size and shape and colour, but quickly detects and throws out every seed that is small or misshapen or badly coloured or in any way wrong . . . In the boxes the women throw rejected seeds into we find 'rogues' of all shapes and sizes, which if allowed to pass would exercise a most injurious influence and initiate a real deterioration. But they are detected and cast out for feeding pigeons and other such purposes.

The warehouses were divided into sections for different types of seed, and one section was used for making up 'selections' for amateur gardeners.

There was much rivalry between the seed companies as to who produced the best varieties, so advice was helpful. The following notice appeared in the *Gardener's Chronicle* in 1857: 'Amateurs and Gentlemen's Gardeners may have a list of the few seeds that are really useful on sending a directed envelope to G. Glenny, Dungannon House, Fulham, SW. "Glenny's Companion" (with portrait) and Garden Almanack. 13 stamps each.'

Books stressed the importance of choosing a reliable seedsman. Elizabeth Watts in *Practical Modern Gardening* gives prices to be paid for various vegetable seeds, which are usually measured by the ounce, or for larger seeds, such as peas and beans, by the quart,[15] but she qualifies her remarks with 'wherever trustworthy seedsmen are within reach'.[16] J.H. Clark, in *The Cottager's Kitchen, Fruit and Flower Gardens*, gives the following 'general remarks to be observed': 'Be careful in your selection of seeds; and, if possible, purchase them of a nurseryman you know well, or you may have the mortification of finding bastard cabbages in your garden, instead of brocoli [*sic*] – and a cross of the savoy and cabbage, instead of Brussels sprouts; or, if the seed be of the right sort, it may be old and unsound and your labour, time, ground, and money, thrown away.'[17]

Seed catalogues in the 1850s and 1860s were still basic printed lists of different varieties with their prices, but by the 1880s the rival

companies were producing sizeable booklets with coloured covers and colour plates showing the best varieties. Cannel's catalogue of 1888 also advertised such requisites as tobacco powder (for fumigating aphids), manure, tiffany, horticultural sand, raffia and bouquet wire, while Carter's sold Stevenson's Abyssinian mixture (tobacco?) as well as rough shag, Boston's 'Ne Plus Altra', 'for the entire eradication of the greatest pests in plant houses', Gishurstine, 'for preserving gardeners' boots', and a ladies' basket stick, which was a walking stick incorporating a basket at the top for holding cut flowers that might be gathered around the garden.

Seed merchants offered prizes at shows for plants grown from their seeds. (Advertisement in *Amateur Gardening*, 18 January 1890, p. 471) (*Amateur Gardening*)

Florists

The word florist today means someone who sells cut flowers and creates arrangements with them. In the nineteenth century such a person would be known as a market florist. The word florist on its own meant someone who grew particular, specialised, plants for competitions held by florists' societies. Florists are mentioned here with nurserymen because by the nineteenth century many of them had become nurserymen, and many established nurserymen had started selling florists' flowers. The most important thing about florists as the century went on was their influence over the nursery trade in that the skills developed by florists in plant breeding helped to create the huge number of flower varieties that became available.

The traditional florists' flowers were the hyacinth, auricula, tulip, polyanthus, ranunculus, anemone, carnation and pink. Some societies specialised in one sort of flower, but most held shows several times a year for different flowers which were in season. Originally, the shows took place at a feast held at a local public house for members of the society, and prizes were usually silver spoons and copper kettles, or sometimes money. However, the real money was made when a florist created a winning plant and could then propagate more plants to sell to other florists. It is also possible that money was gambled on the results of the competitions, as it was on most competitive sports in the eighteenth and nineteenth centuries.

These florists' flowers were hardy plants that had been grown in Britain for centuries. They could be propagated by seed, which was how the new varieties were produced, or their roots or bulbs could be divided and sold to other florists. They did not need to be grown under glass, so were available to even the humblest people. The skill of the florist was in choosing parent plants and creating a new seedling that had a perfectly round flower conforming to the rules of each society. Many types developed for each flower, according to the patterns on the petals, so for instance carnations were divided into picotees, flakes or bizarres, and tulips into bizarres, roses and bybloemens. Names of varieties were usually taken from national heroes, such as Lord Nelson or the Duke of Wellington, from royalty, or from the florist's own family. Flowers were usually exhibited as potted plants or as cut flowers in glass jars. The exception was tulips, particularly in the London area.[18] They were planted in beds, laid out according to variety, and the judges progressed as if 'on circuit', going round the different florists over several days.

Florists' societies were known in Britain from as early as the seventeenth century,[19] and they existed in European countries too. There are different theories about how they originated. They are sometimes said to have been associated with particular trades or guilds, and Huguenot refugees from the Low Countries were thought to have helped popularise the interest. It is certainly likely that they brought over new varieties of plants with them. Another theory is that competitive floriculture developed simply through groups of professional gardeners meeting socially in pubs and putting together shows of their favourite flowers. This then developed into competitive shows, and the rules were drawn up as a standard to comply with. By the eighteenth century, craftsmen and artisans who

Florists' carnations and
picotees were particularly
popular in Lancashire, Sheffield
and Bethnal Green in London,
where many people grew them
in back yards. (Engraving from
Amateur Gardening, 6 March
1886, p. 535) (*Amateur
Gardening*)

worked at home started growing the flowers and entering the
competitions. It was a convenient pastime for people who worked at
home in cottage industries and could keep an eye on their plants
during the working day. Apart from the interest of growing the
plants, there was always the hope of making money if a successful
flower was created. Some plants commanded higher prices than
others: tulip bulbs might cost five or even ten pounds each, a
considerable amount for a working man.

The high value of good plants sometimes led to fraud. In the early editions of the *Gardener's Magazine*, Loudon warned florists about fraudulent travelling salesmen who appeared from nowhere in villages claiming to be selling roots of well-known florists' flowers.[20] The *Midland Florist*[21] cited examples of floricultural imposters, including a man pretending to be a Frenchman who sold 'plants of the most unheard-of colours', which later turned out to be common wild plants. There is also considerable correspondence in the *Gardeners' Chronicle* in the 1840s about new seedling plants being exhibited as perfect new varieties, which when grown on turn out to be leggy weaklings.

The peak of popularity for the florists' societies was between the 1820s and 1850s, but by that time florists had already started experimenting with new plants. This was not surprising: anyone who is interested in plants will want to try growing something new. The only reason florists had restricted themselves to the traditional flowers was that only they were available for them to grow. Once new plants, such as pelargoniums and dahlias, became affordable, they were keen to try them. There was also a new wave of interest from a new type of florist. Employment in factories meant that artisans and craftsmen no longer worked at home, but the amateur gardeners who were being encouraged to grow flowers in small gardens in their spare time could not fail to be attracted by these brightly coloured flowers that appeared relatively easy to grow and were abundant in their variety. Loudon, writing in 1826, had tried to interest 'gentlemen's gardeners' in growing florists' flowers, which he had recently discovered and had been promoting in his *Gardener's Magazine*.[22] They did not seem to respond and he soon lost interest, but the middle-class gardeners of the later part of the century took to them with enthusiasm.

Books on gardening for amateurs contained sections on florists' flowers, showing that they were beginning to be recognised in their own right as garden flowers, but by the second half of the century there was confusion about what a florists' flower was, and they began to be seen as traditional flowers, as distinct from bedding plants. Then, later, even bedding plants themselves seemed to be defined as florists' flowers, as they are hybridised by amateurs and judged by rules as to their qualities.

Jane Loudon referred to florists' flowers as:

> Those which it has been found may be grown to an extraordinary size and degree of perfection by taking great pains with their culture. The Dutch were the first who practised this art with their Hyacinths and Tulips; but their example has been followed by the florists of other countries who, as they cultivate their flowers in the hope of winning prizes with them at flower-shows, may be said to use them as

instruments for gambling . . . It may be observed, that the rules by which florists decide as to the merits of their respective flowers do not depend on any particular beauty of colour, and sometimes not even on form; but on certain arbitrary criteria which they have settled among themselves . . . as it requires to be a florist to know the full merits of florists' flowers, they are of comparatively little interest to amateurs.[23]

That was where she was wrong. Elizabeth Watts, writing in about 1865, described florists' flowers as 'those kinds which can be brought to a great degree of perfection and novelty in size, colour, and other properties, by careful cultivation'.[24] She listed not just the traditional flowers and the chrysanthemums and dahlias which had been included for some time, but also calceolarias, cinerarias, fuchsias, phloxes, verbenas, and even 'American plants', by which she meant rhododendrons, azaleas and other shrubs, and she also included roses. By the end of the century, *Beeton's All about Gardening* included a section on planning a florists' flower garden and also included hollyhocks as well as dahlias and chrysanthemums, 'for florists have largely increased the objects of their care'. It was commented that florists' flowers 'are so rich in beauty that most persons take delight

ALFRED SMEE (1818–77)

ALFRED SMEE lived at Finsbury Circus in London and was admitted to the College of Surgeons in 1840. At the age of twenty-three he was elected to the Royal Society for research in science, especially electricity. He became consultant surgeon to the Bank of England and invented a new method for printing bank notes. He created a garden at The Grange, Wallington, Surrey, in the 1860s. It included several self-contained features and collections of sedums and saxifrages. He intended them to come as surprises as one walked round the garden. He wrote *My Garden: Its Plan and Culture* in 1872, which described not just the plants in the garden, but its geology, and its wild birds, animals and insects. Smee was scathing about florists' flowers, which he thought artificial and worthless. His son, Alfred Hutchinson Smee (1841–1901), was also a medical man and particularly interested in orchids. He also supported the City of London Flower Show, held annually in Finsbury Circus.

Alfred Smee (1818–77). (Engraving from *Gardeners' Chronicle*, 27 January 1877, p. 109) (*Royal Horticultural Society, Lindley Library*)

in them. Indeed it is quite impossible for a garden to be really gay without its share of them.'[25] But one writer did not agree. Alfred Smee (1818–77) seemed to like some flowers grown by florists, but constantly railed against the florists themselves. Of florists' varieties of daisy, he said they were 'immeasurably coarser and less refined in their character than the wild daisy of the fields',[26] and of snapdragons he said, 'Florists dignify the finer kinds with names which are neither worth recording nor committing to memory.'[27]

Even if not all gardeners approved of the florists' methods, they benefited from their skills. When the large commercial nurseries developed to cater for the trade to the middle-class amateurs and the individual florists disappeared, their legacy lived on in the enormous variety of flowers available. Seed catalogues of the late nineteenth century contain long lists of flowers for customers to choose from, far more than we have today. For example, Suttons Flower Seed List for 1892 offered thirteen different types of campanula and thirteen different helichrysums; in 1895 it offered seven different types of cineraria and eight types of gaillardia.[28] The catalogue for 2005 offered only two campanulas, two helichrysums, two cinerarias and one gaillardia. The large number of varieties available may have been a marketing ploy, however. Seedsmen then could not guarantee the germination rate they can now, and offering many varieties made buyers feel that they had more chance of getting a good seed if they chose wisely.

CHAPTER FIVE

The Hardware of the Garden

The amateur needs to invest in tools, pots and containers, composts, fertilisers, pesticides, all sorts of 'sundries', and even buildings like glasshouses and frames, to make a successful garden. Today the composts and fertilisers will be mixed and measured to the amateur's requirements and poisonous chemicals are strictly regulated and labelled. Tools are designed for use by one person and are light and easy to clean. In early Victorian times the 'hardware' of the garden was designed for professionals, and they usually worked in teams. Machinery was often made to be operated by two pairs of hands and sometimes pulled by a pony. A 'professed gardener' would expect to be provided with the right tools for the job and would not be prepared to improvise like an amateur. The foremen would be anxious to make sure all the men were fully employed, even during the quieter periods in winter when nothing was growing and the days were short, and cold. This was the time when double digging and constant raking of leaves would be resorted to to keep them busy, and it would be a welcome break for everyone to work inside, cleaning and mending the tools ready for the following season. Amateur gardeners would be looking for tools that were easy to use single-handedly and versatile enough to have multiple uses. The rise in popularity of amateur gardening in the second half of the nineteenth century coincided with the increase in mass production of consumer articles and the technical advances that made labour-saving appliances possible.

Businesses selling gardening equipment were usually specialised and run by experts. Self-service was unheard of; personal service, usually by recommendation, was all that mattered. Goods were attractive if they were seen to be well made and meant to last. Businesses were usually run by families, and because customers were valued both for themselves and for the recommendations they would pass on to others, good ones were usually allowed to buy on credit. Testimonials were used in advertising: 'I have had 400 feet of your Gutta Percha Tubing (in lengths of 100 feet each, with Union Joint) *in use for the last twelve months for watering these gardens, and I find it to answer better than any thing I have ever yet tried.* The pressure of the water is very considerable, but this has not the slightest effect on the Tubing. I consider this Tubing to be *a most valuable invention for Gardeners*, inasmuch as it enables us to water our gardens in about one-half the time, and with one-half the labour formerly required.'[1] Those were said to be the words of Mr J. Farrah, Gardener to Boswell Middleton Jalland Esq., of Holderness House, near Hull. Boyd's Patent Brush and Croquet Lawn Mowers were advertised with recommendations from no less than both George Glenny and Shirley Hibberd ('Instead of the old bother of scythe sharpening, sweeping, rolling, and loitering, the grass is mown now almost by looking at it').[2]

Ladies were an important market, and much advertising was aimed specifically at them. A leaflet for 'Florvita, The Life of Flowers' was printed on pink paper. It was said to be for stimulating and quickening the growth of plants: 'To ladies who take an interest in their flowers, both indoors and out, Florvita particularly recommends itself; for though chemically it represents a very highly concentrated fertiliser, it has not the appearance or character of what is known under the head of "Flower Manures"; being a delicate pink powder soluble in water, with a most agreeable bouquet.'[3]

By the second half of the nineteenth century, improvements in transport and the postal service meant that goods could be bought by mail order and delivered to virtually any part of the country. Even garden buildings could be delivered to the door 'flat-packed', and there was a willing workforce ready to put them together. Shirley Hibberd, in *The Rose Book* of 1864, encapsulates perfectly the procedure for buying a glasshouse:

Whatever will putrefy and become obnoxious if exposed to the air loses all its obnoxious qualities the moment it is mixed with the soil, which is a natural deodorizer, and all such substances are powerful in stimulating and feeding vegetable growth. You have, therefore, one source of the very best manure in the household, and you must treasure every scrap of stinking rubbish, solid and liquid, and not waste so much as a dead cabbage leaf.

Shirley Hibberd, *Profitable Gardening*, p. 28

I saw plainly that Sir Joseph Paxton's patent was the thing for me to patronize, and by means of two letters to Mr Hereman, to settle the size and the price of the house, all preliminaries were settled, and before the postman who took the second letter ordering the house to be supplied could have fairly rested from his journey, there stood at the frontgate a waggon piled to the height of the first-floor windows with the bran new span lights, all glazed and painted, with the doors, ventilators, bolts, screws, everything down to the penny nails, so that with the aid of a couple of carpenters the house was put up, in less time and with about a fiftieth part of the labour required to print this little book about roses.[4]

Most gardening requisites could be bought through advertisements in the gardening papers. *Amateur Gardening* contained the following:

FISH GUANO
WARRANTED TO CONTAIN 11 per cent AMMONIA
ENTIRELY FREE FROM ACID
In bags 1 cwt, 15s, ½ cwt, 10s. Delivered free
to any station
GIRLING & WOODS
Fish Guano Makers,
LOWESTOFT.

RUSSIA MATS
JAMES T. ANDERSON
Supplies every description of RUSSIA MATS for Covering, Tying, and
Packing, at the very lowest possible prices.
TOBACCO PAPER, RAFFIA, BROWN PEAT,
SILVER SAND, COCOA-FIBRE REFUSE (best only)
And Other HORTICULTURAL REQUISITES.[5]

Some merchants sold an extraordinary mixture of commodities. The John Johnson collection in the Bodleian Library in Oxford has a trade card from Thomas Elliott, dealer in London stable manure, and peat moss manure. He lists grains, raw fish and sugar scum as his other specialities.

Tools and equipment

The hand tools used by the Victorian gardener were similar to those we use today, except that ours are made of modern materials which are easier to clean and lighter to use. Victorian gardening books show a great array of tools which we may not be familiar with, such as a 'turf beetle' (for levelling and consolidating newly laid turf) and a suckering iron (for removing suckers from shrubs). Elizabeth Watts, never afraid to call a spade a spade, suggested at least two for the flower garden:

> Spades are made of three sizes, and it is best to have two for a medium-sized flower garden. The largest, or the second size, may be chosen according to the strength of the hand which will have to use it, for the chief of the digging; and the smallest will be useful among the flowers in rather crowded borders. There is also a deep spade much scooped, which is very good for getting up plants with a good ball of earth. A really good spade will wear with a good edge throughout. A shovel is a kind of spade, broad in make, and rather hollowed in form, and is used for removing earth and such like jobs.[6]

She also suggested rakes of three sizes, as well as a wooden rake for the lawn and a daisy rake. However, Alfred Smee, who was an amateur on a much grander scale, and probably never went out and gardened himself, considered that rakes were more 'ornamental' than 'really useful'.[7] He specified only one spade for general purposes, but emphasised the importance of its being made of steel. He had consulted Messrs Spears and Jackson of Sheffield on the question of tools, who did not recommend weldings of steel and iron. He proudly stated that 'Most of the tools in my garden are made entirely of steel, and have been procured at their manufactory.'

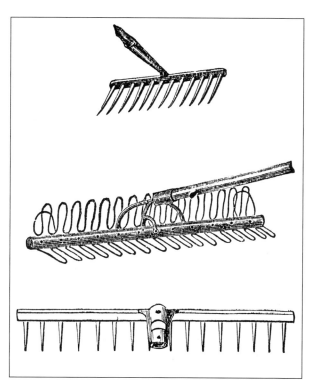

A selection of rakes: garden rake (top), wire lawn rake (middle), steel hay rake (bottom) from *Beeton's All about Gardening*, p. 414). (*Author's collection*)

Elizabeth Watts then went on to hoes and 'the spud', a tool most beloved of all Victorian gardeners. She describes it as 'a wide-made chisel, set on the end of a long handle, and is good for cutting up weeds on grass, paths, or beds. Alfred Smee illustrated the spud and said it was 'for cutting off suckers, or digging out long-rooted weeds'. Mrs Earle apparently loved using it: 'Weeding, if tiring, is also a fascinating employment; and so is spudding. The first is best done in dry weather, the second in moist.'[8]

When it came to forks, Elizabeth Watts again found merit in variety. She recommended:

A light fork, with three prongs, is best for common use. A four-pronged fork is also good for some purposes. A tulip fork – a nice little three-pronged fork, with a handle little more than a foot long – is a most useful tool. It is especially handy for ladies, as with it they can fork as much as is necessary, while they stoop over a bed to plant and arrange it. Where the ground is large enough to require a large assortment of tools, a leaf fork will be found handy: it is a large four-pronged fork, made of wood, shod with iron, and it will enable one person to take up more leaves than two can without its help, as it is large and light, and the leaves do not fix to it as to a common fork.

Luckily, she was content with only one trowel: 'it should be kept clean and bright, and it will have plenty of work to do'.

Cutting tools for the professional also came in great variety, with different knives for budding, propagating and pruning, as well as specialised shears and scissors for thinning grapes and flower gathering. Our universal tool, the secateur, was still written with an acute accent on the first 'e' in the *Gardener's Assistant* of 1904, and was described as 'shears of French invention'.[9] Actually, they had been in use in Britain since at least the 1850s, though in France were mainly used in vineyards, being safer and more convenient than knives.[10] They were ideal for amateurs, as they were versatile and safe in inexperienced hands, but the British saw them as particularly appropriate for women, which probably slowed their acceptance by male amateurs, who thought they should give the appearance of having confidence with a knife. Alfred Smee was quick to condemn them: 'The various forms of pruning shears are not approved, as they bruise the wood when unskilfully handled, and in this respect are inferior to a sharp knife.' Jane Loudon, however, praised them whole-heartedly: 'Every lady ought to be provided with a pair of pruning-shears, so contrived as to make what is called a draw-cut, and thus not to bruise the wood or the bark so as to prevent its uniting again smoothly . . . The French instrument called a secateur is only a somewhat larger and stronger pair of pruning-shears.'[11]

The lawnmower is the tool most identified as an indispensable invention. It is certainly unlikely that the lawn would have become such a feature of amateurs' gardens if the mower had not existed. Before the mowing machine came along, grass was cut with a scythe. William Cobbett in *The English Gardener*, published in 1829, writes that 'the mower can operate only in the *dew*'. This sounds strange to the modern reader who knows only too well that it is the dew which makes mowing with a domestic machine impossible. But in Cobbett's time 'mower' meant the person doing the mowing,[12] and apparently it was usually done on a Saturday morning. During the week the grass was poled or swarded to cut off the daisy heads and remove worm-casts in preparation for mowing: 'A good short-grass mower is a really able-workman; and if the plat have a good bottom; he will leave it very nearly as smooth and as even as the piece of green cloth which covers the table on which I am writing: it is quite surprising how close a scythe will go if in a hand that knows how to whet and use it. If, however, you do not resolve to have the thing done in this manner, it is much better not to attempt it at all. The decay of gardening in England in this respect is quite surprising.'[13] Was there a subliminal message here that mowing should be done by hand and not machine? Cobbett is well known to disapprove of new ideas such as tea-drinking that changed the character of the British countryside. But if this was written before 1829 it is unlikely that he was expressing distaste for the lawnmower, as it had yet to come into common use. It was patented by Edwin Budding in 1830 and manufactured by John Ferrabee in Stroud, Gloucestershire.[14] The idea came from machines in the textile industry for cutting the 'nap' of cloth. A mowing machine could cover a much larger area than one man with a scythe, and it did not require as much skill. A bad scyther would cut unevenly, leaving bare patches, whereas a machine could be mastered fairly quickly by anyone. It could also be fitted with a box to collect the clippings, thereby saving even more labour, although the first machines did usually require two people to operate them: one behind and one in front.

After the initial excitement over the mowing machine, however, it seems to have lost its impact. The *Gardeners' Chronicle* in 1843 rather sneered at it in comparison with the scythe, except in 'very small places, where there is no regular gardener'. This of course is before the watershed of 1858, so they are not yet interested in amateurs. Alfred Smee had no qualms about recommending one in 1872: 'We sometimes cut the grass with a scythe, but prefer the mowing machine, of which there are many kinds now in operation. The one at my garden was made by Green, and has lasted satisfactorily for some years in constant work without any inconvenience. The grass lawn is essentially an English feature, and a lawn may now be kept by a good machine in a state worthy of its English reputation with only a moderate amount of labour.' Elizabeth Watts also saw no objection to the machine, other than its cost ('from three or four pounds to thirty') and stressed that it must be kept thoroughly cleaned and oiled.

It was the rise of amateur gardening in the 1850s and 1860s that created the demand for smaller, lighter mowers that could be operated by one man, or even a woman. Advertisements in the gardening magazines increasingly depicted men and women

TRY THE NEW

"Tennis" Lawn Mower,

A beautifully-designed, well-constructed, and almost noiseless Machine. Durable, easy to work, and eminently suitable for the Tennis Ground, and also for ornamental gardening. Gearing is encased; Steel Cutters, made by a new process, are unbreakable.

NET CASH PRICES,
Complete with Grass Boxes.

6	7	8	10	12	14 in. wide.
23/-	29/-	35/-	42/-	63/-	84/- each.

The 'Tennis' Lawn Mower. (Advertisement from *Amateur Gardening*, 4 May 1889) (*Amateur Gardening*)

speeding along with tiny mowers, wearing smart outdoor clothes and hats, so that you had the impression that they were fitting in a bit of lawnmowing before they went out for the afternoon. By the 1880s it was commonplace for people to use such machines as the 'Victoria Lawn Mower': 'The very shape of the machine suggests its capability for being worked with ease and pleasure by ladies and gentlemen, who are able to enjoy the light exercise its use entails, and thus mow their own lawns themselves. We have to look more to the value of appliances from this point of view, because this journal caters for a class of persons who prefer attending personally to the management of their own gardens, and therefore need such mechanical aids as they can easily make use of.'[15]

Another task which was gradually eased during the nineteenth century was watering the garden. We take it for granted that water can be delivered around the garden now because we are used to a constant supply of tap water and have lightweight hosepipes. In

Victorian times not everyone had tapped water even in their houses, so many had to rely on rainwater from a well or pond. Taking it anywhere meant carrying heavy buckets or cans. Many larger gardens would have water supplied by laying pipes underground and have purpose-made ponds, not as decorative features but as 'dipping ponds' so that gardeners could fill their watering cans near to the flower or vegetable beds.

For moving large amounts of water, barrows were used, like barrels or cisterns on wheels, often topped by a pump, which turned them into 'engines'. These barrows would be heavy before they were even filled and they would therefore require two men or a man and pony to wheel them around the garden.

Elizabeth Watts deemed a good water engine essential, but pointed out that it would be dear to buy: 'a good one will cost several pounds'. A hydropult, the pipe of which could be placed in a tank, was slightly cheaper ('two guineas'), and smaller ones could be used by ladies. She also described the variety of watering cans or pots: 'The roses of some should be finely perforated that the watering may the more nearly resemble rain. Besides common watering-pots of all sizes, there are long-spouted watering-pots for watering the plants on the shelves of a greenhouse; French watering-pots, with zigzag bends in the spouts, to break the force of the water as it descends upon the plants; and shelf watering-pots, small and flat in shape, for watering plants that are high up and in out of the way corners, and near the glass in greenhouses.' Alfred Smee illustrated a pot used in his garden with a long perforated spout 'which throws a fine jet of water over delicate plants'.

The idea of a flexible pipe that could be moved around the garden was not a new one. Hoses had been made in canvas and in leather for centuries, but the materials were stiff and heavy and needed constant maintenance to keep them functioning. Also, before piped water was a reality their use was limited. The first material that made hosepipes more practical was indiarubber. In 1827 Thomas Hancock of Fulham in London introduced the idea and it was taken up by insurance companies for use by the fire brigade. In 1845 Henry Bewley started manufacturing hosepipes for gardeners out of gutta-percha, which was a product from another tree in Malaya, similar to rubber.[16] Both these types of pipe were liable to cracking if not maintained properly. They were also quite heavy, and frames had to be used to enable them to be moved about the garden. Probably professional gardeners running large gardens where much of the area to be watered was away from a piped supply would not see the advantage over the other forms of water carriage. Once again, therefore, the amateur, with his smaller garden, would be more likely to have a piped supply if he

were living in town, and without the help of a permanent gardener, would find the hosepipe more useful.

The more usual watering method for an amateur on his own was the syringe ('of great value to the horticulturalist', according to Watts, who paid five shillings and sixpence for it, from George, at Camden Town). It was used to provide a jet of water, either on its own or mixed with soap or other chemicals. Similarly, sprayers were either fitted to the top of the tanks on water barrows or could be carried about with a small tank strapped on to the gardener's back. Although these were used predominantly for pesticides or weedkillers, it was also common to spray plants with soapy water to clean off the soot.

Moving things around the garden and gathering things, whether weeds or produce, requires containers and transporters. The wheelbarrow is the most useful form of transporter. Victorian ones were made of wood or wrought iron, and the wooden ones often had removable sides which could be built up to make a larger capacity. The advantage to the amateur gardener is that the wheelbarrow is designed for one person to use alone. Jane Loudon recommended them: 'One intended for the use of a lady ought to be made as light

A watering pot for seedlings. (Alfred Smee, *My Garden*, p. 61) (*Author's collection*)

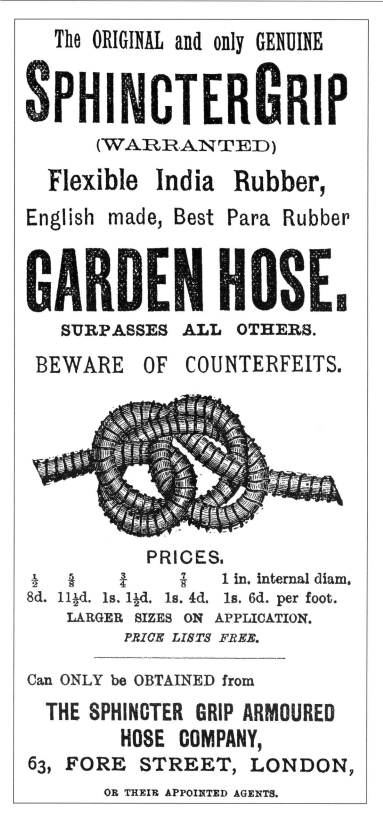

The Sphincter Grip hose made watering gardens easy in towns with a good piped water supply, and saved amateurs the trouble of carrying water pots long distances. (Advertisement from *Amateur Gardening*, 4 May 1889) (*Amateur Gardening*)

To get abundance of Horseradish, it is only necessary to drive an iron bar or stake into the ground, to the depth of eighteen inches or two feet, and to throw bits of a root to the bottom of the holes thus made, and fill them up with earth, and you will soon have a good crop, with long, thick, straight and tender roots; but when once you have it there, it will defy all your efforts to exterminate it.

J.H. Clark, *The Cottager's Kitchen Garden*, p. 121

as possible, and the handles curved so as to require very little stooping.'[17] Professional gardeners made frequent use of the hand-barrow for transporting potted plants or bedding plants to be put out. This could be a basket with carrying poles or like a bench with handles at each end, but either had to be handled by two people, making it less useful for the amateur working alone. For carrying around smaller quantities, baskets would be used, and the traditional trug. In the *Gardener's Assistant* the oval basket made of strips of wood is described as a 'truck-basket'.[18]

Plant pots in the nineteenth century were almost invariably made of fired clay. This made them more breakable and heavier than modern plastic pots, although once broken they were made use of as 'crocks' at the bottom of pots to cover the drainage hole. They came in a bewildering variety of shapes and sizes, partly dictated by use, but also by local custom where they were manufactured. Many writers commented that the sizing and numbers should be standardised, but it failed to happen. Pots were classified according to the number made in one casting, so a number one pot was the biggest and a number 80 (also known as a thumb) was the smallest. However, the actual measurement varied in different parts of the country. *Beeton's All about Gardening* commented: 'This nomenclature is always puzzling to the amateur, who never knows precisely what number he wants, and so can best express his wants by measuring the outside diameter of the sized pot he requires and mentioning the number of inches to the nurseryman, who is at once able to tell what his customer wants, being thoroughly conversant with numbers and their sizes.'[19]

There were pots for forcing rhubarb and sea kale, 'long toms' and shallow pans, square pots for ferns, small ones for alpines, and pots with holes in the sides for crocuses and orchids. How much this was a smokescreen put up by professional gardeners to safeguard the

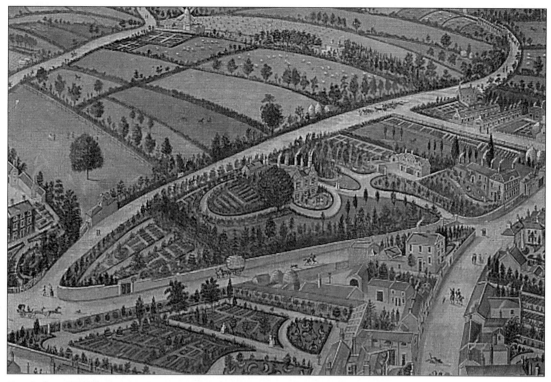

Details from William Brown's *Panorama of Louth, Lincolnshire*, painted in the 1840s from the church spire. The gardens are in the early Victorian 'gardenesque' style with symmetrical or 'tadpole' beds divided by paths or turf and enlivened with statuary and specimen trees. (*Louth Town Council*)

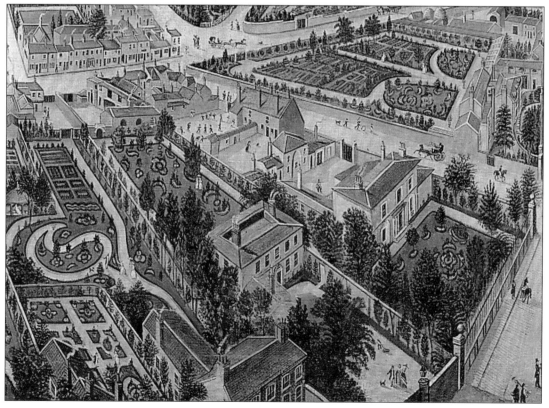

Painting by P. Dommersen (1874) of the Butters' garden at Parkfield, 49 King Edward Road, Hackney, featuring ribbon borders and pincushion beds in patriotic colours. *(By kind permission of George Butters Esq.)*

Painting by P. Dommersen (1874) of the Butters' family garden at 41 King Edward Road, Hackney, with the family seated on the terrace and maids chatting in the background. (*By kind permission of George Butters Esq.*)

Ornamental Foliage Plants, frontispiece to Volume III of *Cassell's Popular Gardening* (1892). By 1892 many amateurs would be growing such exotic plants in greenhouses and conservatories and they were available from specialist nurseries. (*Author's collection*)

H.J. Bidder's rock garden at St John's College, Oxford, built with his own hands in the late nineteenth century. A stone plaque commemorates his work. (*Author's photograph, taken by kind permission of the President and Fellows of St John's College, Oxford*)

An autochome of the interior of the greenhouse of the Gaviller family at 183 Lower Clapton Road, Hackney, in about 1910. Many amateurs would have to cram all their tender plants into one house under the same conditions, producing an exuberant display. (*Hackney Archives*)

An artist's impression of Shirley Hibberd's front garden at 6 Lordship Terrace, Stoke Newington. This coloured version appeared in the *Floral World* in 1870, but the original engraving appeared in *The Town Garden* in 1859. (*Hackney Archives*)

Portrait of Shirley Hibberd (1825–90), commissioned by the Royal Horticultural Society after his death as a memorial to him. (*Royal Horticultural Society, Lindley Library*)

Hand-coloured lithograph of florists' pelargoniums from the *Florist's Journal*, 1840. The aim was to produce a perfectly round flower. (*Author's collection*)

Shirley poppies were selectively bred by the Revd William Wilks in his garden in Shirley, near Croydon, Surrey, from wild poppies growing nearby. Wilks was one of many gardening clergymen who gave much of his time to furthering the interest of amateurs. (Colour plate from *Amateur Gardening*, 5 July 1890, by kind permission of *Amateur Gardening*)

Aubergines, or Egg Fruits, as *Thompson's Gardener's Assistant* calls them (vol. VI, new edn, opposite p. 441), were widely grown in the nineteenth century, and came in a variety of sizes and colours. The white ones were used as ornamental plants. (*Author's collection*)

Growing melons was within the capabilities of keen amateurs, and tomatoes were easier, although until late in the nineteenth century they were not thought worth eating. The melons here are Royal Jubilee (yellow) and Middlesex (green) and the tomatoes are Chiswick Peach (yellow) and Frogmore Selected (red). (*Thompson's Gardener's Assistant*, vol. V, new edn, opposite p. 321) (*Author's collection*)

'mystery' of their craft and how much a merchandising ploy on the part of the makers is difficult to know. Most amateurs probably used whatever pots they had handy unless they were wealthy and trying to impress others. Presumably if you could afford orchids, you could afford special pots to grow them in. Orchid pots had holes in the sides to allow aeration of the roots. *Beeton's All about Gardening* describes how amateurs could convert ordinary pots into orchid pots by drilling holes in them with a brace and bit. A soft pot should be used and during drilling the pot should be filled with a substance such as felt rags. The observation that 'this operation is perhaps somewhat difficult and tedious, but it can be done' appears just as the same thought has crossed the reader's mind. The piece also comments that anyway orchids can be grown in wire baskets or on bits of wood, so orchid pots are not strictly necessary at all.

However much an amateur may have wanted to save money, he was unlikely to make his own pots, but seed boxes and trays were different as they were made of wood. Shirley Hibberd, in *The Amateur's Flower Garden*,[20] explained how to make your own:

Amateurs could make their own seed boxes from waste boxes and cardboard. (Shirley Hibberd, *The Amateur's Flower Garden*, p. 58) (*Hackney Archives*)

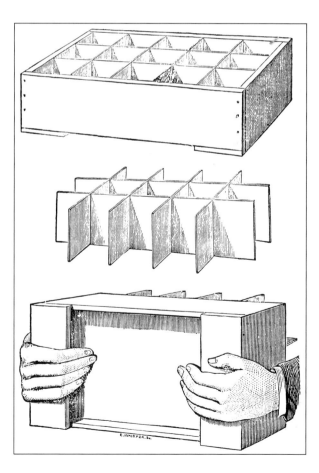

In the diagrams . . . the first represents the box ready for use. Each compartment is filled with suitable compost . . . The little seedlings or newly-struck cuttings are planted in the divisions singly, and at planting-out time each plant is presented to the hand in a single square block; there is no division necessary, not a fibre as fine as gossamer need be injured or disturbed. The sides and bottom of the box are wood; the divisions are thick cardboard. Suppose a fig box with the bottom knocked out. Now, across the bottom, at each end, nail a strip of wood. Next cut a piece of thin wood to make a loose bottom, the full size of the box, and drop it into the box to rest upon the two slips. Suppose the cardboard divisions next inserted, then, by turning the box on one side, and placing both hands against the loose bottom . . . a little pressure with the fingers would thrust out the loose bottom and the cardboard divisions. The two slips over which the hands pass remain firm, because nailed down to the bottom edge of the box. You have only to suppose the divisions filled with plants, and [the figure] would explain the process of 'turning out' not one from a pot, but fifteen from a box. The bottom being loose, yields to the pressure of the hands, just as the large crock in the bottom of a pot yields to the pressure of a finger if the pot is inverted. But the contrivance is not used in such a way at all. It is so engraved in order to convey an accurate idea of its construction. When full of plants it has but to be lifted on to a brick and the surrounding sides drop down and leave the soil divided by the pasteboard in the most handy position possible for operations. These pasteboards . . . are first cut to fit the box, and then are slit half-way so as to fit together firmly, the short cross pieces being slit from the side which forms their bottom edge, and the long pieces from the side that forms their top edge. As they fit together firmly, each division remains intact to the last. Then, to liberate each block for planting, the cross pieces are successively removed, which frees the outside blocks, and, lastly, the two long slips are removed and the remainder are ready. Those who suppose this to be a frail affair are mistaken. The cardboard will last two seasons, and the wood-work a lifetime.

Larger containers might be made of wood. The *Gardener's Assistant* suggests beer casks be obtained from a brewer for a few shillings, cut down and painted brown or green for use in a conservatory. Alfred Smee had such large pots in his garden that they had to be carried about by two men using chains attached to a pole on their shoulders.[21]

Enriching the soil

The Victorian amateur gardener had quite a lot to put up with when he tried to go it alone. He did not have the luxury of pre-packed 'multi-purpose' potting compost and had little hope of enriching his land with manure unless he obtained it fresh and had somewhere to stack it. Fertilisers were not supplied as clean granules in sealed packages with a handy measuring device; they usually had to be obtained as raw ingredients. Books written for professionals gave much information on nitrogen and soil structure and where to choose for a vegetable garden, but of course the amateur had little choice and often little space. Even *Beeton's All about Gardening*, specifically written for amateurs and well into the period where they were accepted as serious gardeners, gives a long list of what a successful flower grower needs always 'to hand':

1. All the leaves which can be got together, except those in the shrubberies, which should be dug in.

H.A. NEEDS (active 1880s–90s)

H.A. NEEDS lived in Catford, south London, and worked in Lombard Street in the City of London in a financial institution. He carried out most of his practical gardening in the early morning, or by the aid of a lamp in the evenings. In his greenhouse he grew ferns, bulbs, roses and a collection of zonal pelargoniums. Outside, in the summer, he specialised in tuberous begonias and won many prizes at the Lewisham and District Floral Society. His great speciality was the chrysanthemum, of which he grew about sixty plants in a span-roof greenhouse supplied by Peel and Sons and heated with a Loughborough boiler, which he thought superior to oil stoves. The boiler ran on sifted coke or 'breeze', which kept up a steady heat from morning until night. Mr Needs and some fellow enthusiasts established the Kent County Chrysanthemum Society in 1888, the first county society for chrysanthemums, of which he was secretary.

H.A. Needs (photographed from *Amateur Gardening*, 22 March 1890, by the author with permission of *Amateur Gardening*).

especially, might contribute to the soil around her, manure worth two millions a year, yet the Boards that manage these things are busying their wooden heads to throw it out to sea.'[25] In 1874 he referred to correspondence in *The Times* relating to the high death rate in London. He said that complaints about sewage farms were unjustified because the farms helped to purify town sewage which could then be used to produce cheap food.[26] When commenting on the drought in the summer of that year he explained how sewage was going into the Thames, polluting the air and being washed up in the heart of London with every tide: 'the waste of sewage is a national calamity . . . The people take it quietly, and die as cholera and typhus require them'.[27] He claimed that sewage farms failed because they were not under the management of competent people; the town council just muddled its way through.[28]

All the above fertilisers were organic, being derived from animal or plant substances, but there were inorganic fertilisers too, from minerals. Many were by-products of industry. Coal ash, peat ash, wood ash, charcoal, burned clay, gas waste, lime, chalk, gypsum, copralites, marl, magnesia and ammonia are all enumerated by

Thompson's Gardener's Assistant. From the 1840s artificial fertilisers began to be patented and advertised. These may have been more acceptable to the amateur gardener as they would come ready packaged, with rudimentary instructions. Of course there were few or no safety regulations to make sure people would not be harmed by using them. John Bennet Lawes was responsible for the introduction of superphosphate in 1843. Lawes inherited the family estate at Rothamsted in Hertfordshire at the age of eight, and after graduating from Oxford started experimenting in using different fertilisers on the land. He followed the theory that if bones were treated with sulphuric acid they produced a by-product called superphosphate, which was an effective manure. Lawes went one step beyond what had been done before and started manufacturing this fertiliser on a commercial scale and patented it before anyone else.[29]

Killing pests

If using fertilisers could be dangerous for the uninitiated amateur, it was nothing compared to using horticultural poisons. However, the Victorians were used to dangerous substances in both the medicine cupboard and the kitchen. Opium, in the form of laudanum, was the universal painkiller and anti-depressant, and arsenic was used as a cosmetic to whiten the skin, as well as a fly-killer. Such drugs and poisons could be bought in the high street from a chemist, with the only formality the obligation to sign a poisons book.

   Nicotine was one of the favourite, and efficient, insecticides. A whiff of smoke from a cigar was recommended as a convenient way to rid the greenhouse of greenfly. Tobacco was sometimes home-grown, for use in gardens rather than to smoke. Fumigators were used to diffuse the smoke. They could be made from an old flower

Slugs and snails should be sought for by lamplight. They can rarely be found during the day, although their trail is very conspicuous. About an hour after dusk they come out of their hiding places, and may then be caught as they are about to commence further mischief. Sometimes they evade detection. It is then advisable to put down little heaps of bran, saturated with vinegar, and examine them late at night.

                          J. Birkenhead, *Ferns and Fern Culture*, p. 126

pot or an old pail with a hole, into which was introduced a pair of bellows. Coal was lit in the bottom, then the tobacco paper (paper impregnated with tobacco water) was added and slowly blown with the bellows. In the palm house in Kew a small portable forge was used.[30] It was said to be harmless to the plants, but what about the gardener? To make tobacco water, one pound of tobacco was dissolved in four gallons of water and a quarter pound of soft soap. This was recommended to deter apple aphis. For caterpillars on cabbages, laurel water was used.[31] In the 1880s *Amateur Gardening* advertised Hughes' aphicide, not a substance, but a bottle with a tube coming out of the top, attached to a mouthpiece, so that the operator blew through it and the liquid inside was sprayed on the underneath of a plant. The liquid used was Fir Tree Oil, one or two tablespoons of which to a pint of water 'will answer for all insects on plants'.[32]

Flowers of sulphur was used as a fungicide in the same way; the bellows was known as a sulphurer. The universal fungicide in the later part of the nineteenth century was Bordeaux mixture (sulphate

Preparing to fumigate plants in a greenhouse with tobacco paper to control aphids. The plants were covered in a 'tent' to prevent the fumes escaping too quickly (and perhaps to help prevent the gardener from breathing in the 'noxious matter'. (From Shirley Hibberd, *The Amateur's Greenhouse and Conservatory*, p. 298) (*Author's collection*) of copper mixed with slaked lime), introduced from France, where it was used on the vines, and adopted everywhere against potato blight. An alternative was carbonate of copper mixed with ammonia or iron sulphate with sulphuric acid.[33] Enticing-sounding pesticides for fruit pests were Paris green and London purple, as well as Gishurst compound. Other useful substances which crop up in books and magazines are ashes, dog dung, soap suds, gas water, train oil, cart grease, hellebore powder, phosphorous paste to poison cockroaches, and boiled potatoes or roasted apples poisoned with arsenic for rats. None sound pleasant to use or store, and many would be hazardous.

Mechanical traps were also used for pests. A Mr Edwards of Birmingham invented an earwig trap, particularly designed for use in dahlia beds, which was recommended and derided in turn by the gardening magazines.[34] Lots of ideas were put forward for getting rid of cats, the gardener's greatest pest. Instructions for an 'anti-cat contrivance' were given by William Charles in *Amateur Gardening*. It was made of 'stout tin' cut into strips diagonally, so that each strip was pointed, and they were arranged in pairs, crossed and soldered on to a flat sheet of tin and the points bent up. The contrivance was then set in the soil wherever cats had been seen: 'No sooner does the cat visit the spot afterwards, and his feet come in contact with the sharp barb-like points, than he beats a hasty retreat. As to their cost that is a trifling matter. I generally get for a few pence the waste cuttings from a tinman's shop . . . I had no previous experience in tin work, and yet could make the contrivances well enough to suit my purpose.'[35] A kinder idea was suggested for getting rid of weasels: encourage owls to take up residence.[36]

The anti-cat contrivance was just one way of trying to combat one of the most reviled pests of the garden. (From *Amateur Gardening*, 17 August 1889, p. 183) (*Amateur Gardening*)

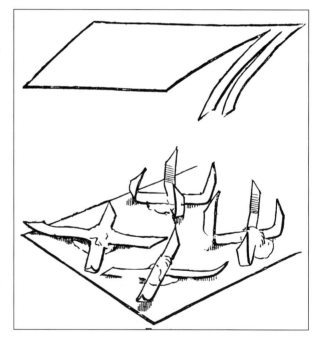

Glasshouses and protection

Glasshouses and conservatories eventually became cheap enough for the middle classes in terraced houses in the suburbs. But there was a great difference between glasshouses for professionals and those for amateurs, as the professionals would have a whole range of houses designed for different purposes.[37] The amateur usually had only one for growing everything, and it would not have provided much scope

Birkenhead's beetle trap was sold by John Birkenhead of Sale, Manchester, an enterprising nurseryman, who published his own book on fern growing. (From *Ferns and Fern Culture*) (*Author's collection*)

for real gardening. Conservatories may have housed some palms or ferns, and perhaps the popular aspidistra (known as the 'cast iron plant' as it was said to be indestructible). Glass was also used on a smaller scale in the form of frames and 'lights'. Patented protectors came in varying shapes and sizes, such as those invented by Rendle, and could be used in combination with wooden frames or turf pits to protect from cold or bring plants on more quickly in the spring.

WILLIAM EDGCUMBE RENDLE (1820–82)

WILLIAM RENDLE was the son of a nurseryman near Plymouth. He took over the business
at the age of eighteen, invented a greenhouse
heating system and expanded into a seed business.
He imported guano from Peru and distributed Lawes
Patent Superphosphates to the west country. In 1852,
when the railway reached Plymouth, he opened part of
the nursery as a public garden, holding concerts and flower
shows for the community. In the 1860s he sold up and moved
to London. He joined the board of several banks, the Langham
Hotel and the Westminster Brewery, but in 1867 lost his
wealth in the stock market crash. Nothing daunted, he invented
a portable glass covering for fruit and vegetables, which when
shown to the chairman of the Great Western Railway was
adapted to be used for the roof of Paddington Station and many
more stations throughout the country.

William Edgcumbe Rendle
(1820–82). (Engraving from
The Garden, 2 September 1882,
p. 217) (*Museum of Garden
History*)

Propagating and overwintering plants called for extra protection
in the form of glass or insulation. Hand-lights and bell glasses, also
known as cloches, were glass covers that could be used outside to
protect young or vulnerable plants. The hand-light was usually
square with a conical top, like a miniature greenhouse. It was made
of a metal framework filled in with panes of glass. The top could
sometimes be removed from the sides for ventilation. The bell glass
was one piece of glass, shaped like a bell, with a knob on the top

Rendle's patent protector was a
useful device for amateurs who
could not afford glasshouses
and wanted early crops like
strawberries. (*Floral World*,
1870, p. 20) (*Hackney Archives*)

which acted as a handle. The English style had a hollow knob which could be pierced for ventilation. The town gardener, usually an amateur, found glass covers to be a good way of protecting choice plants against soot.

Another way of protecting plants in the winter was to put them in a turf or preservative pit, which would be a cheap alternative for the amateur. The pit should be made on a south-facing slope, 12 inches deep and over an area 12 feet long by 5 feet wide. The pit is lined with planks, then turves are laid along all sides, providing walls 6 to 9 inches thick. The finished pit should be 3 feet deep at the back and 2 feet at the front. The pit would be covered with 'sashes', meaning a glass frame, like a window. If glass could not be afforded, oiled calico or tiffany could be used. The oiling mixture was made of linseed oil, sugar of lead and white resin, ground into a paste and heated in an iron pot. The inside of the turf could be 'dressed' with coal ashes to improve insulation and keep out slugs and snails.[38]

Sundries

Many of the 'sundries' the Victorian gardener needed would be recognised by us now, although not perhaps by younger gardeners. Before the advent of nylon and plastic, natural materials were used. Raffia was commonly used for tying up plants, and string was tarred to keep it from rotting. We are so used to white plastic labels that it seems incredible that books should devote pages to plant labelling. The simplest label was pine wood, painted white and inscribed with black lead or red chalk. Permanent labels for trees could be made of lead, punched with letters, which were to be filled with white lead, and a hole should be made for attaching it to the tree with wire.[39]

Tiles came in all varieties for edging paths, such as those made by Ransome's from 'patent siliceous stone',[40] and some that were triangular-shaped to provide a firm retaining wall.[41] Shirley Hibberd improvised in providing plant supports:

> Near London, where people have to pay a shilling a bundle for pea-sticks, and often have to submit to have them carried through the house, and stored in a corner that is already choked up with brooms and trellis-poles, and all sorts of similar roomy lumber, it is sometimes better to trust to the greengrocer for peas that are scarcely eatable, than incur the bother of raising a crop at home. We have found a remedy for this nuisance in the wire hurdles made by Mr T. P. Hawkins of 27, Dale End, Birmingham. These hurdles are very

cheap, and with proper use, will last a lifetime. When done with for
the season, they can be packed together into a small compass, and be
stowed away next the wall in any shed or outhouse, ready for use at a
moment's notice. In a flower garden they are just the thing on which
to train sweet peas, or a fence of roses or chrysanthemums, for they are
almost invisible, are very firm, and admit of being covered with an
even growth of foliage and flowers.[42]

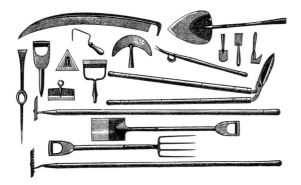

CHAPTER SIX

Societies, Shows and Competitions

In a time before television and glossy magazines were available it was not easy to learn about new plants unless one could see them 'in the flesh'. Apart from visiting nurseries and public parks, the best way for a Victorian amateur gardener to see flowers was to go to a flower show, where the best plants would be, and in perfect condition. Flower shows were one of the spectacles of the Victorian age. In modern times, we often forget the impact of seeing something 'live', whether it is music or drama, sport, wild animals or foreign places. Everything is brought into our living rooms in full colour and we can be fooled into thinking that we have actually experienced the event or place ourselves. The Victorians had to go out and find their entertainment. Visiting a flower show was both a social and an educational occasion as well as a pleasure. One of the biggest impacts on entering the marquee or the hall was the overpowering smell from the fresh flowers on display. In the nineteenth century there would have been the added impact, for many people, of the blaze of light from gas or even the new electricity, for those more used to the dim glow of firelight and candles.

Florists' societies' shows were mainly of interest to the members of the society themselves; when they were still connected with florists' feasts they would probably not have been open to visitors. Each society held shows at different times of the year for the flowers in season, and sometimes they included fruit as well. The Aylesbury Florist and Horticultural Society held the following shows in 1829: [1]

20th April: Auriculas, Polyanthuses, Cucumbers and Apples;
18th May: Tulips and Anemones;
29th June: Ranunculuses, Pinks and Strawberries;
3rd August: Carnations, Picotees, Melons, Currants, Gooseberries and Raspberries; and
5th October: Apples.

When Loudon started the *Gardener's Magazine* in 1826 he said that he had intended to give accounts of all the principal florists' shows in

London and name all the flowers for which prizes were awarded, but he soon realised that it would occupy more space than he could spare, so had to restrict his listings to the main ones. Nevertheless, in his first issue he listed six auricula shows and over twenty tulip beds. The shows also included prizes for potatoes, a pineapple, geraniums, greenhouse plants and broccoli. The Hampton tulip bed was said to be 'one of the most select in the neighbourhood', with a feast day and many men of leisure there, including the Duke of Clarence. Two women florists were also mentioned (at Islington and Lancaster).[2] Loudon, however, was a little scathing about florists' flowers. He visited Mr Groom's florists' garden in Walworth, commenting that floriculture was not as fashionable as it had been but that his main purpose in publicising it was 'in the hope of extending this department among gentlemen's gardeners, by whom, we think, florists' flowers are at present too much neglected'. He continued to report shows throughout the 1830s, from which it can be seen that although traditional florists' shows thrived, they included fruit such as grapes and strawberries, as well as greenhouse plants, dahlias, roses and shrubs. Some featured 'georginas', which were a type of dahlia. There were also general horticultural shows and specialist melon feasts and gooseberry shows.

Like allotments, florists' societies were approved of by many people for their moral tone, in an age when the alternatives to flower growing were cock-fighting and bear-baiting. In 1830 Loudon quoted an extract from the *Stockport Advertiser* publicising a new floral and horticultural society: 'Cultivation of fruits and flowers ought to be encouraged as recreation. It is conducive to health, attaching men to their homes, preventing a life of dissipation: for every rank of person, from humble cottager with his favourite auriculas and polyanthuses, to a lady of fashion with tender exotics; botanists who look closer at plants cannot fail to see the work of the Creator; of all luxurious indulgences, that of the cultivation of flowers is the most innocent.'[3]

General horticultural societies, like other aspects of nineteenth-century life, were defined or divided by social class. Local associations were set up in country towns and villages to encourage amateur gardening, and were usually patronised by the dominant estate owner or gentry. Shows helped to uphold the identity of a town or village, providing something for the inhabitants to be proud of, in the same way that the municipal parks did in cities. The Horticultural Society for Stamford Hill (now part of Hackney in north-east London, but at the time a self-contained suburb) was instituted in 1833: 'This society, which is strictly confined to the Gentry of the vicinity, numbers upwards of 300 of the most influential families among its supporters. Members are elected by ballot, on introduction of a member of the council. The Exhibitions, of which there are three in the course of each season, are held in the months of May, June and July under tents, erected in the grounds of Arthur Craven esq. or Josiah Wilson esq. A full military band attends each show.'[4] A report in the *Gardeners' Chronicle* in 1846 recorded that its first exhibition of the year attracted a thousand visitors.[5] Generally, however, the *Gardeners' Chronicle* did not mention any florists' shows, nor many local horticultural societies, only the Horticultural Society itself, or the other learned societies. In a letter to the paper in the issue of 6 August 1842, 'a constant reader' suggested that they give a list of all the forthcoming shows every week as the *Horticultural Journal* had done, but the editor complained that this could only happen if the secretaries of the societies sent details to him. This they did not seem to do.

Scarecrows are generally so evidently a burlesque on anything real, that birds take pleasure in sitting upon them. Small windmills with rattles upon them, are often very effective; pieces of glass may be hung up in such a way that they will swing and scintillate with the sunlight, and even rattle if two pieces are tied in proximity . . . Incessant war should be waged against the sparrow, the worst of all feathered pests.

Thompson's Gardener's Assistant, vol. 1, p. 75

The new-style societies that took the place of the traditional florists' societies tended to be dominated by professional nurserymen who were competing in exhibitions all over the country. It was the subject of complaint by many people who regretted the changes that were coming about. The view of the *Midland Florist* in 1847 was: 'It cannot have escaped the notice of florists generally, that their community does not contain so many purely amateur exhibitors as it formerly did; and this must be a matter of regret to all, and lead them to the inference that the pleasures in connection with exhibitions have an alloy which makes their pursuit questionable, if not possibly objectionable.'[6] The writer went on to state that in his opinion the subscriptions were too low and the shows were not attracting enough good competitors as it was not worth their while to enter for the prizes on offer. What he seemed to be saying was that the best nurserymen were not attending and therefore only the

inferior ones appeared. The following year there was a discussion about agreeing codes of conduct among exhibitors to prevent dishonesty, particularly in relation to suspicions that plants were not grown by the exhibitors themselves, to which some contributors replied that a good society would not need such rules.[7]

In 1852 the *Midland Florist* gave a list of Floral Exhibitions for the year throughout the country, which consisted of thirty-seven shows, comprising thirteen tulip shows, six carnation and picotee shows, six pink shows, three gooseberry shows, one auricula show and eight general societies or those concentrating on more than one flower. These ranged across the whole country and, although they may not have been exhaustive, they show that the traditional florists' societies mainly persisted in the north and midlands. The thirteen tulip shows are a far cry, however, from the twenty-two mentioned by Loudon in the London area alone in 1826.[8] Times had changed, and as usual, new trends started in London.

An example of a society thriving a little later in the century was the Wantage Horticultural Society in Oxfordshire, run by local

Prizes at flower shows were often sponsored by seed companies, such as Suttons. Here flowers and vegetables have been judged in a local flower show and are awaiting the arrival of the public. (*Museum of Garden History*)

tradesmen with the object of promoting knowledge of and interest in horticulture and encouraging cottagers in the culture of their gardens.[9] The members paid a minimum of five shillings annual subscription. This allowed entry to the show by a member and one other person. A larger subscription entitled a member to bring up to four people. To enter a specimen or collection of produce for a prize at the show cost sixpence for each item. However, cottagers could pay one fee of sixpence for all their entries in the cottagers' classes. These would be exhibited on separate tables, and cottagers could only exhibit by invitation of a subscriber. Professional gardeners were excluded from cottagers' classes, and the classes were limited to those paying not more than seven pounds per year for their cottage and garden. Shows were open to members of the public paying for tickets, as well as subscribers and their guests. The cottager exhibitors were allowed in only for the last hour of the show by producing special tickets.

A similar local society, the Hartwell and Stone Horticultural Society, was founded in 1829 and celebrated its twenty-fifth anniversary on 31 July 1854 with a dinner and gooseberry show. The gooseberries were weighed 'promptly' at one o'clock, to be followed by the dinner at two. Prizes, ranging from twenty shillings to two shillings and sixpence, were given for the four heaviest berries in each of the categories, red, green, yellow, white and named varieties, as well as for the 'best sorts'. Further prizes were given to cottagers for collections of vegetables, fruit, currants, wild flowers and honey. The prizes included a clock, knives and forks and a shoulder of mutton. In addition, a prize of ten shillings was awarded to the best cottager's garden.[10]

These examples show that upper- and middle-class patronage played its part in horticultural societies as it did in the allotment movement. At Stamford Hill the gentry provided the site for the show; at Wantage cottagers were only allowed in by invitation from a member of the society. At many shows local gentry or aristocrats provided prizes and may have attended to present them. They gave an air of respectability and approval to the proceedings, helping to make gardening an acceptable pastime for all classes. Organisers took trouble to encourage attendance by as wide a group of flower fanciers as possible. A notice in the *Gardeners' Chronicle* in 1859 announced the thirteenth annual exhibition of the Stoke Newington Chrysanthemum Society on Monday and Tuesday, 7 and 8 November, the prizes including six silver cups. The doors opened at 12 o'clock on the first day (to allow for judging beforehand) and 9 o'clock on the second. Admission was a shilling on Monday and sixpence on Tuesday, but schools were admitted free of charge by applying to the secretary. Omnibuses were said to have run to and from The Flower Pot, Bishopsgate, every five minutes.[11]

As horticultural societies expanded and florists' societies became dominated by nurserymen, shows became of greater interest to the general public. By the mid-century flowers were an interesting subject in themselves, and the Victorian love of socialising and greater ease of travel made a day or evening out at a flower show a pleasurable prospect. Paxton and the Crystal Palace Company were astute enough to instigate flower shows as one of the attractions at Sydenham when the Crystal Palace was rebuilt. For several years after the opening in 1856 they held three shows a year with over £2,350 in prize money,[12] classes for amateurs and nurserymen being separate. By 1860, however, the company only held one show a year, the amateurs and nurserymen showing together and only £531 in prize money,[13] but the *Gardeners' Chronicle* judged it 'a spectacular show': 'never before perhaps were so many plants brought together on one occasion as there was on this'.[14] The displays included pelargoniums and roses in pots, Indian azaleas, fruit, stove and greenhouse plants, orchids, cape heaths, fine-foliaged plants and calceolarias.

Instead of running the show itself, the Crystal Palace Company then allowed other horticultural societies to hold their own shows at the palace. In 1860 there was the National Rose Show (attended by over sixteen thousand people), the National Hollyhock Show, the Dahlia and Fruit Show and a three-day Amateur Chrysanthemum Show. There was obviously money to be made in bringing these societies in and letting them do the work of organisation, but not everyone agreed it was a good idea. The *Floral World* reported that the Crystal Palace shows did not encourage small growers and that the shows lacked the character of local shows.[15] This was echoed by correspondence from readers in the *Gardeners' Chronicle*, who said that although the show was well arranged and laid out, the vastness of the surroundings and their ornate decoration dwarfed the plants, however spectacular. They did not believe the shows would ever be a success horticulturally. The readers also criticised the Botanical Society's show in Regent's Park for having the tents spread out at random, rather than in an orderly fashion, and for the plant displays being too gaudy and exuberant.[16] It seems that the more ornate and magnificent the displays were to attract the general public, the less the horticultural experts liked them.

There still remained the problem of the professional versus the amateur. As in sport, where the two types of player were kept separate, so in gardening; as it developed in popularity and competitions increased, a complicated structure of rules developed to prevent different classes from competing against each other. In the example of the Wantage show, the professionals were kept out of the cottagers' classes. There were two classes of professional gardeners who might be involved: gentlemen's gardeners who wanted to compete as amateurs when growing their own plants in their spare time, and florists, who may have been self-taught, but who earned some money, if not their total income, from selling plants. There was further controversy in flower shows concerning people competing as amateurs but employing gardeners to produce the plants. The *Gardener's Weekly Magazine* commented:

> By the term Amateur Gardener is commonly understood one who, having a fondness for gardening (flowers principally), cultivates them either solely by himself, or at least with small help from others, and not as a means of obtaining his livelihood. We are aware that it is frequently the case to allow gentlemen such as are referred to by our friend to compete in the Amateurs' class – but would, in such case, prefer to see the professional gardener employed by them receive the honour and the credit that is fairly his due, by the plants being regularly entered in his name.[17]

As gardening developed in towns, societies were formed which held shows similar to those held in the country. The *Floral World* praised the show of the Tower Hamlets Floricultural Society, held in 1860 at the Eagle Tavern, Mile End, because it was mainly patronised by local amateurs: 'A result far preferable to the crowding of the tables with nursery stock, intended much more to advertise trading firms than to promote a genuine love of horticulture.'[18] The Tower Hamlets Society flourished between 1860 and 1875.[19] It began as a chrysanthemum society and held a large show and several smaller shows throughout the year, as well as an annual dinner in the spirit of the old florists' feasts. Fuchsias, dahlias, asters and verbenas were subjects of competition in the summer. Plants were also displayed by local growers as part of the decoration, and no doubt helped to bring in the crowds. They might be exotics, such as ferns and lilies, or impressive curiosities, such as a monster marrow weighing over thirteen pounds. One of the most frequent judges at the shows was George Glenny, and another, an expert in chrysanthemums, was Samuel Broome (1806–70), head gardener of the Inner Temple Gardens. The members of the society were referred to as 'working men' but also seemed to be professional gardeners competing in a private capacity with their own plants.

The Tower Hamlets Society had started as a chrysanthemum society and branched out, but the Stoke Newington Chrysanthemum Society in north-east London remained a specialist

society throughout its existence.[20] The chrysanthemum was regarded as a peculiarly 'metropolitan' flower, having been introduced to Britain in 1790, and appealing to growers in London and other cities. The society was started in a small way by a group of friends, professional gardeners and amateurs who met in a local pub, whose landlord was also an amateur grower. Soon there were regular meetings held throughout the year when members took it in turns to give talks on cultivation, and an annual dinner was held. The exhibitions started to be held in local halls; money prizes and

Chrysanthemums became the most popular flowers to be grown for competitions in the last part of the nineteenth century, when the metropolitan societies replaced traditional florists' societies as the place to see prize specimens. (*Museum of Garden History*)

ROBERT JAMES (*c.* 1801–70)

ROBERT JAMES was landlord of the Rochester Castle, in Stoke Newington, north-east London, where the Stoke Newington Chrysanthemum Society was started in 1846. He was born in Downhampton, Gloucestershire, and was described in the *Gardener's Magazine* in 1871 as 'a big handsome man, of generous rosy face . . . a first-rate host, an enthusiastic and able florist'. He grew twenty-five sorts of chrysanthemums himself. The first competition for twelve blooms was held in an upstairs room; the following year it was held in the skittle ground at the back of the pub, and specimen plants as well as cut flowers were displayed. After an acrimonious split in 1858, when two societies were formed, and a reunion in 1862, the society became a national one in 1884. Robert James was treasurer of the society for many years and when he died on the eve of the annual show in 1870, the event was cancelled.

some trophies were presented and growers began to come from all over London and the south of England. By the 1870s interest began to wane as there were so many other societies, but the audiences returned when fruit and foliage plants were introduced to the shows, which created a greater spectacle. By the 1880s the Stoke Newington Society was the most important chrysanthemum society in Britain, with seven hundred members and an income of £850 per year. It resolved to name itself the National Chrysanthemum Society, following other societies such as the National Rose Society, which had been created in 1876. Shirley Hibberd, who had been a member of the society in the 1860s, went so far as to say that chrysanthemum shows held on dark November evenings actually lowered the suicide rate, as they cheered people up so much: 'Chrysanthemum growing became a metropolitan floral fashion – perhaps a mania, and a very good one, for it appears that from the date of the dethronement of Louis Philippe [1848], and the first multiplication of chrysanthemum societies, November suicides began to decrease in number, so that now every well-intentioned city, town, and village has its annual show, the month of November is found to be less characterised by suicides than any month of the year, because, of course, it is the most cheerful month in all the year.'[21] This may have been something of an exaggeration, but it illustrates the dramatic impact of the golden flowers with their characteristic scent on a foggy November evening.

EDWARD SANDERSON (active 1840s–80s)

EDWARD SANDERSON was president of the National Chrysanthemum Society for twenty-five years, having started as a member of the original Stoke Newington society in 1848. He first grew plants outside his home in Dalston, east London, bringing them inside to flower on a drawing-room table. As his business affairs prospered, he moved house, always keeping his plants growing under improvised structures, and constantly winning prizes. He was also a founder member of the Hackney Horticultural Society and a star player in the Middlesex Amateur Racquet Club. At his home in Harlesden Park, Willesden, in the 1880s he grew 160 plants in a moderate-sized greenhouse, consisting of forty-six varieties of the 'incurved' sort. They were all grown from cuttings in a mixture of topsoil and cow dung and watered with 'pure water'.

Edward Sanderson. (Engraving from *The Gardening World*, 15 November 1884, p. 169) (*Museum of Garden History*)

Shirley Hibberd was also instrumental in starting the Guildhall Flower Show, held at the Guildhall in the City of London, and continuing until the end of the twentieth century. He wrote in the *Gardener's Magazine* in 1890 that November 1865 marked the first occasion that chrysanthemums were the main exhibit in a big London flower show:

On my own share in the business I say nothing, save that, although the task was tremendous, all the workers worked with such a will that probably all enjoyed it as I did . . . The life and soul of the concern was Mr James Crute. With Mr Crute and myself rested the whole of the negotiations with the Lord Mayor, the Common Council, the Guildhall officials, and all the parties concerned with the decoration of the Guildhall for the mayoralty banquet . . . Mr Forsyth, of the Brunswick Nursery, Stoke Newington, exhibited an enormous collection of superbly grown chrysanthemums; Mr George, of Stamford Hill, a group unequalled amongst all the competitors of the season in size, finish, and splendour of bloom. Mr Crute, of Tufnell Park, not only made a gorgeous bank of 'long-rod' chrysanthemums, but in the centre of the hall constructed a beautiful flower bed. This was made on a convex mound of grass mowings, enclosed in a stone moulding supplied by Rosher and Co. and encircled without by a gravel path. The bed had for a centrepiece a noble fern, then a broad circle of chrysanthemums, trained down to fit the regular convex surface of the bed, next a circle of Iresines, next a circle of *Centaurea plumose*, and outside of all a lovely margin of white and crimson Chinese primulas.[22]

The trend to form national societies for all popular plants fitted conveniently with the policy of the Royal Horticultural Society, which was gradually becoming accepted as a national society with provincial branches, and whose rules governed the shows of affiliated societies. The society's financial problems came to a head in the 1850s and 1860s and it was forced to sell its herbarium, premises and, eventually, its library. The difficulties sprang from disagreement among members as to where subscriptions should come from and who should be allowed to visit the gardens and attend the shows. Once again, the issue was the differences of opinion over accepting the lower classes and the professionals, and whether they could be regarded as respectable gardeners.

New administration and the patronage of the Prince Consort, leading to a royal charter in 1861, helped the society's fortunes and by the 1860s it was replanning its gardens in both Chiswick and Kensington and organising conferences for delegates from abroad as well as from Britain. Royal patronage clearly helped the

REVD WILLIAM WILKS (1843–1923)

WILLIAM WILKS was secretary of the Royal Horticultural Society for over twenty-five years, working in conjunction with the president Trevor Lawrence, son of Louisa Lawrence, whose garden Loudon so admired in the 1830s. Wilks was vicar of Shirley, near Croydon in Surrey, from 1879 to 1912, where he worked to improve the village amenities and the church. In the garden there he discovered a wild poppy with a white edge to the scarlet petals. From the seeds he started to breed a new strain of poppy, known as Shirley poppies, over a period of ten years, gradually eliminating the black at the centre of the flower and producing a white centre with golden stamens and flowers ranging from white through all shades of pink to deep scarlet. He also bred a Shirley strain of foxgloves, and a cooking apple is named after him.

Horticultural Society in encouraging gardening as a leisure activity among all classes. Prince Albert's involvement showed that gardening counted among the other arts that the prince was interested in and practised himself. It was not just royal patronage that helped the RHS, but also the respectability conferred by several clergymen, many of whom proved to be efficient organisers. The Revd William Wilks (1843–1923) was a Fellow of the society from 1866 and in 1888 became the honorary secretary, in which position he remained for over twenty-five years. Other clergymen played important parts in establishing and running national societies, like Samuel Reynolds Hole and H.H. D'Ombrain in the National Rose Society. Many also took part in running allotment societies and window gardening for cottagers. The Revd T.H. Parkes started the idea of a flower show for the poor of London in 1860, when he was a curate in Bloomsbury. The *Illustrated London News* featured the fourth annual show on 21 July 1866. Four hundred and sixty plants were exhibited by three hundred exhibitors in a marquee 100 feet long. Similar shows were organised by the East London Window Gardening Society and the

The Bloomsbury Flower Show in Russell Square, London, became an annual event for the poorer inhabitants of the parish. In 1864, 400 people competed with flowers grown on window sills and there were also prizes for the tidiest rooms. (Engraving from *The Illustrated London News*, 23 July 1864, p. 84) (*The Bodleian Library, University of Oxford*)

Society for Promoting Window Gardening among the Working Classes, which organised the Westminster Flower Show in 1874 and 1875.[23]

By the later part of the nineteenth century magazines were using shows for their own publicity. *Amateur Gardening* gave away prizes of bound volumes of its magazines at flower shows. At Buxted in 1889, it presented a bound volume for the best collection of potatoes and took the opportunity to emphasise the virtues of gardening:

> It was won by a hardworking, industrious painter named J. Hollobon, who, until last year, had taken but little interest in gardening. He strove hard to win the prize, and this stimulated him not only to produce a first-class crop of potatoes, but to cultivate other vegetables as well to such a high state of perfection that he was able to gain a few pounds as prizes for these also. With the money thus creditably earned he was able to provide himself and his family – a large one – with good boots and some useful articles of clothing, and he, moreover, had a better and greater supply of vegetables and fruit in his garden for the purposes of food.[24]

PART THREE

Creating the Garden

CHAPTER SEVEN

The Front Garden

Victorian suburban and town houses were usually terraced or semi-detached, and their gardens had well-defined 'front' and 'back' sections which could be separately designed. The front was on view to the world, which restricted its use as a leisure space for the family, unless a tall hedge was allowed to grow. The design was intended to soften and individualise the front of the house but at the same time to show that the inhabitants were well-behaved, clean and tidy people who could keep up to the highest standards in the neighbourhood. Therefore the appearance was usually formal and predictable, as well as easy to manage.

H.J. Dyos, in his study of Camberwell, a south London suburb, surmised that neighbours could judge a home by the appearance of the front garden.[1] He compared the use of aspidistras behind lace curtains in the windows in one situation to clumps of shrubs and stone urns set among lawns and gravel drives in another to show that there were different levels of decoration and taste. However, Shirley Hibberd, who lived in the suburbs in the 1850s, had slightly different ideas as to how a front garden should be arranged:

The front of the house seldom has such a range of garden as the back, and as a south or south-west aspect for a garden is preferred, the front usually faces the north or north-east. Here is just the place for some bold masses of evergreens, with a few deciduous trees on the border next the footway. A breadth of lawn, with a bold walk or drive to the house, may be graceful in themselves, but in front of portico, steps, and windows, there is a thin look about it unless shrubs be added. A central compartment of the lawn is usually allotted to hollies, laurustinus, aucuba japonica, tree box, rhododendron, common and Portugal laurel, snow-berry, and such like shrubby-growing evergreens, and these look rich when they get to their full size, and well massed together. The borders, if there are any, may be edged with brick makers' 'burrs', or, still better, Hogg's tiles, or if a live edging be preferred, common ivy is just the thing. The borders may also be of shrubs, for this front court should present a *fullness* of character, to give the house a substantial aspect, but all must be as trim as the Corporal's boots; no ugly branches straggling out of the line, no rampant growth to shut out light and suggest that you can't afford to keep a gardener. You need not lavish much upon the forecourt, but what you have must be in first-rate order.[2]

So the garden should be generous in its planting, but restrained, and kept tidy so as to suggest that you can afford proper help in the garden. He goes on to emphasise the quality of the planting:

Then for the border next the public path what can be better than limes, or a pair of the rose-coloured horse chestnut, with a mixture of almond, lilac, laburnum, lady birch, and acacia, or even apple and pear, all planted out in order, and with a facing of hardy rhododendrons on the side next the house to cheer the eye from the windows with their lovely purple blushes in June and July. The Irish yew and evergreen cypress look well in single plants or pairs on a trim lawn, but all these are better suited for planting apart from clumps and borders, either on grass or gravel, and as they are somewhat gloomy, though very substantial and respectable, must not be chosen without at least some consideration.[3]

The exuberance, however, should always be toned down, though there was no harm in sharing an abundance of flowers if the conditions were right:

In a north or east aspect such a mode of planting a forecourt would afford shelter for flowers, which, of course, should be grown on those borders which were quite within view of the windows. The flowers most suitable for this purpose are the old fashioned perennials, with a few bedded greenhouse plants, such as geraniums, fuchsias, calceolarias, and myrtles, but high-class flowers or glowing masses of contrasted colours are, in my opinion, quite out of place here, as much so as wire arches and rustic baskets would be. Architectural embellishments are admissible, but they should be sparingly used, for what gives perfect grace and luxuriance to the private grounds has an air of ostentation when exposed to the daily gaze of an 'admiring public'. Spring flowers are unquestionably as much for the joy of the wayfarer as for the proprietor of the house. The invalid who creeps out in spring on the first day that the weathercock indicates a change to a warm quarter, the artizan plodding to work at daybreak or returning fatigued at dusk, nay even the overworked postman and newsboy hurrying to your gate with glad or sad tidings, are entitled to a little of the cheerfulness which you can give them by displaying some of those precious snowdrops, crocuses, hyacinths, and tulips that are never out of place anywhere.[4]

Hibberd's own front garden in Stoke Newington appeared in the revised edition of *The Town Garden* in 1859. It shows a tidy forecourt with a large, formally planted 'jardinet' made of 'Ransome's patent siliceous stone – a material equal in appearance to the finest sandstone'. This was matched by the white edging tiles, said to have the appearance of stone moulding, and kept bright with the occasional washing with 'mason's dust' (no doubt to keep off the soot). The jardinet was first planted with blue and scarlet bedding plants, such as geraniums and lobelias. Later Hibberd seemed to favour bulbs and ferns. He used the container for his experiments with 'the plunging system' of perennials as an alternative to bedding plants. He recommended it as particularly suited to amateurs of modest means who could not afford to grow their own bedding plants, or buy them in huge quantities. He advised them to use shrubs or perennial plants in pots which could be 'plunged' into a bed of coconut waste (coir), still in their pots. Then, as they faded, another set of plants could be brought out to replace them. A good display could thereby be achieved all the year round, berried evergreens replacing flowering plants in the winter. Density of the planting was one of the system's main features.[5]

Plans for front gardens are generally uniform for houses in the same group or terrace. The usual layout consists of gravel paths and shrubbery. *Amateur Gardening* in 1888 was strict on what should be used: 'The shrubs used ought not to be flowering ones, or, at any rate, if they are, not choice kinds, as these are tempting to boys and others to often sadly disfigure them by stealing the blooms. Aucubas, hollies, conifers, box, laurel, mahonias or euonymus, that have nice foliage would perhaps be as suitable as anything.'[6] Thus the same traditions carried on: safe, but dull. One wonders who the 'others' were who stole choice flowers. *Amateur Gardening* also went on to explain the importance of hiding the tradesmen's entrance with shrubs and the inevitable privet hedge, and the space thereby hidden away could conveniently be used for storing fuel and 'soils', which presumably means ingredients for compost.

Cassell's Popular Gardening, published in about 1892, went into such detail about how to design and plant even the smallest front garden that it must be assumed it expected the readers to be totally deficient in experience. How different from the attitude of writers earlier in the century! The reasons not to use grass in a small space are spelt out at excruciating length:

> It would not be advisable to lay any of it down in grass, as it would of necessity be so small a piece that when requiring to be mown, no machine, if ever so small, could be worked with any comfort. The use

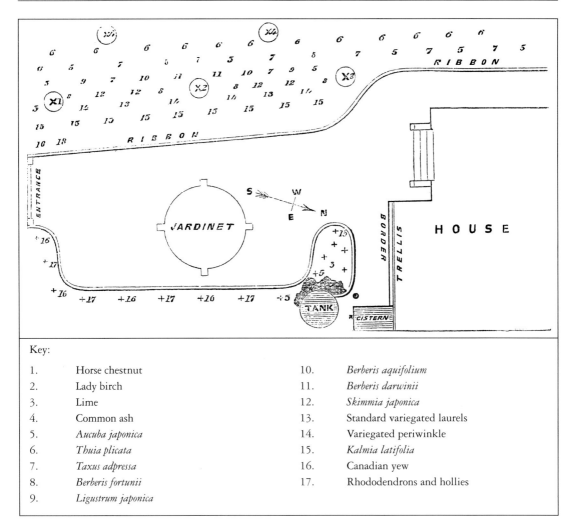

Key:

1.	Horse chestnut	10.	*Berberis aquifolium*
2.	Lady birch	11.	*Berberis darwinii*
3.	Lime	12.	*Skimmia japonica*
4.	Common ash	13.	Standard variegated laurels
5.	*Aucuba japonica*	14.	Variegated periwinkle
6.	*Thuia plicata*	15.	*Kalmia latifolia*
7.	*Taxus adpressa*	16.	Canadian yew
8.	*Berberis fortunii*	17.	Rhododendrons and hollies
9.	*Ligustrum japonica*		

Shirley Hibberd's planting plan for his front garden at 6 Lordship Terrace, Stoke Newington. (*The Town Garden*, 2nd edn) (*Hackney Archives*)

of the scythe requiring some practice to manipulate it in a skilful manner, almost forbids the use of that implement, and recourse would have to be had to garden shears, which would be found rather back-aching work to those who are not accustomed to the use of such tools. There is a more modern invention for small pieces of grass, after the pattern of horse-clipping machines, but of this we cannot speak from experience.[7]

The alternative to grass provided an extremely low-maintenance garden consisting of shrubs, hardy ferns and gravel. Dwarf box hedging was mooted, but it was decided that edging tiles were better in polluted atmospheres, and the best sort to use were 'blue cable

pattern', particularly if of terracotta ware, which would withstand frost and would be found the cheapest option 'in the long run'. Box was also rejected on the ground that it harboured slugs and snails. An alternative to flower or shrub beds was said to be a 'vase' as a central arrangement, but this should only be considered if it were convenient to water it frequently. The planting was similar to that suggested by Shirley Hibberd with his jardinet: changing it with the seasons and surrounding the main plants with creepers at the edges.

A further caution was to avoid any plants of 'robust growth', as they would need frequent pruning, 'unless used as a boundary line to the next garden', when apparently you could let them grow as wild as you liked. However, as to boundary walls at the front of terraced houses, the writer James Hudson was of the opinion that it would be far better to do away with them, as then the garden could be dealt with as a whole, but he felt that it was impracticable 'in the present state of society and customs'.

Mrs C.W. Earle had no pretensions and had no time for people who did. Her comments on front gardens were typically down to earth and practical:

> Many of the houses built round the neighbourhood of London in the early part of the century were built close to the road, and have a ludicrous and pompous approach of a drive passing the front door, with two gates – one for entrance and one for exit. Surely this is a great

Shirley Hibberd's front garden featured a 'jardinet', which would be filled with seasonal plants in pots, 'plunged' into coir fibre, which became one of the sights of the neighbourhood. (Frontispiece from *The Town Garden*, 2nd edn) (*Hackney Archives*) waste of ground with no proportionate advantage. Most places of this kind would certainly be improved if the two gates were blocked up, the drive done away with, and a straight paved or bricked path made from the door to the road, with a shelter of wood, or even of corrugated iron, painted to match the house, and creepers planted along the posts that support it. The space on either side of this path could be planted with low-growing shrubs, or in some instances laid with turf.[8]

For some people the front garden was the only garden, and for others there was not even that. The *Floral World* in 1871 gave advice on 'Gardening without a garden' for those who only had balconies, 'areas' or 'flats'. An 'area' is the space in front of a basement at the bottom of the outer steps leading down from the front of the house. Presumably a 'flat' was a flat roof accessible from a window higher up. W.D. Prior, who wrote the piece, assumes that the people doing this type of gardening would be cooks or other servants, who would not have had the chance to use the main garden and had to make do with the space they had: 'The gratification of this addition to urban pleasures, will be duly appreciated by all who are capable of estimating the difference between a look-out upon bright foliage and flowers, or upon stucco fronts and brick walls; and of comparing the fragrance wafted through windows so adorned, with the natural whiff of the streets.'[9] He advised that planting in these situations would have to take place in containers, though plants could be trained up the house on wires. The plants would probably have to be bought from nurseries as the person with such limited space would not be able to grow them himself. Pots could be bought, of all dimensions and materials, but should not be too ornate: 'They require considerable taste and judgment to fill them to advantage, their brilliant colours and ornate patterns having a tendency to make them principals instead of simple accessories, and to *kill* the flowers, unless ingeniously harmonized or contrasted therewith; indeed they may be termed too ornamental in themselves, and are only suitable for positions of pretension.'[10] Instead they could be home-made from 'fir cones, crooked lengths of wood, oak varnish, and a wooden framework', perhaps with the addition of 'virgin oak', an article recently introduced.

Another idea for a front garden appeared in *Gardening Illustrated* in 1879. It suggested growing trained fruit trees, apparently all the rage in France, which always appealed to William Robinson, who ran the magazine. It was an opportunity to grow something edible as well as to get away from the conventional front garden: 'The market distribution of the good things produced by our fruit growers is so very imperfect that it behoves the owner of even the smallest garden

to secure as far as possible his own supply. We may even say that much of the monotonous entanglement now known as shrubbery might well be exchanged in small gardens for well-grown and well-chosen fruit trees.'[11]

Whatever the books said, people probably dealt with their front gardens in whatever way they wanted. Cottage gardens were frequently mostly at the front, and were filled with flowers and sometimes vegetables. A photograph in the Museum of Garden History taken in the late nineteenth century shows a couple standing proudly in what appears to be their front garden (as there is a number on the cottage door), with pots of ferns in the window and raised beds made of planks filled with flowers, which look like nasturtiums. A wooden box acts as another plant pot, a slug trap in the form of a pot inverted on a pole guards against the worst evils of vermin, and a display of shells on the window sill adds an artistic touch. Within the bounds of their resources, and perhaps without a back garden, they have followed Hibberd's advice and kept everything in 'first-rate order'.

Many people in towns had only front gardens, and therefore had to grow as much as they could in them. These raised beds are probably resting on paving, but still provide an opportunity to grow flowers every summer. (Photograph taken in Bradford) (*Museum of Garden History*)

CHAPTER EIGHT

The Pleasure Garden

The term 'Pleasure Garden' conjures up elegance, flowers, garden parties and romance. It was used in early gardening manuals describing great gardens to distinguish the ornamental garden from the kitchen garden. In a modest Victorian middle-class garden 'taking pleasure' could encompass anything from sitting quietly reading, to rolling up one's sleeves and getting on with the digging or watering. We have some photographs of people in their gardens in the nineteenth century, but they are usually carefully posed and take the form of family groups or studied views of flower beds, although from literature and diaries we know that games were played and meals were enjoyed outside, just as they are now.

One garden that is unusually well documented, appearing almost frozen in time, is that of the Butters family in Hackney, east London. There were two gardens, at numbers 41 and 49 King Edward Road, owned by the same family, and the ends of the gardens were joined together behind the intervening gardens, producing a U shape. The whole street had been built by Charles Butters, who reserved two of the houses for himself and his son, Walter.[1] In 1874 both gardens were painted and they were also photographed extensively by the family in the last two decades of the century. They show the family in the garden, with their pets and servants, playing, gardening, picking fruit, picnicking and literally 'taking pleasure'. There were also two accounts of the garden in the *Gardener's Magazine* in 1876, describing the planting: these are referred to and illustrated in Chapter Eleven. Although the family business provided a good income, the Butters' wealth did not meet country-estate standards, and the garden is a good example of a town or suburban middle-class garden. The length of the plots on which each house was built was about 200 feet, and the width 40 to 50 feet, and although professional gardeners were employed, the family were believed to have planned the garden and directed the work themselves. The houses have now disappeared, replaced by a housing estate.

Another well-documented garden, also in Hackney, is that of the writer Shirley Hibberd. He supplied two, slightly different, accounts of how he renovated his garden when he took it over in 1858, in *The Town Garden* and the *Floral World*.[2, 3] His plot was about 280 feet long and 35 feet wide, and the garden stretched towards the north-west behind his house, which was at 6 Lordship Terrace (then called Meadow Street). Many illustrations of the garden, in the form of engravings, appeared in the *Floral World* and the *Gardener's Magazine* throughout the 1860s, and most were used again in Hibberd's books. Some even had a new lease of life in *Amateur Gardening* in the 1880s. In about 1870 Hibberd moved to Bridge House, Hermitage Road, slightly further north. The garden there was also described, but was

> The spacious lawn, with not a tree or interruption of any kind, is the very first necessity for promotion of garden games. My croquet lawn would accommodate one hundred pyramid pear trees, and thus profitably occupied would make me miserable. Its nice green carpet gives me a twofold pleasure – as grass turf it is beautiful in all seasons; as a playground it is the scene of joyous assemblages in the pleasant days of summer.
>
> *Floral World*, May 1875, p. 138

not as extensively illustrated. However, it is clear from his writing that his friends and family enjoyed croquet, boating parties on the lake, strawberry picking and skating, although Hibberd himself seems to have limited his pleasure to gardening. Both these gardens have also disappeared under later housing developments.

A mid-nineteenth-century middle-class town garden that has been reconstructed is at Peckover House in Wisbech, Cambridgeshire, owned by the National Trust. It is slightly larger than those already mentioned, but similar in layout and appearance. It is predominantly lawned, with a network of paths linking the separate areas and features. There are specimen trees, shrubberies, beds of tender annuals, glasshouses, roses, a kitchen garden and even an authentic, restored rustic summerhouse. Walking around there gives one a feel for what those disappeared gardens must have been like.

Early Victorian gardens were usually laid out in the so-called 'Gardenesque' style, vividly brought to life by Loudon's account of Mrs Lawrence's villa garden in his *Gardener's Magazine* in 1838, mentioned earlier in Chapter One.[4] This garden has been described many times, so does not need another repeat, but the same style is beautifully illustrated in two paintings by William Brown of Louth in Lincolnshire. Brown's 'Panorama' was painted in the 1840s from the top of Louth's church spire when scaffolding was erected for repairs. He sketched his view in all directions and later turned the sketches into two paintings which fit together either way and thus produce a panorama. The main purpose was to record the prosperous town itself, which became the third largest in Lincolnshire in the 1850s, but the paintings incidentally depicted many of the gardens enclosed behind buildings. Most are laid out with lawns and geometric beds, though some have the curious swirling 'tadpole'-shaped beds popular at the time. There are arbours and arches, statuary and paths, with identifiable people walking and sitting in the gardens. Every corner of the town that is not brick seems to be cultivated.[5]

To learn how middle-class amateurs directed the work in their gardens, we can turn to their own writing. Elizabeth Watts is a good example of a woman writer who explained gardening techniques to amateurs. Nothing seems to be known about her, but she published three gardening books in the 1860s 'for the use of persons who require information on the management of their own gardens . . . It embodies the actual experience of the Author, and will, it is believed, show that moderate economy and very good gardening are by no means incompatible.'[6]

Elizabeth Watts describes how to make a pleasure garden interesting for walkers and visitors in the 'Landscape' style:

Trees and shrubs planted in large or small groups, or singly; tasteful openings to show distant peeps of scenery, wherever such happen to be at command; promontories reached by rough rustic stairs, now seen, now hidden; faces of cliffs, in some parts densely draped with foliage, in others shaped into little flats, planted with groups of plants of bold foliage, hollowed out into caverns and grottoes, adorned with picturesque erections, or left in naked ruggedness, helped by the hand of man to an angle taking the finest sunset tints, – will lead on such a bit of ground to a very beautiful landscape garden. The top of the height may be shaped into terrace walks, approached from below at intervals by gradual ascents and rustic stairs; and half way up and near the bottom, summerhouses, aviaries, grottoes, little caves, arbours, and seats of various form, may at once please the eye and utilize the position by offering pleasant places for rest, and cool or warm refreshment to suit all seasons. Little hills can be tinted and varied by winding devious gravel paths, and diverse vegetation; and flat parts may have ponds for water fowl, surrounded by rising ground planted as shrubberies.[7]

As an alternative, she offers 'gardens in the Italian style', which also need sufficient space so as to avoid 'degenerating into a tea-garden-like assemblage of fountains, parapets, and pedestals, or at any rate of incurring the odium often bestowed on Cockney gardens'.[8]

For a more modest garden nearer the end of the century, we have only to look at the winning essay in the 'Cheap Gay Garden' competition in *Amateur Gardening* in 1884. Mr J.F. Rayner of Southampton received £5 for his contribution. It began: 'Let us imagine our garden ground as we generally find it, oblong in shape, and in size much nearer to the eighth than the whole of an acre, walled on three sides and the house at one end. We lay this out very simply. A long oval bed occupies the centre, with a three or four foot gravel path round it, and outside that a border, or rather three borders, which are at least four feet wide at their narrowest part – which of course will be at the centre of each – and widest at the corners.'[9] Rockeries are to be placed in each corner, of 'a few shapeless stones', and in the shady ones he grows ferns 'collected in a country excursion in March or April', periwinkle and creeping jenny. In the sunny rockeries he grows sedums, sempervivums, saxifrages and snowdrops. He suggests improving the soil with decayed manure, sifted ashes 'or better, with road scrapings'. The paths may have a base of cinders under the gravel, if desired. The edgings of the beds could

A family examining a recently planted parterre; they have the added luxury of an observatory in the garden. (*Museum of Garden History*)

be thrift, 'found growing on most sea-shores', or pinks, which could probably be had from a friend. For the walls, winter jasmine or ivy would grow in the shade and Japanese quince or weigela in the sun. The house, having a higher wall, could support Irish ivy or Virginia creeper, the sight of which in autumn would never be forgotten. Over a bay window could be grown Chinese wistaria and, over a porch or arch, Gloire de Dijon rose, *Clematis jackmanii* or Japanese honeysuckle. However, if it were not possible at the time to 'lay his hands on the plants', a temporary climber such as nasturtium, sweet pea or canary creeper could be used. Such a 'cheap gay garden' can still be found all over towns and suburbs in Britain where gardens remain from the nineteenth century. The plants are versatile and hardy and are still being bought in garden centres today.

Elizabeth Watts worked her way through all departments of the garden, starting with paths:

> The paths should be wide, if space can be spared. For the main paths, ten or twelve feet make a pleasant promenade. Any width between that and three feet may be chosen, but the last is sadly too narrow, and should not be fixed on unless the room that better ones would take is a very great object. They should be straight, as they necessarily will be if the beds are rectangular, and they should be of gravel if any can be procured in the locality. Mark them out with lines, and dig out the earth to a depth of one foot: this earth, if it be pretty good, may be thrown upon the beds. Let the trench thus made be square and smooth, and if the locality renders draining advantageous lay down draining tiles at each edge; but whether this be necessary or not depends on the dry or retentive nature of the soil. Lay in a good thickness of the coarse stony gravel used for road-making; if this be scarce in the neighbourhood, any collected rubbish consisting of broken crockery, oyster-shells, and all hard refuse, or the burnt clay so much used in railway construction, will do. If you can get a sufficient quantity, fill the trench nearly to the top, and then let the path that is to be remain for a few weeks, trampling it often and rolling it from time to time. When this is well settled and firm, spread a layer of coarse gravel: let it be a week, rolling it several times. Then add a top of fine binding gravel, and keep it constantly rolled until it is hard and smooth. One coat of gravel over the foundation of rubbish or stony gravel will do, if two be thought too expensive or troublesome. Before the last gravel is laid on, the edges should be fixed.[10]

She therefore advocated the use of the road grit that we have heard so much about already, or alternatively anything else that was locally available. Shirley Hibberd explained how his walks were laid out when his garden was drained: 'Simultaneously with the draining, the walks were laid out, and six inches of rubbish laid down for a bottom; the rough wheeling during the winter settled this firmly for gravelling in spring, and it is now the best walk in the neighbourhood. For the walks and the drains five and twenty loads of rubbish were used, at the somewhat extravagant price of three and sixpence a load.'[11]

Lawns were the next essential in the pleasure garden: 'Amongst the earliest recommendations in this volume is one in behalf of the greatest possible breadth of well-kept turf consistently with the area enclosed for purposes of pleasure. To ensure the luxury of a "velvet lawn," is, to speak generally, a most easy matter, and, though it may be comparatively costly in the first instance, it will prove in the end one of the best of investments of gold in gardening.'[12] Hibberd recommended using turf for a new lawn, unless the area be more than an acre; meadow turf was perfectly adequate: 'We have formed many lawns from meadow turf, which in the first instance appeared far too coarse, and they have in the course of three years acquired a beautiful texture fit for the foot of a princess in a fairy tale.'[13] He had obviously discovered this by experience because some ten years earlier he had said: 'Turf from a meadow is utterly unfit for any garden, and the reason for obtaining it from a "high and dry common", or, in any case, a poor, sandy soil, is, that you may make sure of the fine grasses that thicken below into a sort of felt.'[14]

Watts was happy with meadow grass, and explained exactly how to cut it as well as how to lay it:

> The turfs are cut a foot wide, a yard long, and as nearly as possible an inch in thickness.[15] Before cutting them the ground should be marked out, and cut downwards with a racer or rutter – a thin sharp instrument with a rounded edge, like a cheese-cutter, fixed to a handle about four feet long. They should then be raised with a turfing iron – an implement with a flat arrow-shaped blade, for cutting up the turf, fixed to a handle which goes straight from the blade for several inches, then turns at an angle and turns again at a second angle, so that the handle is above the ground, while the blade is at work beneath it. As one man cuts the turfs, another should roll and remove them. They are unrolled as they are laid, placing edge to edge with great exactness, and mending and filling in the broken parts as they are laid. As soon as the grass is laid, it should be beaten flat, rolled repeatedly, and watered if the weather be dry.[16]

Hibberd explained that there was a third way of forming lawns, known as 'inoculating', which consisted of planting tufts of grass a foot apart, which would spread during the summer and form a lawn. Weeds could be killed by depositing a small quantity of phospho-guano on them, if 'spudding' them out was too much trouble, but this must be done carefully. As to mowing, he explained that machines came in two types, those that cut and carry and those that cut and scatter. Which you used depended on the soil and weather conditions: 'In the excessively hot and dry summers of 1868 and 1870, we constantly employed the "Archimedean," which scatters the grass and our lawns were as green through all the burning drought as in the cooler days of spring. In the moist summer of 1871, it would have been necessary to sweep up the grass, had the scattering machine been employed on our strong land, and therefore we kept our trusty "Shanks" at work, cutting and carrying and had to mow twice a week through the whole of June and July to keep the grass down.'[17] Hibberd gives the usual advice about not cutting the grass too short and goes on to caution against too free a use of the edging iron:

> The man who persists after warning and explanation in chop, chop, chopping at the edge, as if it were necessary to construct a gutter of mud on each side of a walk, deserves to hear an opinion of his procedure that will make him tingle from head to foot with shame. The jobbing gardener is the master of this chop-down-gutter-forming business, and will always be ready to advise the employment of gravel to fill up the trench that should never have been made . . . A gardener who cuts into the turf on the edge of the lawn to make a finish ought to be compelled to eat all that he removes.[18]

Lawns, however, did not have to be grass. Even with the benefit of the lawnmower, Victorian gardeners, like modern ones, dreamt about doing

H.J. ELWES (1846–1922)

HENRY JOHN ELWES was a Gloucestershire country gentleman, the oldest of seven children, whose first career was the army. When he retired to the country, he took up natural history and travelled the world in pursuit of plants, birds, butterflies and big game. He published *A Monograph of the Genus Lilium* in 1880, illustrated by W.H. Fitch, and later wrote a study of trees of Great Britain and Ireland in collaboration with Augustine Henry. The *Botanical Magazine* published ninety-eight plates, from 1875 to 1877, of plants he introduced or cultivated in his own garden, and *Galanthus elwesii* is named after him. Elwes was an incurable collector: his plant collections included succulents, bulbs and alpines, and he also collected breeds of sheep, having clothes made up entirely of wool from one particular breed.

away with grass and replacing it with something that did not require cutting. Most people have heard of camomile lawns, but these in practice are hard to establish and maintain in anything but well-drained sunny conditions. The Victorians developed an interest in spergula lawns in about 1859. Brent Elliott, in his article on the novelist R.D. Blackmore,[19] points out that the spergula lawn was a short-lived fashion due to the inability of the plant to cope with the English weather. The nurseryman E.G. Henderson introduced it and Elizabeth Watts used it:

> *Spergula pilifera* forms a moss-like carpet, which is said by many to be better than grass for a lawn. Where is takes well, it maintains a bright uniform green; in shade, where grass often will not thrive, it does well, and on hot sunny banks it will do with watering. It has the advantage of not requiring mowing, and its pretty little flowers are very fragrant, and are great favourites with bees. The surface to be planted with it should be manured, and then prepared as for another lawn, and gently rolled. Break up the spergula turf into bits two inches square, or rather less; plant the bits two inches apart, roll the ground and give one good watering. Keep the surface weeded, roll it once a week, and when it has taken, it may now and then have a watering with liquid manure. It may be grown from seed. It is especially good for small lawns, borders, and banks. The Messrs. Carter, of Holborn, sell the turf in small quantities, 2 shillings for enough to plant a square yard, and, I believe, charge less for a large surface. They supply the seed also.[20]

Shirley Hibberd also latched on to it and even featured his spergula lawn in an illustration of his own garden, calling it his 'magic ring'.[21] However, by the date of *The Amateur's Flower Garden* he was advising that it should not be employed for 'general usefulness'.

Once the paths and lawns were laid out, the beds had to be defined by some sort of edging. Hibberd gave several alternatives:

> In open breezy places, dwarf box makes the best edging in the world, and the cheapest in the end, no matter what its cost in the first instance. If a green edging is desired in a spot shaded by walls or trees, box is useless, but common evergreen euonymus will take its place tolerably well. Grass verges are beautiful, if well kept; but they entail a lot of labour to keep them trim, and it is always a question if the time spent in clip – clip – clipping them might not be devoted to something better. Well-made edgings of ivy have a solid, rich appearance; but it would render a large garden heavy in character, and an example of a good idea overdone, to employ ivy edging everywhere.[22]

He then went on to recommend, as an alternative, 'handsome stone moulding or its equivalent in some imitative material such as

Ransome, Rosher, or Austin can supply'. Elizabeth Watts assumed edgings would be made of box, and suggested that one yard of old box edging could make several for replanting by digging it up, choosing the less woody stems (not 'thicker than a crowquill') and trimming the roots to provide suitable small plants.[23]

Elizabeth Watts' advice on choosing ornamental trees for a 'dwelling of moderate pretension' was to pick trees that were not too large, had pretty foliage and could put up with smoke if grown in London. What seems slightly strange is that she usually explains how to grow the trees from seed, which would imply that she expected her readers to retain the garden for some considerable time. One of the more unusual trees she mentions is the Osage Orange (*Maclura ponifera*) from North America, said to have ornamental orange-like fruits on which silkworms can be fed. She recommends for planting on lawns the Cedar of Lebanon (used also by Shirley Hibberd as a specimen tree outside his drawing room), the tulip tree and the weeping ash. She also suggests the *Wellingtonia gigantea* as a specimen on a lawn, but here she seems to have departed from gardens of 'moderate pretension'. The evergreens she recommends are the typical sorts of the Victorian garden: common laurel, Portugal laurel, holly and aucuba.[24] Having dealt with trees on lawns, as an afterthought she recommends yucca and pampas grass as other specimen plants.

The design for a villa garden in *Amateur Gardening* in 1888, referred to in Chapter Seven, recommended the use of shrubs to divide the front garden from the back, providing a screen for the tradesmen's entrance. They are also used to break up the back garden, particularly where changes in level occur, and privet hedges again appear to be one of the shrubs of preference. Elizabeth Watts also recommends hardy foliage plants for a permanent backdrop to

Design for a villa garden, 80 by 200 feet. This is a sizeable suburban garden with a lawn large enough for tennis and a kitchen garden hidden behind some hedging. C is a flower bed, 'which may be of any design'. (*Amateur Gardening*, 27 October 1888) (*Amateur Gardening*)

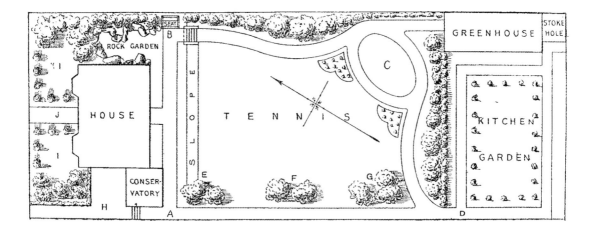

the flower garden and a 'verdant screen' in winter. 'Foremost in the beauty of foliage must therefore ever stand our evergreens.'[25]

As to the use of the pleasure garden, thanks to the lawnmower it was possible to provide a level, close-textured lawn suitable for summer games such as croquet and lawn bowls. Archery might also be attempted where space allowed. Tennis, of course, eventually became the favourite summer game for social events, but not until the end of the century, into the Edwardian era. The *Floral World* suggested another use for the lawn in winter if it were based on clay soil and had a good supply of water:

> All the summer long this is a croquet ground or bowling green, a place for lawn billiards, and many more good games. Very early in the winter it becomes a skating rink, when the weathercock veers to some point of north you turn on the water and flood the ground, and next morning there is good skating ice for your money. You rejoice in your possession, and you score its face with your elegant evolutions, and when dusk stops your sport, you flood the ground again, and next morning you have a new surface, smooth as glass, and so safe that it will be quite a delight to fall on it.[26]

Simply walking in a garden could be considered pleasant and interesting exercise, particularly for ladies. Considering that their clothes may well have weighed about thirty-seven pounds (and ours are typically two pounds),[27] it may be imagined that getting round a garden of any size could be considered the Victorian version of 'working out' in itself.

A larger country garden might have space for a croquet lawn. Here onlookers take the opportunity to examine the roses, and a pergola provides shade for the ladies. (Alfred Smee, *My Garden*, p. 38) (*Author's collection*)

CHAPTER NINE

The Vegetable Garden

We probably know more about the kitchen garden in Victorian times than we do about any other part of the garden. So many walled kitchen gardens have been restored or re-created, most of which date back to the nineteenth century, that hardly anyone interested in garden history can claim not to know what they were like. However, although these gardens are interesting and pleasurable to visit, they cannot re-create the 'actuality' of the Victorian garden because many of the real working practices of that time would breach modern health and safety regulations and produce conditions that most visitors would not want to endure.

We have already seen how many nineteenth-century pesticides and manures were dangerous to handle, and it can be imagined what sort of conditions were usual for professional gardeners and the young boys working as apprentices. The professional kitchen garden should be considered as a food factory, similar to any other factory, and factories in Victorian times were fairly evil places to work. Spending day after day in glasshouses, hot and humid by their nature, pruning and tying vines, for instance, or taking endless cuttings and potting them up, was in reality repetitive and exhausting in hot summer weather and often involved revolting conditions. At Clumber Park, Nottinghamshire, a shelf high above the vines growing in a lean-to glasshouse, just underneath the roof itself, was used to hold a trough full of urine in which pots of tomatoes were put for ripening to prevent insect damage. Apart from the unpleasant smell for the gardeners working there, and the risk of accidents when they assembled the contraption, one wonders whether the prospective consumers would have enjoyed their salad if they had known how it had been raised. Kitchen gardens in country estates were situated well away from the house, and out of sight. The boilers used to heat the glasshouses were fuelled by coal. There would have been coal heaps outside the walls and smoke belching from the chimneys for a large part of the day and night, throughout most of the year. Stable manure and spent tanning bark were essentials for the hotbeds, and other manures and fertilisers would all be stacked up ready for use. It all smelt unpleasant and attracted flies and rats.

The reason for this mass production of food was that it was the best, and sometimes the only, way to get what was wanted. Fruit and vegetables were not imported on the large scale they are today, freezing was unheard of and only seasonal, local produce could be bought in the markets. The methods of preserving then available – drying, bottling, canning and making jams and jellies – produced a fruit or vegetable that was sometimes barely recognisable as the real thing. Nothing compared to the taste and texture of fresh fruit and vegetables. If you were rich enough you would employ staff to grow exactly what you wanted, throughout the year. Skilled gardeners

The addition of a table vegetable of this delicious and nutritious nature – the food of millions of the human race – and yet, for want of experience of the sorts adapted to our climate, so strangely unappreciated here, seemed of no inconsiderable importance, the more so as it ripened in the late autumn, reproducing then the lost flavours of the early pea and of the asparagus.

Revd T.C. Brehaut, 'Maize: Its Use and Culture',

Floral World, 1871, p. 87

were trained to extend the growing season to produce early and late crops by using glass, by controlling temperature and humidity, and by using the different parts of the garden to accelerate or retard growth. Hotbeds and cold frames, pits and forcing rooms, they all had their uses and were controlled to within days or even hours to produce delicacies for the table. The amateur had a daunting task if he tried to compete with the skilled professional.

Inevitably amateurs did try to compete. By the 1850s books and magazines were being published with instructions for amateurs to follow, but growing vegetables is a craft all of its own. All plants grow in the same way, and all gardening is artificial, but vegetable gardening is the most artificial of all. Whereas in the flower garden you can get away with the odd weed, and often things grow reasonably well in average soil without much feeding, with vegetables, every weed consumes food the vegetables should be getting and vegetables not grown in sensible rows or groups are much harder to weed and harvest. Vegetable growing, therefore, is where the amateur needs most guidance and where there is most mystery attached to getting it right. It is also the area where the most satisfaction and pride are derived from being successful. From early times working people enjoyed competing to grow not just the biggest vegetables, but also the best quality of some of the most difficult and time-consuming edible plants, such as blanched celery and melons, and they probably relied on skills handed on from their relatives and neighbours to learn to do so. As amateur gardening began to be popular with the middle classes and publications were produced for them, instructions began to appear to teach them the skills of kitchen gardening in a methodical way. These were often accompanied by instructions on the best way to cook the produce thus grown.

The first vegetable most people think of as being grown universally is the potato, but in fact the one that seems to figure most frequently in illustrations of working people's gardens is the cabbage. Cabbages are not particularly easy to grow well because they are susceptible to a lot of pests, and they require extra care in being started off in a seedbed and then transplanted to a well-firmed permanent bed. But cabbages are important because the various varieties span the whole year with their growth, and the winter varieties will stand in the ground throughout frost and snow. Beans and peas have a short season, although they can be dried for winter use, and root crops can be stored if you have the space and the right conditions, but cabbages can be eaten fresh throughout a large part of the winter, providing greenery and flavour, although not everyone liked them. Nathaniel Paterson, in *The Manse Garden*, regarded the cabbage as 'excellent for a cow or such of our own species as have the like powers of digestion . . . the main fault of the early cabbage is that it usually comes not till far on in May, when the sun checks its growth and hardens its fibre into wood'.[1]

Elizabeth Watts gave instructions for choosing the best cabbage plant on the plot and marking it out as a source of seed for the next season. She said that the soil for cabbages could not be made too rich. She lists among 'the cabbage tribe' spring cabbage, Savoys, or winter cabbage, red cabbage, kales and Brussels sprouts. She is not keen on the Egyptian kale or kohlrabi: 'the greens from it are coarse, and the portion of the root which is good to eat has a strong flavour which is not very nice'.[2] Alfred Smee agreed: '[it] is sometimes grown at my garden for the cattle. Occasionally we have cooked it by way of experiment, but it is, at best, an indifferent vegetal.'[3] Cauliflower and broccoli, on the other hand, were considered delectable, and of the two, broccoli was advised for the amateur with a small garden because it was easier and quicker to grow. The cauliflower would take up the ground for a longer period and was more difficult to get right. The *Gardener's Magazine* gave cooking instructions: 'This noble vegetable [broccoli] is one of the easiest to cook, yet it is often brought to the table in an unsatisfactory manner, through being slowly cooked in a spoonful of water, instead of being quickly and completely cooked in plenty. In common with all other vegetables, broccolis should be quite fresh when cooked, but they may be kept a considerable length of time after being cut, by laying them on damp stones or bricks in a still dark place.'[4] The instructions continued by saying that broccoli should be cooked whole unless too large, but that sometimes the ones the writer had to deal with weighed over twenty-one pounds!

The recipes for cauliflower included serving with white sauce or cheese sauce, a more elaborate cheese sauce flavoured with onions and cayenne pepper, called 'Cauliflower Compliqué', and a sauce made of the cauliflower itself, to be served with turkey or cutlets.

So to the humble potato. They certainly were grown in cottage gardens and allotments, but in Jeremy Burchardt's study of allotments in the middle of the nineteenth century it is revealed that potatoes were closely followed by wheat as the favourite crop to grow. There are many reasons for this, one being that for good results potatoes had to be grown in rotation with other crops, and another being that wheat had an important morale-boosting quality among the poor, who were proud of being able to grow the raw ingredient for good-quality bread. Once wheat and potatoes were accounted for, however, only a small proportion of the ground was used for other vegetables, such as beans and peas, cabbages and turnips. Considering that some of those would have been grown as animal food, it seems that the British reputation as meat-eaters was well founded.

The potato was one of the staple foods in the nineteenth century, as it is today, but the Victorian gardener was only too aware of the difficulties of growing potatoes: the blight or 'murrain' which had caused the great Irish potato famine of 1845 periodically returned and wiped out the whole crop. Although gardeners knew that blight was made worse by damp weather, they did not know that it was caused by a fungus and that there was no cure. It was only in about 1888 that French farmers discovered that Bordeaux mixture, the fungicide used on grapevines, could be successfully used on potatoes to prevent or lessen the effects of blight. Therefore, in the early part of the century, theories abounded as to how to prevent it and new varieties of potato were produced every year to try to beat it. Shirley Hibberd wrote extensively about growing potatoes, trying out new varieties every year and recording the results for readers of the

ROBERT FENN (active 1880s–90s)

ROBERT FENN started his working life as a watchmaker, but soon realised his vocation was in gardening. He made some experiments with using house sewage as a fertiliser, became an expert at fruit winemaking, and promoted the keeping of bees as an essential part of any garden, before taking up potato breeding as his speciality. Fenn made it his life's work to develop new strains of potato resistant to disease, using American sorts crossed with those of his own raising. He chose appearance and quality above mere size, and his success at producing many good varieties encouraged others to develop a huge variety of shapes and colours by the late nineteenth century. From the time when disease resistance had been the desire of all potato breeders, Fenn's work in producing perfection encouraged many other growers to experiment and produce more varieties than could ever have been imagined.

Robert Fenn. (Engraving from *The Gardening World*, 4 October 1884, p. 73) (*Museum of Garden History*)

Gardener's Magazine and the *Floral World*. He said that by 1868 he had tried out over 250 sorts on his trial grounds at Stoke Newington. He believed that potato disease came from the sun, but that on his soil he could obtain twenty tons per acre in a good season. His 'secret' was to grow the potatoes on tiles. Ordinary roof tiles could be used, but he had specially shaped ones made. He dug a trench, put down the tiles, and then grew the potatoes on top, covered over with soil, the theory being that the air trapped underneath helped drainage and kept the plants warm.[5] In *Profitable Gardening*, published in 1884, he advocates good soil preparation, early planting and early lifting, saying that it is during storage that potatoes develop disease.[6]

Hibberd was always ready to try something new and in *Profitable Gardening* he also extols the virtues of the Chinese yam as an alternative to potatoes.[7] It was not all that new when he was writing in the 1880s, as it had been mentioned in the *Gardeners' Chronicle* in 1858: 'That this esculent is of excellent quality when properly boiled is now admitted; that a fair crop of it may be obtained has been here and there sufficiently proved.'[8] The Chinese yam had been introduced at the time that blight was thought an insurmountable problem, but it did not catch on as a realistic proposition for British gardeners. Something that did catch on for a while, however, was salsify and its frequent companion (though not relative), scorzonera. Both were large roots, grown like carrots or parsnips, which could be boiled and served with melted butter or white sauce, or made into fritters. The stalks could also be eaten like asparagus, or raw in salads. Salsify is a yellowish colour on the outside and white inside, while scorzonera is black. Mrs Earle gave a recipe for cooking salsify in vinegar and water, cut into small slices and served with a white sauce 'in shells, like scalloped oysters. Add a little cheese and breadcrumbs and brown in the oven.'[9] That must have been how salsify came by its alternative name of 'vegetable oyster'.

Elizabeth Watts considered scorzonera and salsify old-fashioned in the 1860s, and linked them with chicory, rampion and skirrets. She said they were 'still used on the Continent. They are wholesome, make a change with other vegetables, and are eaten boiled tender, and covered with white sauce, or with various vegetables in stews, fricasees, and other made dishes'. She advised, however, that the black skin should be scraped off the scorzonera (also known as 'viper's grass') 'before it is seen at table'.[10] But she did favour the Jerusalem artichoke, saying: 'It imparts a delicious flavour to stews and hashes, and is very good boiled as a vegetable, although a little watery. It is so nice, and so different from other vegetables, that it seems quite to deserve more general cultivation than it gets, especially as any spare corner will do for it, and it requires little care in the cultivation.'[11]

The other roots 'less in general use' that she included were the root of chicory, succory or wild endive ('eaten in France, and there is no doubt but that it is very wholesome. That old-fashioned writer, Culpepper, attributes to it beneficial action on the liver, and other vital organs, and mentions it as a remedy in ague'), the rampion ('a radish-like root which does best in a moist shady border, where the earth is rich and very light'), skirrets ('grow something like dahlias. An old root or two may be left to ripen seed in autumn, or the seed may be bought') and the oca. This she compares to the Chinese yam ('another root which there has been much talk about cultivating for a vegetable, and some persons like it very much . . . in Belgium the leaves are used as sorrel, and the flowers are put into salads').[12]

The more usual roots were carrots, turnips, parsnips and beetroot. Poor Nathaniel Paterson, whose garden on the Scottish Borders does

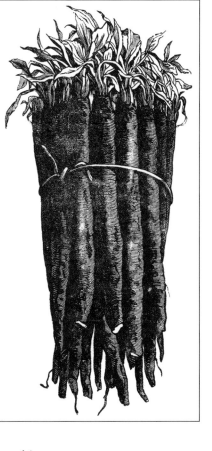

Scorzonera was one of the root vegetables that provided variety in the Victorian diet. (*Thompson's Gardener's Assistant,* vol. 6, p. 514) (*Author's collection*)

not seem to have been very productive in spite of all his attempts, said that carrots were 'the greatest trial of the gardener's patience and skill' because of 'the worm',[13] by which he presumably meant the carrot fly. He gave detailed instructions as to how to 'annoy the enemy'. Carrots came in handy in various guises because of their sweetness. We are now used to carrot cake, and some of us may have old recipes using carrots in Christmas pudding, but Mrs Beeton also gives a recipe for 'Carrot jam to imitate apricot preserve'. The boiled carrots were puréed through a sieve and then boiled with sugar, lemon rind, almonds and brandy.[14] Elizabeth Watts mentioned carrot wine, though said she had never tried it. Pests of the turnip seem even more numerous than those of the carrot, and amateurs were warned against growing the larger turnips, such as swedes. Being part of the brassica family, turnips were also susceptible to clubroot. Dusting with soot, charcoal or hydrosulphurate of lime from the gas works was recommended as a deterrent.[15] The parsnip, however, was recommended as useful and virtually pest-free, although some people did not like the taste. Beetroot was recommended as a summer salad, and some kinds could be used as a leaf vegetable.

The scarcity of interesting food in the winter was what made the early summer crops all the more exciting and luxurious when they first appeared. We are now so used to seeing every variety of vegetable available in the supermarkets all the year round that we forget how dull food must have been in winter and how important the race must have been to produce the earliest crops. The Victorian vegetable year began with asparagus, a vegetable that is only normally available grown outdoors in Britain in May and June, which is why it was considered so special. If you have only ever eaten asparagus from a supermarket you probably do not understand why it is so special: there is a subtle change in the flavour of the shoots within hours of cutting, so only by growing it at home can you really taste asparagus as it should be. The problem for many amateur gardeners both now and in Victorian times was not so much the skill of growing it as having the space to set aside for the crop, which has to be in a permanent bed several metres long and must be grown for two or three years before it can be cut, and thereafter weeded and cared for assiduously. And all this for six weeks of pleasure each year when it can actually be eaten. Only the relatively wealthy would have the space to grow it and the time to care for it.

Thompson's Gardener's Assistant, written for professionals, devotes over seventeen columns of text to growing asparagus.[16] It goes into detail about different methods of cultivation, manures to be used, forcing, and the correct method of cutting. An amateur reading this would probably be put off by the thought of preparing the soil by first using the bed to crop peas, then a bed of celery, and finally planting asparagus the following year. After that, two or three years would elapse before the asparagus could be cut for eating. Many ordinary people would have moved house by then! Asparagus was a chief source of income for many market gardeners around London and Paris, but their methods could not be recommended for amateurs. Shirley Hibberd advised:

> In a private garden the endeavour should be to produce plump, short, tender, and highly-coloured stalks; not the rank growth (in the fashion of drumsticks) that too many people are ready to pronounce 'fine.' The market-grower knows pretty well how to grow it; he is obliged to produce it for market in a way not promotive of its highest excellence at table; but as you have nothing to do with professional packing and market usage, you can have it doubly delicious from your own bed by taking the crop just at a certain moment of its perfection, which the market-grower dare not do.[17]

Hibberd recommends growing from seed for 'the best bed of asparagus ever seen by gardening eyes' and also says that for 'the private table' the proper way to cut asparagus is to wait until the shoot is six inches high and then cut it level with the soil, rather

I have grown Cardoons (*Cynara cardunculus*), but never will again, as whether I have tasted them from my garden, or whether I have obtained them abroad, they appear to be unworthy of cultivation. The blanched ribs of the leaves are eaten, but are infinitely inferior to stewed celery.

Alfred Smee, *My Garden*, p. 116

than cutting below soil level as done by market growers. The main controversy over asparagus, however, proved to be on the question of blanching. Blanching involved growing stems of plants without light so that they stayed white. It was commonly done with celery, cardoons and seakale.[18] William Robinson, who had spent years travelling in France and liked anything French, praised the white asparagus produced there and claimed that it was better than the green asparagus grown in Britain. The French type of asparagus tended to be much thicker than the British. When Hibberd had described asparagus disparagingly as 'fine' he was using a pun: fine asparagus meant very thin green shoots, which were inferior in flavour and would be produced if the asparagus beds had been cut over too long a period or not fed enough.

Asparagus may have been a luxury only available to the relatively wealthy or the dedicated amateur, but reading between the lines it seems that once the first excitement was over, there may well have been rather too much of it about, and it was relegated to being used as a substitute for the real delicacy of the early summer table: the pea. The general usefulness and popularity of the frozen pea, now always available as an accompaniment to anything and at all times of year, has debased the most exquisite of summer vegetables for ever. All gardening and cookery writers speak of the first fresh green peas of summer as the holy grail of vegetables:

> When a City man first owns a garden, perhaps there is nothing which pleases his fancy so much as the hope of giving his friends fresh-gathered peas.[19]

> Nothing can be more idle than to study the endless varieties of peas. To collect parcels, label, sow in patches, keep tallies, boil in several pots, and write the taste in separate pages, is scarcely consistent with the use of ordinary intellect, or with the idea that life has other ends than eating.[20]

> Without a good supply of peas, gardening is but sorry work, and the finer the peas the more we rejoice in the glorious summer weather that brings so many blessings with it for both mind and body.[21]

Loudon describes how to use 'fine' asparagus chopped up into pea-sized pieces as a substitute for the real thing before peas were ready in the garden. Mrs Beeton gives a recipe for 'Asparagus peas' to be served as a side-dish.[22] Asparagus cut up to the size of peas was parboiled and drained. Then it was stewed with butter, parsley and onions. Once cooked, the sauce would be thickened with flour and sweetened with sugar. The parsley and onions would then be removed and the dish enriched with egg yolks and cream. It seems a lot of trouble to disguise asparagus. The *Gardener's Magazine* gives a recipe for duck with green peas stewed with butter, bacon, onions, parsley and bay leaf, as a change from roast duck.[23]

Another substitute for real peas were 'pea-tops', which could be made into a mock pea soup. The pea seeds were sown in a box and grown until about four inches high. They were then cut down and the whole plant was boiled and puréed and mixed with cooked dried peas, a dish which 'will rather surprise even the epicure'.[24]

Beans closely followed peas both in popularity and growing season. Nathaniel Paterson advised that as broad bean seeds were slow to germinate and often eaten by mice, they were best soaked in train oil first.[25] He classified all other beans as kidney beans, then divided them into French and scarlet runners ('worthy of notice as a beautiful flower, and useful by its rambling growth, for ornamenting any object which in itself might be a deformity').[26] Elizabeth Watts praised both the eating and the ease of growing ('Forcing French beans is easy from the manageable compactness of their growth; and there is no vegetable more esteemed or more *recherché* than a dish of French beans, come when it may').[27] The scarlet runner was popular with cottagers and city dwellers alike, and Shirley Hibberd did not worry about having too many ('Anybody will accept a dish of French beans or runners; and if you have plenty it will not be a labour lost to gather as the plants require it, and give to your neighbours what you do not want yourself').[28]

Recipes abounded for cucumbers, stewed, fried or cooked in sauces. Perhaps their cucumbers were more bitter than ours, or perhaps the Victorians preferred more labour-intensive dishes. They were suspicious of eating anything raw, perhaps wisely, as their water was often contaminated. Tomatoes were also suspect. Here the reason

> Boil marrows sharply for three-quarters of an hour, scrape from the skin, strain from the liquor and mash like turnips; the great objection to them is a kind of stringiness which the flesh acquires after the fruit has reached a certain size; but at sea, or under any circumstances rendering vegetables scarce, one might be very glad of a store of them. Small ones make a very delicious pickle.
>
> Elizabeth Watts, *Modern Practical Gardening*, p. 111

may have been the close connection with potatoes. The fruits which sometimes developed on potatoes were poisonous, and tomatoes looked very much like them. Also, tomatoes were considered fit only for the wealthy because in Britain they only ripened reliably under glass. It would not be worth the trouble to try to grow them unless you were sure you really wanted to eat them. Loudon gave recipes for 'tomatas', as he called them, in 1826. They were mainly used for

sauces, made by puréeing boiled tomatoes. For a sauce for cold meat
he added garlic, shallots, vinegar and chillies. It then had to stand
two days before corking. 'Potted tomatas' were made by boiling and
sieving, then adding 'glaze' (probably a thick meat stock) and then:
'Put them in a white earthen pot; when cold, cover them with
writing-paper dipped in brandy; pour over some warm hogs' lard,
and cover all over with a bladder tied quite tight; a small piece added
to a little gravy or melted butter will make an excellent sauce for
cutlets or chops.'

Loudon also gave sweet recipes for tomatoes. A 'towit of tomatas'
could be made by reducing a pint of tomatoes with a pound of fine
sugar and juice of a lemon, as if making jam.[29] 'Tomatas as dried
fruit' was made as follows: 'The pulp may be reduced; say a pint with
a pound of fine sugar, till quite stiff; pour it on your tin; it must be
dried in a stove; when nearly dry, cut it into what shape you please, it
does for ornament in the dessert.'[30]

If tomatoes did not ripen, Mrs Earle suggested: 'All gardens at
this time of year are full of unripe green Tomatoes; they are generally
left hanging on the plants till the frost touches them, and then
thrown away. If picked and stewed in a little butter in an
earthenware dish, they are excellent. They have not quite the same
flavour as the ripe ones, but still they are very good, and some people
think them nicer than the red ones when cooked.'[31] She was writing
late in the century, when tomatoes were not such a novelty. Shirley
Hibberd commented in 1877 that the tomato had 'of late years
passed from the rich man's garden, in which it was exclusively
located, and has become a citizen of the world, the welcome guest of
every household, and the subject of the poor man's special care . . . it
suits every garden and every table, and, strange to say, gratifies every
taste, for it was never heard that, when fairly presented, this noble
fruit displeased anyone.'[32] Hibberd went on to say that whatever
variety was chosen, all tomatoes made good sauce, which still seemed
to be the primary reason for growing them. At that date they were
available in many different shapes and sizes and in all shades of
yellow, orange and red. In the same article Hibberd went on to
describe egg plants, or what were described in culinary terms as
aubergines. Again, they were grown in the nineteenth century in
many more varieties than we usually see them today. The small white
ones were popular as decorative plants, but the larger purple ones
were used for cooking. They were still something of a novelty in the
kitchen, but Hibberd recommended them sliced 'as thin as lemon
peel', fried in fresh butter and served with lemon and cayenne.[33]

Salads came in great variety in Victorian times. Nathaniel
Paterson mentions dandelions, endive, cress (grown on the

mantelpiece on a piece of flannel), 'coss or ice lettuce' and cabbage lettuce.[34] Elizabeth Watts listed plants alphabetically from borage and burnet to rocket and scurvy grass, followed by a whole chapter on radishes. Alfred Smee included corn salad or lamb's lettuce, which he described as 'most disagreeable . . . utterly worthless; it should be exterminated from a garden as a useless weed' (whereas Elizabeth Watts called it a 'useful little salad plant . . . It makes a very nice salad with beetroot'). Watercress was popular because it came early in the year, but generally needed running water in which to grow. It was sold in the London streets by the poorest of street sellers, usually children or old women, who bought the small bunches from market gardeners who carted them in from the country. Shirley Hibberd had a stream at the end of his garden and grew his own cress, but as pollution became more of a danger in the suburbs he began to worry that although he knew his water was clean, some of his friends might be wary of eating the cress. So he experimented with growing watercress in pots in town gardens and published *Watercresses without Sewage: Home Culture of the Watercress*, in 1878.[35] He was given a medal by the RHS for his work.

Other popular vegetables were those of the marrow and pumpkin family. We are now more familiar with courgettes or zucchini, which are baby marrows, but in nineteenth-century Britain they seem to have been eaten when fully grown. The marrow, so named after the long, hollow marrow bones of beef, which would be served on toast and the inside eaten with a spoon, was grown with abandon, and eaten stuffed, boiled or fried. Illustrations in gardening books show all sorts of gourds, squashes and pumpkins, some grown to eat and some for decoration. They were a popular subject for competitions, as they could be grown outdoors and looked impressive. They could also be preserved with sugar and ginger. However, the three days to let them soak up the sugar, and the week to leave them after boiling but before the adding the final syrup, may put off modern cooks.[36]

Herbs were essential for the Victorian cook, and would not have been so readily available dried and pre-packaged as they are today. Some were still commonly used medicinally, and far more baking and pickling went on at home, requiring many herbs not now commonly grown in gardens. J.H. Clark, in his *Cottager's Kitchen, Fruit and Flower Gardens*,[37] mentioned balm, camomile, hyssop and pennyroyal as medicines, dill for cucumbers and soups, fennel for salads and fish, the seeds being useful in winter. Parsley was said to be a diuretic, but also good eaten with bread and butter, like watercresses. Elizabeth Watts included angelica for confectionery,[38] although she says it was formerly blanched for eating. Anise she recommended for seasoning and balm for tea and to treat sick

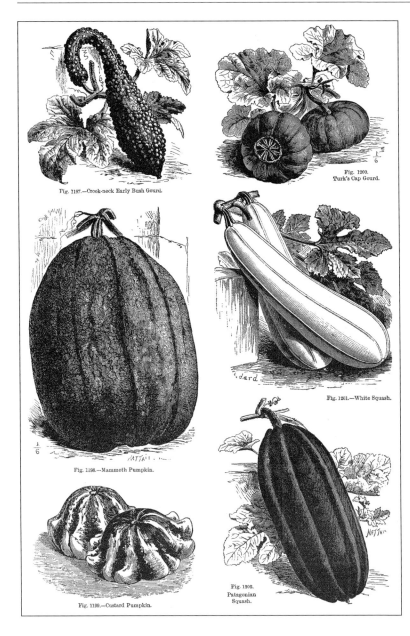

Fig. 1197.—Crook-neck Early Bush Gourd.

Fig. 1200.
Turk's Cap Gourd.

Fig. 1201.—White Squash.

Fig. 1198.—Mammoth Pumpkin.

Fig. 1199.—Custard Pumpkin.

Fig. 1202.
Patagonian
Squash.

Gourds and pumpkins were popular vegetables because they were easy to grow in a good summer and spectacular to look at. (*Thompson's Gardener's Assistant*, vol. 6, p. 447) (*Author's collection*)

animals. Sweet basil and knotted marjoram were useful for mock turtle soup. Caraway she used for confectionery, flavouring and for a cordial, and coriander she used in curry powder and on cakes. Horehound was used for cough candy and drinks. She also included samphire, as a pickle and salad, tansy as a vermifuge, and tobacco for fumigating the greenhouse, frames and pits. She lists three members of the wormwood family, *Artemesia absinthium*, 'the splendid bitter of which makes a nice liqueur, the *absinthe* of the French', southernwood and tarragon, for vinegar and pickles. Alfred Smee did not agree about the absinthe:

> Dr Gros, in a letter to myself, states that on the Boulevards of Paris, between four and six o-clock, glasses of absinthe are to be seen on every coffee-house table and at all wine-merchants'. The workpeople frequently take absinthe. They make what they call *les tournées*, each one wishing in his turn to treat his comrades. The middle class and the army drink it more frequently mixed with water, though the latter do not object to it pure, and the Parisian alcohol drinkers take absinthe as a rule. Physiological experiments show that in small doses absinthe causes giddiness, and epilepsy in larger. The mischief which is being done by this plant is incalculable, and I grow the plant to point it out to my English friends, that they may never use so hurtful a drug in this country.[39]

Smee listed among his herbs 'hot Chilis and Capsicums'. He made cayenne pepper by beating dry chillies in a pestle and mortar with a little salt: 'This is far superior to anything which can be obtained in the shops; and it should therefore always be grown in first-rate gardens.' He intended to try growing ginger for preserving in his fernery or cucumber house. His other herbs included woodruff, which he grew for use in claret cup: 'It grows well with me, but some time ago I nearly lost the whole, as a stupid labourer was carefully picking it all out as a useless weed. This is really one of the greatest difficulties with which a cultivator of plants has to contend, as *employés* destroy the loveliest plants, and only preserve some florist's worthless monstrosity.'[40]

CHAPTER TEN

The Fruit Garden

Fruit has always had a special place in people's gardens. Generally, fruit is a luxury, something extra special that is only available fresh in the British climate in the summer and autumn. Its seasonal quality has made the first strawberries of the year still considered special. As with vegetables, extraordinary methods were developed to 'force' early rhubarb, that strange hybrid food, neither fruit nor vegetable, that seems to be the first item in the year that can be cooked as a dessert. Many methods, of course, also developed to preserve summer fruit for the rest of the year, so that the weeks when soft fruit and tree fruit were suddenly ready to pick produced a frenzy of activity in both the garden and the kitchen so as not to lose any of the precious harvest.

Fruit in British gardens was strictly divided along class lines until well into the second half of the nineteenth century. Only the wealthy could grow fruit under glass, so generally only they could eat grapes, peaches and nectarines, and of course the famous pineapples grown in the stove houses of the ultra-wealthy. Apples, plums, cherries, gooseberries, red- and blackcurrants and hedgerow fruit like blackberries were the fruits of the working people in the countryside.

The mere cost of glass is not the only impediment to its use in places kept by humble people . . . there must be good carpentry, good brick walls, and a certain completeness about the structures that of necessity makes them expensive. Tiffany is so light that the merest skeleton of a structure is sufficient to carry it; and for every kind of garden stock which needs partial protection only, it answers not only as well, but better.

Floral World, May 1860, p. 92

Town-dwellers would be able to buy seasonal fruits sold in the streets, even if they could not grow them. But there was a curious anomaly: melons. Melons appeared at florists' feasts from very early in the nineteenth century when the florists branched out and started exhibiting fruit at their shows. How was this? We think of melons being grown in hothouses with a lot of skill and fuss, but actually they are closely related to cucumbers, and though they need warmth to germinate and sun to ripen them properly, they can be grown in a sheltered place outside, with care. In a cottage garden they could be grown on the heat of the dung heap, which would have the same effect as a hotbed. It would therefore be possible for someone with the skills of a florist to grow one or two melon plants if he had the space and the time; the dung certainly would not be a problem.

Nathaniel Paterson listed melons with vegetables ('Great chieftan of the fruit race'), but was not sure whether it was worth growing them:

Whether the melon ought to be admitted into the manse garden is a question which the following may help to solve . . . The breadth of glass seemed not very formidable, and the requisite heat is not that of actual combustion . . . A dunghill must ferment somewhere, and its heat is dissipated. Instead of giving this warmth to the unthankful winds, why not apply it to the production of the rich odour and nectarine juice of the melon? . . . Then came something about the convenience of a cart road leading to the interior, namely of the 'melon garden', another staggerer. But still a wheelbarrow road might do; and 'melon garden', after all, might signify only a part of the garden separated from the rest by a holly hedge. But next came the various sets of hot-beds and hot-ridges, the one-light and two-light frames; the thermometrical trials; the decay, the revival, and the preservation of heat; the opening of the glass for air, and the hazard of a shower; the awnings for the sun and the mattings for a frost; the constant waterings, with the cautions not to wet a leaf; the drying of the seed by animal heat, that is by carrying in the pocket, and keeping it till five years old; the cautious turning of the fruit, like a patient in a bed; with this greater care, that whereas if the patient may at any time be turned either way, the last turning of the melon must be remembered in order that the next day may observe a contrary direction, lest by several turnings in one way the head should fall off; and with this care of turning the fruit, the contrary caution is necessary with regard to the leaves, which must not be permitted to turn by the natural breeze, but must all have their faces set full to the sun, and be kept in that position, for which purpose a liberal use of pegs is recommended . . . at this stage [the writer] was arrested by a considerable commotion of disgust, not only with the pains necessary to produce the fruits, but with the fruits themselves, and scarcely failing to include the eaters.[1]

He concluded that the cost of rearing a melon was in the amount of care needed, which was the same for one as for a hundred, and that therefore it was a hundred times cheaper to buy a melon than to grow one. Shirley Hibberd tried to dispel the fear of melon growing by an article in the *Floral World* on frame culture of the melon in 1874. He claimed that melons could be grown in frames on hotbeds only three feet long by two and a half feet wide, but they would have to then be moved to another bed for fruiting. It still sounded complicated, with ridging up with tiles and turf, and constant vigilance with shading and watering. If this was not thought feasible by many amateurs, they may have been more encouraged by a later article he wrote in the *Gardener's Magazine*, called 'Melon Culture in Open Ground': 'Those who simply plant out melons and hope for the best are very likely indeed to go unrewarded, for systematic cultivation is required, and the principal object of all the arrangements must be to make the best of the climate to carry the plants safely through a period of trial, or enable them to derive the fullest possible advantage from a long spell of bright warm weather.'[2] The melons were to be grown on hillocks made of fermented stable manure and then covered in bell glasses. He went on, 'If the sun shines fiercely, lay a rhubarb leaf over the glass, and tilt it slightly to give a little air.' The glasses also had to be set on notches made in stakes of deal so they could be raised or lowered 'as changes of weather may render necessary'. It still wasn't easy.

Hibberd was determined to teach ordinary people the skills of gardening to enable them to have luxury fruit just as the wealthy did. He produced a series of articles in the *Floral World* called 'Grapes for the Million' in 1866, saying that he had grown eighty bunches of Black Hamburg grapes, averaging one pound each, in his conservatory in Stoke Newington, only ten feet by six foot six inches: 'If eighty bunches of Black Hamburgs, when ripe, are not worth a five pound note, then this number of the *Floral World* is not worth a farthing, and my name is not Shirley Hibberd.'[3] He also wrote about pot culture for strawberries as another way to make fruit more accessible for the millions. The young strawberry runners could be put into pots, firmly rammed with soil, and set in a frame or in any space available in a glasshouse, and so would be ready before plants grown in open ground.[4]

Raspberries and redcurrants were other fruits that were grown in great gardens on a vast scale, and ordinary people coming to gardening for the first time were put off because they thought a lot of complicated pruning and training was required. Shirley Hibberd pointed out to his readers that these fruits had been grown for generations in cottage gardens with very little attention, and that much of the supposedly difficult and skilful training was simply for decoration or because it was more convenient to the gardeners:

> It must be confessed that the raspberry plot in a first class garden usually presents a very pretty appearance. We see the canes trained to wire arches forming a labyrinth of festoons like a fairy bower in a pantomime . . . the universal practice of supporting the raspberry canes in some way or other suggests that they need support, or the practice would be a libel on the common sense of mankind. But the matter cannot be disposed of by such a simple consideration. The necessity for training the raspberry arises in great part from the faulty culture of it, the result of this faulty culture being weak, wiry canes that are unable to carry their fruit fairly, and so support is given to prevent the spoiling of the crop by contact with the ground. When well grown the raspberry does not need support of any kind, and as good cultivation results in an augmented crop, so it obviates the necessity of training and there is a double advantage therefore in the adoption of a natural system of cultivation.[5]

Similarly with redcurrants:

> There is something to be said in favour of leaving currant trees unpruned. In the first place, the labour of the cultivation is reduced to a minimum, and the production of the fruit is raised to a maximum. The fruit, indeed, is smaller than pruned trees produce, but it is of a higher colour and a fuller flavour, and as regards this particular fruit, bulk is of more importance than sample size, when the destination of it is the preserving pan . . . it will be supposed that unrestricted growth will render the trees gigantic and unmanageable, but the truth is, their immense fruitfulness is a check to their growth, and to keep them in order is a very simple matter. The subject is agreeably illustrated by the currant trees trained to the walls that we meet with occasionally in villages . . . it is not unusual to meet with a cottage adorned with red currants, the trees attaining a height of twenty feet, and producing fruit in abundance.[6]

Elizabeth Watts thought red- and whitecurrants more useful than blackcurrants, and advised that though red- and whitecurrants could be left to hang on the bushes, blackcurrants must be picked immediately they were ripe.[7] She also considered gooseberries very useful, and they were the first fruits of the season, other than rhubarb. Victorian gooseberries were a class of fruit all their own. They came in many different varieties, and were classified as red, yellow, white or green. They were also described as hairy or downy. Some varieties were bred for cooking or bottling, others for eating as

FIG. 235.—Melon Apple.

FIG. 236.—Cox's Orange Pippin.

FIG. 237.—Golden Pippin.

FIG. 238.—Court of Wick.

FIG. 239.—Coe's Golden Drop.

FIG. 240.—Court-pendu Plat.

FIG. 241.—Manning-ton's Pearmain.

FIG. 242.—Northern Spy.

FIG. 243.—American Newtown Pippin.

FIG. 244.—Reinette of Canada.

FIG. 245.—Golden Harvey.

FIG. 246.—Early Nonpareil.

Apples came in a huge variety, for eating and cooking, and some to be kept through the winter. (Alfred Smee, *My Garden*, p. 146) (*Author's collection*)

dessert. Competitions were held for the biggest gooseberry and also for the finest-flavoured ones, especially in Lancashire. To grow prize gooseberries, young bushes were used and only two or three fruits were allowed to ripen in each of the five or six branches. Bushes would be well watered in hot weather and shaded during the hottest part of the day.[8]

It was not only gooseberries that came in abundant varieties. Victorian gardening books listed large numbers of all fruit varieties, making us realise just how much we are missing in the modern age. As with vegetables, for most people fruit was essentially seasonal and varieties were developed to provide early and late crops, and, with apples and pears in particular, varieties that were good for keeping through the winter. All great gardens had specially designed fruit rooms for storing fruit in optimum conditions, but it was only worth storing fruit if it was in good condition when picked. According to Elizabeth Watts:

> The good keeping of fruit greatly depends on the care with which it is gathered, as the slightest bruise will spoil the keeping. Many amateur fruit-growers gather their own fruit, and unless the gardener be unusually careful and dexterous, there is scarcely a job in the whole garden on which a gentleman can better bestow his own personal work and attention.

R.D. BLACKMORE (1825–1900)

RICHARD DODDERIDGE BLACKMORE, author of *Lorna Doone*, spent over forty years as a semi-professional fruit grower. He was born in Berkshire, and was educated in Devon and at Oxford. He qualified as a barrister, but gave up through ill health. He taught classics for five years, before receiving a legacy which enabled him to buy a small estate at Teddington, Middlesex, where he set up a fruit farm. He wrote a dozen novels and translated Latin while he ran his business, specialising in pears. Blackmore sat on three RHS committees for fruit conferences in the 1880s and lectured on pests of the vine at the Grape Conference in 1890. He contributed to Robert Hogg's *Fruit Manual*. He was criticised for not taking fruit growing seriously as he collected old varieties of pear trees rather than growing commercially profitable ones, but was the first to admit that his novel writing subsidised the fruit farm.

The fruit should, one by one, be quietly removed from the tree and gently laid, not thrown, into the basket. Apples and pears should never, on any account, be poured from one basket to another, or on to the floor, but gently removed, if necessary, by hand. It is advisable not only to pick the fruit with the greatest ease and gentleness, but to avoid shifting it from basket to basket. Lay it softly in the first basket, in that convey it to where it is to be spread out to dry, and with equal care lay out all that are sound and good, and pick out for immediate use (for self or friends or pig, according to degree of damage) all that are touched by an insect, even in a slight degree, and all that have a suspicion of a bruise.[9]

She considered the pear to be the most popular fruit in England and the apple the most useful. She described over twenty varieties of pear, another thirteen for keeping through the winter, and devoted a further chapter of *Modern Practical Gardening* to pears for baking and quinces. In addition, she gave a list of eighty-four pear varieties known before 1765. This is a heritage that we have irretrievably lost.

All cookery books on English food list more recipes for apples than any other fruit, and no doubt it is the first choice when a fruit tree is sought for the garden. In Victorian times fruit tree growing was a far more complicated business than it is for us now. We can simply go to the garden centre, buy a container-grown tree and know that, even when planted, it will remain the right size for our garden. This is the result of all the hard work put in by nurserymen in the nineteenth century. All books on Victorian gardening, even for amateurs, give

long instructions on budding and grafting trees and the correct way to
prune. Now, trees are grafted on to suitable stocks for small gardens
and not much pruning is needed, but then, a gardener was expected to
graft his own tree, having first found the right sort of stock. He then
had to cover it in a mixture of beaten horse droppings, clayey loam and
fresh cow manure, kneaded with a little 'road drift' to make a paste.[10]
Vigorous pruning had to be carried out every year, and trees were even
dug up annually to prune the roots. Trees grown against walls were
trained in a variety of forms, such as espaliers, fans or cordons, to
encourage fruiting and keep them compact. The amateur was expected
to master all this, and that was apart from the trouble he might have
when taking over a new garden with overgrown cankerous trees left
behind by the previous owner or tenant.

Shirley Hibberd had several revolutionary ideas about fruit
growing, one of which he called 'pulley pruning'. He lectured on it
to the Society of Arts in 1876, under the title 'Fallacies in Fruit
Culture'. He went against the common method of drastic pruning
usually practised at the time, reasoning that when fruit trees
naturally bore a good crop of fruit, the branches were weighed down
with it, ripened well and then produced more new shoots, which in
turn bore fruit: 'Many years ago I adopted a practice of attaching
pebbles and other handy weights by means of string to my long rods,
so as to draw them gently to a horizontal position.'[11] He also
invented a way of growing fruit against a wall, without the wall:

Shirley Hibberd's idea for
'reversible fruit walls' was
supposed to help nurture the
trees in summer and protect
them in spring, but an amateur
would find a huge amount of
work in moving the fence
panels every time the weather
changed. (*Floral World*,
June 1872, p. 168) (*Hackney
Archives*)

The walls are made of wood, the trees are trained on wires; and the system affords the cultivator a choice of three conditions: the walls can be removed and stored away; they can be attached to the supporting posts on the north side of the trees to ensure them a maximum of exposure to sunshine; or they may be attached on the south side to exclude the sunshine, and keep them in a comparatively dormant state until the season is sufficiently advanced to permit the reversal of the walls, and the exposure of the trees to the stimulus of solar heat.[12]

Some fruits that the Victorians used are not often grown by us now. Quinces have been mentioned with pears, and they were good for preserves. Medlars were another fruit hardly seen now, and, according to many, not much of a loss. William Cobbett said, 'it is hardly worth the notice, being, at best, only one degree better than a rotten apple'.[13] Barberries are mentioned in several places. They are the fruit of the berberis. Mrs Beeton said they were very acidic, but made good preserves when boiled in sugar. She gave a recipe for a barberry tart and for preserving whole bunches in syrup.[14] Henry Bright had a barberry bush in his garden, the blossom of which attracted bees, and the fruits he used for crystallising for *bonbons* and also to be preserved in salt and water as a garnish for game.[15] Another useful tree for him was the mulberry: the fruit made delicious ices.[16]

The Queen pineapple was so good that Alfred Smee said a pound of it would go as far in flavouring ices as half a dozen pounds of any other sort. (*My Garden*, p. 207) (*Author's collection*)

By the late nineteenth century it had become more common for amateurs to afford modest glasshouses in which they could grow fruit. Paxton's portable fruit house was used by many who were tenants, as it could be dismantled and moved at the end of the tenancy, and Mr Rivers' orchard house could be used for growing dwarf fruit trees in containers. It was therefore tempting for some amateurs to imagine that they could even try growing pineapples themselves. An article in the *Floral World* in January 1868 attempted to give guidance as to whether it would be worthwhile. The writer explained that his pine pits covered an area of 500 square feet, divided into a first and succession pit, and a fruiting pit. There were

136 plants, of which forty-two were showing signs of fruiting, and it was expected that at least fifty fruits of three and a half to four pounds each would be produced that year. The average yearly outlay for maintaining the house was just over £27 for coke, tan, soil, sand, rotten dung, pots, and painting and repairs. In addition, the cost of labour of two hours a day throughout the year was at least £15, so totalling over £42. The writer further pointed out that he was lucky that the necessary materials, such as tan, were all close at hand and therefore he did not have to pay much for carriage, but on the other hand his boiler was larger than necessary, so he used more fuel than he would with a smaller one. Lastly, he pointed out that although it would be possible to grow pines on a smaller scale, in all cases it would be necessary to engage the services of a man who was experienced in growing them and consequently remunerate him accordingly. The conclusion was that if the pines were calculated as costing £1 each, they would probably be worth more than that in the market.[17]

CHAPTER ELEVEN

The Flower Garden

Victorian flower gardens are usually thought of as consisting entirely of geometric beds of pelargoniums and other brightly coloured tender plants, interspersed with rose trees and foliage plants. It is then imagined that these plants were swept away in the later part of the century and replaced by herbaceous borders, as designed by Gertrude Jekyll, and inspired by cottage gardens. It is true that the fashion for bedding plants gripped the nation from the mid-1850s onwards, but this does not mean that it totally superseded everything that had gone before, nor does it mean that the herbaceous border was invented in the 1880s. Most gardening writers in the nineteenth century constantly reminded readers not to neglect hardy perennials, but to make them the mainstay of the garden. Also, the popularity of florists' flowers as garden plants is plain from reading the gardening magazines of the time, but seems to have been largely ignored by all modern writers on Victorian gardens.

Flowers had many important roles to play in Victorian times. They were not just found growing in the garden or as cut flowers in vases inside. Fresh flowers were used decoratively, pinned to ladies' clothes and hats, and in gentlemen's buttonholes. A bouquet or posy was an important way to show affection for or interest in a lady, and the 'language of flowers' was as interesting to young women then as astrology or the influence of crystals is to many people today. Flowers were not universally available all the year round as they are in shops now, so certain flowers represented the change in seasons. The scent of violets or primroses heralded spring, the rich fragrance of roses characterised summer evenings and the pungent smell of chrysanthemums penetrated damp autumn twilight. The pine-scented boughs of fir trees, mingled with spices and citrus peel, would be a familiar smell for Victorians lucky enough to live in comfortable homes where Christmas festivities took place.

The scent of flowers was important where cramped housing had been constructed hurriedly with inadequate drainage, which was unfortunately the normal situation in towns in the mid-nineteenth century. Most people did not have the facilities to wash either themselves or their clothes as often as we do now, so entering a crowded room, lit by candles or gas flames, whether for an evening party or an afternoon lecture, or climbing into an omnibus or a train carriage, full of people in heavy, possibly damp, clothes, might be something of a faint-inducing situation where the welcome scent of the fresh flowers pinned to one's front would help to ward off the realities of human flesh. There were no regulations preventing picking and cutting of wild flowers, and it was traditional to go into the countryside to gather them on holidays. This made the sight of fresh flowers sold in the street reminiscent of happy days and fine weather.

Amateur gardeners in the nineteenth century tried to imitate the gardens of the wealthy that they increasingly saw depicted in magazines, and they also copied planting ideas from public parks. That planting, still in public gardens today, is one of the last remnants of Victorian style and makes us believe that it was all that Victorian gardens were about. Unfortunately it is rarely done as extravagantly as it was then. Parks departments do not have the vast teams of gardeners that would have provided the workforce a

GEORGE McLEOD (b. 1859)

GEORGE McLEOD was born near Glasgow and was an amateur florist, specialising in pansies from a young age. In the 1890s he was employed in London and lived at Chingford on the borders of Epping Forest. In the summer he would get up at 4 a.m. to work in his garden, which contained over two thousand pansy and viola plants, the best of which he sent out into commercial cultivation. He was a Fellow of the Royal Horticultural Society and an executive member of the National Amateur Gardeners' Association, for which he delivered lectures on the culture of his plants. The Association was formed partly to further the interests of amateurs in shows and uphold their rights to exhibit their plants in separate classes from the professionals. It held an annual dinner in the City of London at the Guildhall Tavern.

George McLeod (photographed from *Amateur Gardening*, 12 September 1891, by the author with permission of *Amateur Gardening*).

hundred and fifty years ago, and probably cannot provide the variety of plants that would have been used then. The schemes we see, though sometimes detailed and original, are not usually as intricate and scientifically worked out as the Victorian originals. Perhaps most modern gardeners do not have their hearts in it in the way that the pioneer gardeners of the mid-1800s did.

The idea of using tender plants as temporary displays in geometrically shaped flower beds started in the 1830s in the great country-house gardens. It was taken up enthusiastically by Donald Beaton (1802–63), 'Flower Garden' editor of the *Cottage Gardener*, but reached a much wider audience when it was used as the major design theme by Sir Joseph Paxton in 1856 when he created the Italian gardens for the Crystal Palace at Sydenham. Then thousands of middle-class and working-class gardeners took the brightly coloured flowers to their hearts and all wanted to make mini-Italian parterres in their own suburban plots. All sorts of theories abounded as to how these beds and borders should be designed. 'Colour theory' became a popular talking point. Gardeners were encouraged to look at the colour wheel, where colours were divided according to their place in the spectrum and rules were expounded, or created, about how opposite colours were complementary and should therefore be used together.[1] However, they should also be divided by neutral colours such as white or silver. In the context of a garden design, green, as an overriding background, also had to be taken into account. In order to keep to the rules, bedding plants had to be carefully bred to provide not only a good selection of colours, but also good-quality, compact plants that could stand up to the weather.

Magazines and books provided designs that could be copied. At first they were geometric, but later they became figurative, and the more life-like, the better the trick worked. In 1876 the *Gardeners' Chronicle* provided plans for the famous butterfly beds at Crystal Palace. There were six in all, each depicting a real species of butterfly. It was only possible to do this once enough different-coloured plants had been provided to fit the scheme.

These carefully crafted designs could only be carried out properly by professional gardeners. Not only would the garden have to be spacious enough and the gardeners skilled enough to put the plans into effect, but they would also have to spend the time trimming, feeding and dead-heading the plants to keep them in good condition, and that apart from the initial cost of either buying in or raising the plants themselves. The *Floral World* constantly advised amateurs not to be taken in by the bedding system alone. In 1866 it published an article once again trying to persuade readers to look at other garden plants, stating that this had been its aim virtually since the magazine began:

But having expressed ourselves in this way, we left our readers to consider the matter as it pleased them; and as a large majority of our supporters were practitioners of bedding, we always offered them the best practical information respecting the relative merits of bedding plants, and the treatment they severally require to bring them to perfection. We blew hot and cold; but whether hot or cold, we always blew in earnest. We believe in bedding, and always did; in its place and well done, it is the grandest of all possible embellishments. A pavement of gems could not glow with such brilliancy as a well-coloured parterre. But it is very much to be regretted that, in small private gardens where promenade displays are not wanted – where, in fact, they are as much out of taste as liveried servants and a military band to play during dinner would be within the residence, that bedding plants should reign supreme, not only to the exclusion of numerous beautiful hardy and tender ornamental plants, but to the detriment of the kitchen and fruit-gardens, which are robbed of the labour they require.[2]

It was then resolved to start a new section in the magazine called 'The Choice Garden' to guide readers towards the best hardy herbaceous plants to use in their gardens.

An amateur could not hope to accomplish intricate designs by himself, but still the books provided them, although sometimes simplified for those gardening on their own. Elizabeth Watts provided some examples for what she called 'the set garden'. She considered the constant attention necessary to keep the beds in good condition a suitable occupation for ladies,[3] and provided plans for them to follow, combining florists' flowers with bedding plants, foliage plants and shrubs. She recommended pegging down flowering plants with twigs to cover the beds more quickly. The Watts system of bedding was therefore not bedding in the purest sense, but was probably more successful and easier to manage for the amateur. Another relatively simple system for flower beds was provided by *Cassell's Popular Gardening*, which gave a diagram for three neighbouring terraced-house gardens of uniform length.[4] Each consisted of beds, and/or gravel and grass, in different layouts with suggestions for planting. It tried to steer the readers

Elizabeth Watts's plan for a 'set garden'. A is pampas grass surrounded by lavender phlox; B is myrtle mixed with scarlet salvia; C is myrtle mixed with blue salvia; D is purple petunia; E is white foxgloves surrounded by scarlet geraniums. (*Modern Practical Gardening*, p. 280) (*Author's collection*)

away from bedding plants in favour of hardy shrubs with variegated foliage. One more alternative to fill up beds quickly, and replace the colour of the plants in the winter months, was to use coloured stones, sand or gravel. This was the ultimate low-maintenance garden, but was thought just too feeble by some people:

> The working out of a great design in coloured earths and flower beds is the most complicated, and, generally speaking, perhaps the least satisfactory, form of the parterre. It has this advantage, that, during the winter, it affords 'something to look at,' but the corresponding disadvantage is that nobody wants to see it. A favourite idea with artists in this line of business is to draw out, on a gigantic scale, a group of rose, shamrock, and thistle in coloured earths and box embroidery, and while the thing is new it looks tolerably well; but the majority of people do not keep themselves sufficiently under control when tempted to indulge a smile as they admire it.[5]

One of the most popular plants for bedding was the 'geranium', properly called pelargonium, but the modern perception that it

ARTHUR LAUNDER (active 1880s–90s)

ARTHUR G.N. LAUNDER was born in Plymouth and was a government clerk in London in the 1890s. He had grown pansies and auriculas since childhood, progressing to zonal pelargoniums, fuchsias and other half-hardy plants by the time he was working in London and living in Clapham. His six prize-winning zonal pelargoniums each measured a metre in diameter. He also won prizes for the best seedling tricolour pelargoniums. He became a frequent contributor to *Amateur Gardening* and was a committee member of the National Amateur Gardeners' Association, which was formed when the editor of *Amateur Gardening* called together a dozen amateur growers to a meeting at the Corn Exchange Tavern, Mark Lane, London in 1890. Arthur Launder believed that visiting nurseries, public gardens and parks added to his knowledge of plants and the best conditions in which to grow them.

Arthur G.N. Launder (photographed from *Amateur Gardening*, 11 July 1891, p. 108, by the author, with permission of *Amateur Gardening*).

was just like the modern one is wrong. The scarlet geranium was what the gardeners yearned for, and the florists tried to breed it throughout the century, but it was only produced in a reliable form as a bedding plant right at the end of the century. Before that, larger, much more variable plants, of different sizes, colour and foliage, were used. In the 1860s a craze developed for the coloured-leaved varieties introduced by Peter Grieve (1811–95), gardener at Culford Hall, near Ipswich, Suffolk.[6] To produce these he hybridised plants with the typical dark zone on a green leaf with the already popular variegated varieties, which had either golden or silver edges. The combination produced leaves where the mixture of the dark zone, which appeared brown on a green leaf, came out red on the white or cream part of the leaf. Thus leaves were produced exhibiting green, brown, red and white or cream. Some of the best known were Mrs Pollock, Mrs Henry Cox, Dolly Vardon and Miss Burdett Coutts, which are all still available today.

Shirley Hibberd provided a spectacular way of using pelargoniums, in what he called the Geranium Pyramid.[7] This required a large stock of plants in pots, which in his own garden he kept throughout the winter under glass so that some were four or five feet high. He built up the plants using the tall ones in the centre, surrounded with a framework of chicken wire, into which he put smaller plants in pots, embedded in moss. The whole structure would involve a huge amount of care and maintenance, but it provided a fantastic centre-piece for a circular path. A similar effect, which is easier to accomplish, can be produced by using metal frames holding a series of flower baskets in descending circles of increasing size. These were also depicted in Victorian books.

Formal flower beds in Victorian gardens often fell into two categories: pincushion beds and ribbon borders. Pincushion beds were circular beds raised in the middle and so shaped like a pincushion. They gradually replaced the swirly pointed bed that appeared in the 'Gardenesque' style of planting typified by Mrs Lawrence in the early part of the century, seen in the Louth 'Panorama' and sometimes described as 'tadpole' beds. A circle would certainly be easier for an amateur to manage. In *Handy Book of the Flower Garden* pincushion beds are described as 'beds that are planted with a self colour as a ground, and dotted over with contrasting plants'.[8] Several combinations are suggested, such as a groundwork of blue lobelia, edged with *Cerastium tomentosum* and Mrs Pollock geranium, planted regularly at intervals. Another combination was *Viola cornuta* as groundwork with yellow calceolaria as the 'dot plant'. As with all bedding, amateurs were probably unable to keep it

The geranium pyramid in Shirley Hibberd's garden. It was made of four-feet-high plants kept though the winter, with smaller plants packed in moss surrounding them. (Engraving from *Amateur Gardening*, 20 July 1889, p. 133) (*Amateur Gardening*)

simple, and the pincushion bed was frequently referred to jokingly as being so called 'because you could stick anything into it'.

In ribbon borders the plants were placed in contrasting colours in parallel lines along the length of the border. The idea supposedly originated in parks to encourage people to keep walking along the paths, rather than stopping to look at circular beds, the lines psychologically encouraging them to keep going. The Butters' gardens seemed obsessed with ribbon planting, which appeared in

both the circular (or pincushion) beds and the borders. They all seem to consist of the same limited palette of bright red, white or pink, which unfortunately Shirley Hibberd considered quite out of place: 'The stereotyped repetition of scarlet geraniums and yellow calceolarias is in the last degree vulgar and tasteless, and the common dispositions of red, white and blue are better adapted to delight savages, than represent the artistic status of a civilized people.'[9] Hibberd wrote that opinion in 1871, but probably had to keep quiet when he went to visit the Butters' garden a few years later to write about it for the *Gardener's Magazine*. He then described it as 'an example of private endeavour, crowned with complete success . . . wherein horticulture is ably vindicated and refinement and finish are conspicuous throughout'.[10]

The classic bedding with brightly coloured flowers gradually gave way to a more intricate form of bedding, known as carpet bedding or tapestry bedding. Instead of the interest coming from the bright colours of the flowers, a more subtle effect was achieved with foliage plants, and eventually the texture of the leaves came to dominate when succulents like sedums and sempervivums came into prominence. The effect was dramatic, especially when three-dimensional living sculptures started to appear. More than once

View of the Butters' garden in Hackney showing pincushion beds and ribbon borders. The potted aloes in the foreground give a subtropical air. (Engraving from *Amateur Gardening*, 23 June 1888, p. 90) (*Amateur Gardening*)

'carpet' bedding was used to create a mock carpet being unrolled: the Victorians loved their puns. Again, the amateur could scarcely compete with such professional work.

When Shirley Hibberd had been criticising the gaudy colours often used for bedding he had gone on to compare the more tasteful effect of using coloured foliage without flowers. In another article in the *Gardener's Magazine* he featured the Butters' garden in connection with tapestry bedding, a form of which he claimed had been invented by Walter Butters:

Detail of the Butters' garden in Hackney, showing formal flower beds surrounding a planted urn, with shrubbery in the background. (Engraving from *Amateur Gardening*, 26 May 1888) (*Amateur Gardening*)

There is no box edging required to define the pattern, no fanciful walks made of spar, or shells, or complicated mixture of stone, slate, or gravel. The whole of the pattern is cut in the grass turf, and, hence the entire design has a green ground-work, and must be coloured accordingly. We begin, therefore, with a piece of fine turf, and, having the design drawn to scale, it is carefully pegged out on the ground and cut with precision. The fine lines are well adapted for cerastiums, lobelias, alternantheras, and such-like, and the beds will require plants of more distinctive character, the smaller zonals or leaf plants of decisive colours being suitable furniture. In any case the colouring should be bright, but there need be no flowering plants employed, and, generally speaking, it would render a scheme of this sort the more novel and entertaining to colour it well with leaves only.[11]

They seemed to have produced a flower garden without any flowers.

Formal gardens began to lose appeal as the 1870s wore on. Henry Bright in *A Year in a Lancashire Garden*, which appeared in the *Gardeners' Chronicle* in 1874, said: 'To tell the truth too, I am heartily weary of the monotony of modern gardens, with their endless Pelargoniums, Calceolarias, and Verbenas. Some few such beds I cannot of course dispense with, but I am always glad when I can *reclaim* a bed for permanent herbaceous plants, as in this case of the *Primula japonica*.'[12] Canon Ellacombe agreed: 'To me a bedded-out garden gives little pleasure, and I see little beauty in "carpet beds" and "pincushion borders", but the flowers which compose these beds and borders have each their own charm and beauty, and we cannot do without them. I would not willingly be without the sweet scent of the heliotropes; and I use largely geraniums, calceolarias, and begonias, but I use them as single plants to fill up many gaps, and to brighten up many an odd corner, and for such purposes they are most useful, and do what I ask of them most effectually.'[13]

William Robinson is credited with the change in planting ideas, but in reality all writers had cautioned gardeners not to forsake the mixed borders, which relied on shrubs and perennials for the seasonal wonders of formal bedding. Bedding plants were certainly useful in

HENRY ARTHUR BRIGHT (1830–84)

HENRY BRIGHT was educated at Rugby School and Cambridge and worked in the family shipping firm specialising in importing goods from Australia. He lived and gardened at Ashfield, Knotty Ash, near Liverpool, which he described in *A Year in a Lancashire Garden* in the *Gardeners' Chronicle* in 1874. He also contributed to *The English Flower Garden* and the *Christian Reformer*. He was a friend of the American novelist Nathaniel Hawthorne, with whom he travelled around Wales in 1854. Bright followed the William Robinson style of gardening, trying to get away from formality and the 'bedding system' and allowing plants to be seen for themselves. He preferred to employ unskilled labourers whom he could instruct himself, rather than trained gardeners whom he felt spent too much of their employer's time growing plants for exhibition, and taking the credit for themselves.

towns where pollution caused all plants to discolour and eventually
suffocate in soot. As bedding was only there for a season it would be
dug up and thrown away when it was past its best anyway. This
'throw-away' mentality could be perceived as characteristic of the
Victorian age itself, in the way that lesser members of society were
used up and thrown away by the wealthy. Servants and soldiers alike
were taken from poorer families who needed jobs and could not pick
and choose where they worked. If dismissed without a 'character'
they had little hope of another respectable position. Perhaps it was
not by coincidence that the return to permanent plants in the garden
that needed constant care and nurturing came about when working-
class activists began to demand better conditions and higher wages
for their fellow workers, and the workers themselves started to see
more value in permanent features. The movement to provide parks
and open spaces for recreation had developed in the early part of the
century when those in power had felt intimidated by the masses who
threatened to take their land if it was not given willingly. It is
unlikely, however, that the move away from formal gardens was
strengthened by any guilt feelings on the part of the wealthy about
the way the lower classes were treated. The spectacular herbaceous
borders created in the later part of the century, which culminated in
the great gardens of the Edwardian era, required just as many
gardeners as bedding plants did, and only fell into ruins after the
First World War when the labour force was massacred in the
trenches, in many cases after serving less time even than bedding
plants to which they might be compared.

The more informal style was easier for amateurs to manage once a
collection of plants had been established as they did not need
replanting every year; the main work was to keep away the weeds
and periodically divide the clumps to keep the more rampant ones
from taking over. It worked best on a large scale where expansive
'drifts' could blend together and there was enough variety of plants
to provide colour and interest throughout the season, but with
careful choices, an amateur could produce a good display. What
seems to have been forgotten by contemporary writers who dictated
the fashion to eager readers, and by present-day writers who try to
explain the revolution Robinson brought about, was that many of
these flowers had existed in amateurs' gardens throughout the
century under the guise of 'florists' flowers', and now they started to
come into their own again, mainly because they were reliable hardy
plants that were easy to grow. The florists had started to latch on to
the more exotic flowers like pelargoniums, dahlias and
chrysanthemums as they were brought into the country, then they
turned their attention to the existing 'cottage-style' plants like

hollyhocks, pansies, phlox and gladiolus. Once they were conquered, there seemed to be total confusion about what to call verbenas, petunias, calceolarias and the like, which were all being marketed as florists' flowers to the undiscerning public. But what did it matter, as long as they filled the amateurs' gardens with colour? There were numberless varieties of all these plants, and only the purist cared what they were called.

The 'Cheap Gay Garden' (described in Chapter Eight) shows what people really put in their gardens in 1884. For the north or shady border the recommendation for the back is 'old white lilies', tiger lilies and orange lilies, with Michaelmas daisies and tansy (the roots to be confined in an old drainpipe). These should be supplemented with hardy fuchsias, monkshood, white and pink Japanese anemones, and foxgloves: 'Three pennyworth of seed will produce a considerable variety of colours, and no plant thrives more satisfactorily in a shady border or looks better in all stages of its growth.' In the middle row should be planted peonies, day lilies, geum, iris, *Dicentra spectabile*, Solomon's seal and mimulus should not be forgotten. The front row should include primroses, polyanthus, cowslip, alpine auricula, forget-me-nots, double daisies, in patches of four or five together, but only one colour. The Christmas rose, *Helleborus niger*, should be in a snug corner with violets and lily-of-the-valley: 'In close town districts violets are useless, but the lily-of-the-valley will grow in any confined spot, and will even thrive in a gravel path.'[14]

For borders in a sunny position, chrysanthemums were considered 'easy doers' and should be placed in the back row with a small selection of dahlias, single and double. Herbaceous phloxes are 'too splendid to be dispensed with', and delphiniums should have gladiolus dotted among them. Carnations and columbines (aquilegia) grown from seed were suitable for the middle row, with English or Spanish iris ('remarkably beautiful and wonderfully cheap'). Ranunculus, *Sedum spectabile* and striped ribbon grass, 'with its roots cabin'd, cribb'd, confin'd', made up the middle row. In front was suggested patches of pansies and poppy anemones, raised from seed, with rock cress, saxifrages, *Campanula carpatica*, as well as lamb's ear, 'with its thick furry leaves like white plush'. Here appears a rather irritated editor's note: 'The importance of attaching the botanical name is illustrated in this mention of Lamb's Ear. What is it? There is a scabious so-called. Does the author refer to *Verbascum thapsus?*'

Lastly comes the description of the central bed, which is rather a surprise after the gay exuberance of the informal planting so far suggested. This, it is said, calls for a different approach. In the centre

Take red or scarlet, dark pink, pale pink, and white, place them in the order named, and a pleasing harmony from red to white is the result. The transition is gentle and beautiful – like a plaintive melody in music . . . take a purple-flowering plant with a shade of red in it, and place it near a crimson, or let a golden-leaved pelargonium be associated with lovely silvery-foliaged plants, and a delicate harmony is produced.

David Thomson, *Handy Book of the Flower Garden*, p. 319

should be a large oval patch of scabious, round which should be a belt, two feet wide, of French and African marigolds, alternating with antirrhinums. Round that, a band of convolvulus minor and sweet williams, which should be arranged so that the convolvulus is next to the antirrhinums and the sweet williams next to the marigolds. Similarly, the next row consists of asters placed next to the sweet williams and wallflowers next to the convolvulus, and the following row stocks and Canterbury bells, with the stocks next to the wallflowers. Round the edge were to be *Phlox drummondii* and mignonette at intervals. When the annuals had finished, the instruction was to fill the bed with bulbs and replace the biennials with new seedlings. It was even suggested which bulbs to place in which gap, but suffice it to say the bulbs consisted of daffodils, tulips, hyacinths and crocuses.

The incongruity of this planting makes it difficult to judge exactly what the typical amateur had gained from all the advice meted out to him in the preceding three decades. No doubt the garden was very gay with its colourful planting, and fairly cheap if much of it was grown from seed, or gathered from the wild and friends' gardens, but what was the reasoning behind setting out the central bed so artificially when the borders and corners were filled so successfully with informal perennials? Perhaps there was a lingering hope in the hearts of all modest gardeners that they could yet produce something to equal the formal parterres of the wealthy that had never been quite forgotten. There was yet another alternative. Canon Ellacombe admitted that he actually liked weeds in his garden:

Some weeds are so beautiful that I should certainly grow them in the garden, if only they could be kept in their place, and if they were not already too abundant. I should be sorry to banish from my walls the creeping toad-flax and the yellow fumitory, and as long as they keep to the walls they do no harm. But there are two plants that are sad weeds, but which, if lost, would be sorely missed. The dandelion is one . . . Surely no other flower can surpass it for beauty of foliage, beauty of shape, and rich beauty of colouring. The second weed that I often wish to transplant into my garden, but dare not, is the goose grass, or silver weed . . . Its beautiful leaves have a silver sheen that make it very attractive; but it is far better kept outside the garden, and it grows everywhere.[15]

CHAPTER TWELVE

The Natural Garden

The Victorian era was a time of extremes. The rigid formality in style in one part of the garden could be offset in more secluded places in the opposite direction. The carefully dressed lady or gentleman with outward respectability was known to enjoy discovering wilder tastes in both garden and the wider world. As usual it was the wealthy who set the trends. The rock garden or rockery was a Victorian invention, and was supposed to re-create the majesty of wild landscapes, but unfortunately it was not always possible to maintain the grandeur and artistry when the concept was adapted to the capacities of a smaller garden.

Although the earliest rock gardens were constructed of real rocks on a huge scale, even those of the 1840s were not true reconstructions of nature, but contained artificial arches and 'windows' to give delight to the visitors. This is the garden as a work of art, trying to improve on nature. After all, if people wanted to see real rocks they had only to go out into the surrounding countryside. The best-known Victorian 'rockwork' is Pulhamite, which was developed by the Pulham family in Broxbourne, Hertfordshire. It consisted of clinker and brick 'rubbish' moulded together with Portland cement, giving a realistic stone appearance, in both colour and shape. It involved practised skill to produce something that looked like a real outcrop of rock, but the principle could be used on a smaller scale by anyone in his own garden, and very soon it was. Shirley Hibberd constantly suggested making use of 'burrs' or 'brickbats', which were misshapen or broken bricks rejected by brickmakers, for small-scale rockwork. In the early nineteenth century there were brickfields all over the areas surrounding London and other big cities, so that the rows of terraced houses were actually built out of the ground on which they stood. Rejected bricks were plentiful and cheap and were used to fill garden walls and other structures.

An amateur's questionable skills at bricklaying or construction would soon by covered with greenery if the right plants were chosen,

REVD HENRY JARDINE BIDDER (1847–1923)

HENRY BIDDER was born in Mitcham, Surrey, the son of an engineer. He became a Fellow of St John's College, Oxford, and took over the management of the garden, which became, in the words of the *Gardeners' Chronicle*, 'one of the most beautiful places in the world'. He helped to establish a professorship of Forestry and secured Bagley Wood as a training ground and arboretum. He became particularly interested in growing alpine plants and in 1893 started to build a rockery in a secluded corner of the college garden to show off the plants. He constructed much of it, made of large blocks of stone, with his own hands. Bidder was also a keen musician and trained a local choir. His advice was to remember the three 'p's of horticulture: 'Propagate, propagate, propagate!' The rockery remains as a monument to him.

Revd Henry Jardine Bidder (1847–1923). (St John's College Archive, PHOTO 128, by kind permission of the President and Fellows of St John's College, University of Oxford)

so many did try building rockeries with their own hands. The Revd Henry Jardine Bidder (1847–1923) was responsible for the garden of St John's College, Oxford and wrote: 'I have built, bit by bit, and chiefly with my own hands a rockery, small indeed in extent, but so constructed as to provide suitable tenements for a large number of species.'[1] His rockery consisted of large, real rocks, built in a terraced formation in a corner of the garden, and still looks elegant and realistic today, even when bare of plants in winter. There is no suspicion of broken bricks and cement.

Shirley Hibberd also built some rockwork with his own hands, in his fern house:

The finish of the work I did myself, and it occupied me, at odd times, about four months, the work being essentially amusing, though attended with an occasional abrasion of the knuckles. The task I had was to make the 'pockets' – openings for the purpose being left at intervals in the work. I made the 'pockets' and planted the ferns at the same time. Some of the larger ones are planted in projecting receptacles, just as the bricklayer left them; but generally speaking, I found it the best plan to stuff the necessary soil into a chink or gap, then place the fern in it, and, lastly, to introduce a piece of burr of suitable size to close it in, and this was done with the help of cement. I do not think I can profitably occupy further space with remarks on the formative part of the affair; details of this kind do not admit of being described minutely; all I can say in concluding this part of the history is this, that I never did a better job in my life; for not only have the ferns and mosses planted in it thriven amazingly, but the scene produced is exquisitely beautiful and affords more than a suggestion of the 'Negligence of nature, wild and wide'.[2]

But even in the 1850s, rockeries had acquired a certain reputation. Hibberd wrote in 1856:

> The mere mention of rock-work is usually sufficient to raise a smile on the face of an enthusiast in gardening; for of all the mistakes that are made by amateurs, and even by professed gardeners and landscapists, the Rockery is but too frequently the most ridiculous . . . Now between rock-work and a Rockery there is the greatest possible difference. Rock-work of a certain kind is admissible almost anywhere . . . But in every case the material must be adapted to the work, and in all coloured and formal scenes the rocks should be used in huge blocks in piles and mounds, not to imitate caverns and rude cairns, but strictly as ornaments to set off the beauties of other objects, or to give light or shadow as the case may be. This is rock-work, not Rockery, and it involves the disposal of rough blocks in symmetrical masses or groups, not in wild and fantastic outlines . . . Wherever you want a bit of rock-work build it up with one kind of material only – no mixtures of colours, no shells, no gingerbread of any kind. Let the mass be sufficiently bold, but subordinate to the general scheme of the garden, for it is not in any case to form a special object of attraction, but is intended only to diversify the colouring and character of the scene. Within a considerable distance of your house it ought to be impossible for you to say to a friend, 'come and see my rock-work,' because it should have no special importance at all.[3]

He gave the impression that although 'rock-work' could be used anywhere, if properly constructed, a 'Rockery' was something trivial and frivolous that should not be contemplated in a 'Home of Taste'. Far from it, however: he then went on to explain how to build a rockery from 'large brick clinkers' or even 'bricks and mortar' if real stone were not available: 'This may sound odd to many readers, but I can assure those who may feel inclined to smile that an artificer possessed of genuine taste and judgment could erect a noble Rockery of any material that could be stuck together with a common cement.'[4] He then describes what mighty feats of engineering may be contemplated and how they would be planted:

The ugly abominations used for rockwork, of which the chief is a product of the brickfield, called burrs, should not be allowed a place inside any decent garden, as they generally convert what might be made a nice place into a brick-yard. Very rarely is stone used, and when it is, it is put together like a rubbish heap. Rockwork is entirely out of place in a small garden, and should never be allowed.

W.J. May, *Villa Gardening* (undated)

Where a considerable elevation can be attained, a dark cave may be constructed, both for general effect and for the growth of mosses and ferns, which may be made to depend from the roof in rich beards of green, and grey, and gold. Around the cave ivy, honeysuckle, Calystegia, Virginia creeper, and Stauntonia may be thickly twined, and the face of the rock-work and each side of the cave planted with the gayest alpines, let into chinks in the blocks of stone. The Scotch Thistle will be an appropriate and noble addition, if planted in the most elevated spots. Willow, birch, and mountain ash trees would add to the completeness if judiciously placed with reference to their effect on the water. A few birds might be domesticated in such a cave; a pair of owls, for instance, whose hooting at night would be no unpleasant music.[5]

Elizabeth Watts had a similar attitude to the perception of the rockery in some people's minds, but she seems to have fallen into the trap of confusing the two terms:

Rockwork is a very favourite decoration for gardens and pleasure grounds. Some people may call it a Cockney fancy to pretend to bring wild nature into trim gardens,[6] by building up stones, and planting ferns, trees, sedums, and appropriate vegetation among them, but what matter if the owner like it, he may do what he likes with his own; and it might be better for us if we would be contented to admire all that is good and admirable in our neighbour's garden, aye! And in his character too, without ultra criticism . . . When the arrangement of the stones pleases, fill up between with rough mortar, except in the case of the interstices or pockets, which are wanted for planting, mix Roman cement to the consistence of thick paint, taking care to mix only a little at a time that it may not set more quickly than it can be used, and, by means of a large painter's brush, cover the surface of the rock-work with it. This will join all into one mass.[7]

She also described how to create a grotto:

> The ruder the rockwork for the grotto, and the larger in character, the better, and the outside should be so concealed as to give the idea of an excavation, not of an erection. The sides of grottos are generally made of rough stone or brick covered with spa, shells, madrepores, corals, &c., with a pebble pavement, in a pattern for the floor. Beyond everything the roof must be weather tight. Earth thrown on the top, if its weight can be borne, and planted with periwinkle, ivy, or low evergreens, rather hanging forward, looks well, or if the grotto be against higher ground the top can be turfed over, so as to give the appearance of a grass knoll from behind. For a grotto to be of any use it must be in so dry a situation as to be quite fit to sit in, and in that case the refreshing coolness of its shade is welcome in hot weather.[8]

The plants for rockeries varied from ferns and ivies to alpines and herbaceous plants. Bidder's list includes many large perennials such as astrantia, geums, geraniums, penstemons and herbs, like borage, small-leaved mint, cotton lavender, prostrate rosemary and many kinds of thyme.[9] *Amateur Gardening*, in 1885, implies that rockeries exist purely to provide a place to grow plants that need to be grown in raised beds or are better seen close up. Trying not to antagonise its typical readers, it hints that some taste is required in planning rockwork:

> A well-made and judiciously-planted rockery is one of the noblest adornments of a garden, and may afford unceasing pleasure to the lover of beautiful plants. But the average rockery, or thing so called, is but a poor toy, and unworthy of consideration in this connexion. The formation and disposition of natural rocks must be borne in mind in the formation of a rockery, for though we cannot command either the space or the materials, or the surroundings of Nature's rockeries, we can with little difficulty imitate the *method*, and, above all, ensure the *unity of expression* proper to such an imitation . . . An artificial ruin is by no means despicable if well done, and may be made wonderfully useful for the accommodation of rock plants, as well as to serve for a distinct and beautiful feature of the garden.[10]

The popularity of using rockwork to display ferns created such an obsession, known as pteridomania, that it permanently affected the native British flora:

> It is not many years since I saw amongst a heap of dried mosses, ferns, grasses, &c, in the possession of a lady, a *sheet* of Tunbridge fern nearly a yard square. This had been torn from its native site, carefully

JAMES BATEMAN (1811–97)

JAMES BATEMAN was born in Lancashire into a prosperous family, and started gardening at his father's house, Knypersley Hall, Cheshire. He persuaded his father to send out collectors for orchids, which Bateman described in his *Orchidaceae of Mexico and Guatemala* (1837–41). In 1838 he married Maria Warburton, who encouraged him to take an interest in hardy plants, and together they moved to Biddulph Grange and created one of the most extraordinary English gardens of any time. Distinct areas such as 'China' and 'Egypt' were planted appropriately and included characteristic buildings and ornaments. A grotto, stumpery and rootery all provided habitats for different plants, and a bowling green and quoit ground provided recreation. In the 1860s the Batemans moved to Worthing and they created a rock garden for alpine plants.

rolled up like a piece of old blanket, and put away, and was afterwards brought forth as a trophy, and preserved as a memorial to the days 'when we went gipsying'. The value of that sheet when fresh might have been about £5, and no doubt any nurseryman could make a larger sum of a good square yard of Tunbridge fern. Such reckless destruction, such base contempt for the value set upon a rare fern by those who understand its history and its habits, and appreciate the interest that arises out of its beauty and rarity combined, is to be considered as a crime; and although there is no law to punish the perpetrator, except in cases where there might be an action for trespass or wilful damage, it is the duty of every conservator of our native flora to visit crimes of this kind with the sternest disapprobation, accompanied with truthful explanations of the injury done alike to the natural scenery and to science by such acts of spoliation.[11]

Ferns seemed to suit the Victorians: there were no flowers to be spoilt by soot and they thrived in subdued light and damp, which were the prevailing conditions in many urban gardens. Perhaps their ancient character suited an age just becoming familiar with fossils and archaeology. They also had an air of the exotic; though native ferns were hardy, they looked very much like the rarer tropical ferns and palms kept in hothouses with orchids. There were some dangers attached to gathering ferns in wild and rocky landscapes, however:

Miss Jane Myers, a young lady, fell over the rocks at Craighall, Scotland, and died at Blairgowrie, three days after, of the injuries she sustained. The most serious wound was on her right leg, the ankle-bone of which was dislocated and protruded several inches through the flesh; but her whole system had received a shock from which recovery was impossible. The lady stated before her death that having wandered up to the cliff, intending to proceed to the waterside, and being fond of botanical specimens, she had stooped to gather a fern, when some loose earth gave way, and allowed her to fall to the bank. She had only a dim recollection of being sorely tormented with flies and other insects, swarms of which had gathered round her as she lay for five or six hours in that dreadful place; and in this plight she was discovered by some visitors. A line hung over the edge of the crag to the bank where the lady fell was found to measure 170 ft, the remaining distance to the water making the entire height of the precipice almost 200 feet. The melancholy occurrence has created a gloomy sensation in Blairgowrie and neighbourhood.[12]

Alfred Smee's fern glen. (*My Garden*, p. 40) (*Author's collection*)

Ferns could be displayed in other 'natural' habitats, such as rooteries, as described by Shirley Hibberd:

I had, in a yard adjoining my garden, a large stock of faggots, tree loppings, bean-sticks, roots, and other forest refuse, and amongst

them a number of old unbarked blocks, on which some fine ferns were
rooted and flourishing. Setting to work one day to put the stack in
order, and having a number of ferns for which I had no room in the
garden, I placed several dead trees of large girth to form the outlines
of a large space. Within this I placed the roots with no particular
order, and at the back I piled up a mass of rotten wood and moss,
which had been collected for cultural purposes. I roofed the whole lot
with loppings and bean-sticks, so as to construct a sort of
extemporaneous hermit's cell, or grotto of wood, into which no
perpendicular light could fall, but the light entered freely at three of
the sides. Here among the roots, on the ground, and on the bank of
rubbish at the back, I planted my spare ferns, and left the rest to
nature. Sufficient rain gained entrance through the interstices of the
roof, the ferns flourished, and a number of pretty wildings sprung up
from the mosses and peat used in planting, and in this way I came
into the possession of one of the prettiest ferneries I have ever seen,
though it was in a position quite unsuited to it, and at a distance had
no more romance about it than belongs to any stack of faggots in a
farmer's yard.[13]

He went on to describe how he would build it again at the time of
writing with more forethought, using 'fast-growing hard-wood
climbers' running up posts, making a fernery and bower combined.
Ever practical, he explained that if you became tired of fern-growing,
'You might pull down the structure, and get back the cost of the
timber by turning it into firewood; and as the ferns and other plants
would increase considerably, the nursery stock would be worth more
than it was at starting, so that a fernery of this description is cheap
enough for the poorest lover of the beautiful, and choice enough for
the most wealthy connoisseur of taste in gardening.'[14]

Henry Bright had a 'loggery' in his garden, which he used as a
setting for *Saxifraga crassifolia* (bergenia), which he considered too
coarse to grow in the border. He also covered the loggery with
bindweed in the summer, 'which rambles about at its own will, and
opens its blossoms, sometimes a dozen at a time'.[15]

Elizabeth Watts suggests a 'root-house', made with pieces of root
'of fantastic shape' or a wood-house made of tree branches with bark
still on, 'ornamented with pines of different sizes', and in yet more
detail she describes a moss-house, which would be a wooden house
lined with a variety of different mosses.[16] This would require some
skill at building, or what we would now call 'do it yourself'. The
Victorians often indulged in woodwork, as well as brickwork, and for
them it was a matter of mastering more skills than are necessary in
the modern day, where we have power tools and easy-to-use glues,
varnishes and paints. *Amateur Gardening* in 1884 gave illustrated

instructions for making rustic tables, said to be 'exceedingly appropriate and pleasing appendages to those useful and necessary places of retreat, for be the garden large or small, it can hardly be considered perfect without some retreat into which the family may escape from the stifling air of sitting-rooms during the fervid glow of the dog-days'.[17] The oval, deal table on a circular pedestal was edged with pine and larch cones, the top being laid with split hazel rods. The pedestal was then covered with 'gnarled knots from the stem of an old grape-vine or those from a whitethorn hedge that has been repeatedly clipped'. This is reminiscent of the legendary words from Mrs Beeton's recipe for jugged hare: 'first catch your hare'. In this case you could say, 'first find your whitethorn, then repeatedly clip it'. But, just a moment – the article continues with an alternative 'designed to suit such persons as cannot readily procure the cones necessary'. For this variation is needed 'oak wrongs', which may or may not be easier to find, as I have no idea what they are, but apparently it does not matter whether or not they have the bark on. A 'nice oak stain' could be used for the 'Vandyked rim', which consists of 'small oak wrongs split, and thinner at the outer point than at the centre of the table'. At this point, I

would imagine the readers would go off in search of fir cones to do the other version. If they battled on, however, they would then be required to look for 'knots from a thorn hedge' to be strung on fine wire to 'depend' in festoons round the edge. Perhaps they would be better off buying a table from one of the 'miserable incapables' mentioned in the *Floral World* as being responsible for the low-grade furniture frequently available.[18]

Diagrams accompanying instructions for making a rustic table from deal, decorated with fir cones and gnarled vine stems. (Engravings from *Amateur Gardening*, 17 May 1884, p. 35) (*Amateur Gardening*)

A rustic table would be used in or near a rustic building, such as the 'Garden-house and Prospect-tower' also depicted in *Amateur Gardening*.[19] Such ideas had originated in eighteenth-century landscaped gardens, where hermitages were built with real-life hermits

employed to inhabit them. Alfred Smee seems to have managed to get one to stay on in his garden, if the illustration of his summerhouse is to be believed.[20] The prospect tower had embellishments similar to those found on the 'cottages ornées' depicted in Loudon's *Gardener's Magazine* in the 1830s, in which people were actually expected to live. By the mid-century these buildings were being produced in suburban gardens for decorative effect, although they could be useful as well. Mr Pickburn's rustic plant house was a conservatory and smoking room combined,[21] while Shirley Hibberd used his rustic summerhouse not just as a reading room, but also as a bee shed. For those contemplating something simpler he had plenty of advice, but seemed even more disapproving than he was of rockeries regarding the questionable taste exhibited in some gardens:

> As to summer-houses and arbours generally, there never was so much ugliness scattered about the world as of late years has been sprinkled over suburban gardens under the vain pretence of ornament and use. The majority are like toll-houses, or beer-shops, or sweet-meat stalls, destitute of all elegance, use, and propriety. A summer-house need not

This 'rustic garden house and prospect tower' is more elaborate than most summerhouses, but shows that decking was popular long before the late twentieth century. (Engraving from *Amateur Gardening*, 14 June 1884, p. 78) (*Amateur Gardening*)

be utterly hidden, but it ought not to stare straight out upon us from a back wall, its ugly lattice-work without one creeping tendril to cool and comfort it, and its interior visible to every gazer, as if it were anywhere but a place of shade and rest. Though you never use it, it must appear fit for use or it is no ornament. It should be well shrouded with greenery, be easy of access, sufficiently inviting to attract a stranger, yet quiet in tone, and of a chaste pleasing outline. Some of these suburban retreats look very much like the little cabins of the fly-boats on the junction canal; and one always expects to see a head pop up above them to take hold of the rudder and steer them into port. Arbours indeed! What a perversion of language, they are *h*arbours for

Alfred Smee's summerhouse with what looks suspiciously like a resident hermit. (Engraving from *My Garden*, p. 267) (*Author's collection*)

earwigs, cats, and other vermin, not tree bowers and trellis shelters, as their philology imports.[22]

A rustic building might be a little ambitious, but a temporary 'wigwam' could be knocked up for the summer season quite easily by making a light framework, filling it in with wire netting and growing annual climbers, such as runner beans or sweet peas, over it and then disguising the whole with ferns and tree stumps.[23] Ornamental grasses could also be used to add a rustic effect. Although we tend to think of them as a modern discovery as they are so popular in a 'minimalist' setting, they were popular in the nineteenth century. Pampas grass, ribbon grass and similar-looking plants like phormium, or New Zealand flax, made spectacular effects where space permitted.

'Wild gardening' was a fashion that began with the publication by William Robinson of *The Wild Garden* in 1871. Bulbs planted in grass or on outcrops of rocks with alpines were ideas he must have acquired in his travels in France and the Alps, and they provided swathes of seasonal colour in distinct areas of large gardens. In the smaller suburban or town setting, however, they often looked mean and sad, interspersed with too many other features. The amateur had to be careful when trying to imitate new ideas and use them effectively, rather than dot everything about and hope for the best. Even the wealthier amateurs, like Mrs Earle, who could afford paid

MARIA THERESA EARLE ('MRS C.W. EARLE') (1836–1925)

MRS EARLE was born Maria Theresa Villiers into an aristocratic family, but lived unconventionally, spending much of her early life travelling in Europe and later attending art school. She married Captain Earle (ex-Indian army) when she was twenty-seven and both became free thinkers and agnostics. After the birth of three sons, she gradually became interested in gardening as part of country life. Her first book, *Pot-Pourri from a Surrey Garden*, was published in 1897, when she was almost sixty-one. Her husband reputedly offered her £100 not to publish it. However, it was followed by six more books (including three more *Pot-Pourris*), which possibly helped to keep her sane after the sudden death of her husband in a bicycle accident and one of her sons in the Boer War. Her books show an academic as well as practical interest in gardening and supply us with detailed information about gardens and interiors at the turn of the century.

professionals to do it properly did not always agree that it should be done at all: 'In spite of all the charming things Mr Robinson says about it, "wild gardening" is, I am sure, a delusion and a snare. I live near one of the most beautiful so-called wild gardens in England, but it requires endless care, and is always extending in all directions in search of fresh soil. What is possible is to have the appearance of a wild garden in consequence of the most judicious planting, with consummate knowledge and experience of the plants that will do well in the soil if they are just a little assisted at the time of planting.'[24] She was also less than enthusiastic on the subject of rockeries: 'The great point in making a rockery is to have large mounds of good earth, and then lay stones on them, making terraces and little flat beds, stoned over to retain the moisture and prevent the earth being washed away. The old idea was to have stumps of trees or mounds of stones and brick, and then fill in the interstices with earth. This is no good at all; the plants have no depth of earth, and perish. The trouble of such gardening consists only in the constant hand-weeding that it requires.'[25]

CHAPTER THIRTEEN

The Rose Garden

On first thoughts it might seem that the rose garden would be something an amateur could start and maintain relatively easily in Victorian times: it would simply be a matter of choosing popular plants and setting them out in a pleasing way, learning to prune at the right time and making good use of the aphicides and syringes available from the magazines. However, contemporary books, even those written for amateurs, make it sound as difficult and technical as any other aspect of gardening contemplated in the nineteenth century. The Victorian gardener was lucky in relation to roses: it was a time of innovation and excitement in rose breeding, and commercial exploitation meant that dozens of new varieties became available in a very short space of time. On the other hand, he was expected to master quite complicated gardening techniques and, if he lived in an urban environment, he would have to equip himself with a glasshouse if he wanted to grow many roses successfully.

The varieties of roses available at the beginning of the nineteenth century were very limited as garden plants. The old gallicas, damasks, albas and moss roses, grown in Europe for centuries, were beautiful, tough and easy to grow, but they only flowered for a short summer season and their colours were confined to white, deep purply reds and pinks. The introduction of the China roses from 1789 brought a revolution in rose growing and breeding. The Chinas flowered from May to October, so they provided interest over a much longer period, but they were delicate in character and difficult to grow successfully in the British climate. At first, they would only be available to the wealthy. The cottagers would still grow the old roses. Flora Thompson in *Lark Rise to Candleford*, describing life in the 1880s, mentions Seven Sisters, Maiden's Blush, moss rose, cabbage rose and York and Lancaster, as growing in the best garden.[1] The obvious aim of the nurserymen was to cross the Chinas with the older roses and produce something robust with a long flowering period. This produced many hybrids in the noisette and Bourbon groups and eventually the hybrid perpetuals, which became the favourite rose of the up-to-date Victorian gardener. Not all, however, lived up to their name. Dean Hole described some of them as 'Perpetuals by courtesy, seeing that many of them score 0 in their second innings, and but few resume their former glory in summer'.[2] A further introduction from China was the tea rose, which brought the colour yellow to garden roses, but it was a soft pale golden yellow, not the harsh, bright yellows that developed into the oranges and scarlets of the twentieth century. Thankfully, the Victorians never saw them. A Victorian rose garden, therefore, was far more delicate and subtle in colour than a modern one. The roses themselves also had a characteristic shape, without the pointed bud of the hybrid tea, yet to be produced. Their attraction was in the full-blown phase, sometimes with dense quartering, and often surrounding a button eye.

Many of the newly produced rose varieties came over from France, but the best-known rose breeders in nineteenth-century Britain were Thomas Rivers and William Paul. Rivers ran his nursery at Sawbridgeworth in Hertfordshire. He was also one of the most important fruit breeders of the time,[3] but in respect of roses published *The Rose Amateur's Guide* in 1837. William Paul set up his rose nursery at Waltham Cross, and published *The Rose Garden* in 1848.

In the mid-Victorian era, when formality was at its height, gardeners liked to grow roses in self-contained rose gardens, known as rosaries (sometimes spelt rosery) or rosariums. This was probably because of the short flowering season, but may equally have been because the Victorians liked to classify their plants and create different areas of the garden in which to show them off. Shirley Hibberd advised that the rose garden should be well away from the house: 'A rose garden should be in its season a wonder to be sought, as, when its season is past, it is a wilderness to be avoided.'[4] In *The Amateur's Flower Garden* he gave a plan of a rose garden to be used as it stood or 'modified by a little careful manipulation', though he stated that it was a real plan that he had carried out in his own garden 'sufficient for our own enjoyment, and the satisfaction of a few critical friends who are known to be half mad on the subject of roses'.[5] The book was published in 1871, so gives a good idea of what was expected of a rose garden at or shortly before that date.

Hibberd's rosarium was on a plot measuring 140 feet by about 100 feet, surrounded by hornbeam, clipped yew or a mixed plantation. The middle of the plot was an oval with three concentric walks dividing it. The basin of water in the centre was 15 feet in diameter, surrounded by trained 'common' China roses (now known as Old Blush China Rose).[6] From the centre, eight walks radiate out

Shirley Hibberd's design for a rose garden with a central basin of water and complicated scroll beds for China roses. (Engraving from *The Amateur's Flower Garden*, p. 203) (*Hackney Archives*)

to the next concentric circle, and this is enclosed within a trellis, with arches over the north and south walks to allow access to the outer walks. The space within the eight inner beds was turfed, but each of the four larger beds had a small semi-circular bed cut into it, containing dwarf China roses. The trellis was to be clothed with

MARY RUSSELL MITFORD (1787–1855)

MARY RUSSELL MITFORD was author of *Our Village*, sketches of
village life based on Three Mile Cross, Reading. She was a keen amateur
gardener and prolific letter writer, corresponding with Elizabeth Barrett
Browning and John Ruskin, among others. Miss Mitford was the daughter of
a naval doctor and his older, richer wife. Her father was a gambler and
spendthrift, who frittered away the family fortune, as well as the £20,000 he
won in the Irish lottery in 1797. They lived in reduced circumstances in a
crumbling cottage, but their flowers were a continuous source of pleasure and won many
prizes in competitions. Miss Mitford sent her correspondents seeds and cuttings of her
own plants and plenty of information and advice on how to grow them. Her writing
paints a vivid picture of country gardens in the early nineteenth century before the
bedding craze took hold, when florists' flowers were still grown for pleasure.

about forty plants of hybrid perpetual, noisette and tea-scented roses
of the reader's own choice. Between the trellis and the outer
concentric walk were 'scroll-shaped' beds, and here fancy really does
take over. The scroll shapes were to hold 'dark dwarf China roses in
distinct masses of colour on a flat groundwork of light China roses of
only four sorts, one sort in each compartment'. Not content with the
twelve different roses for the eight scrolls and four backgrounds, he
also specifies a noisette rose[7] or 'the crimson miniature China rose'[8]
for the small shield-shaped beds in between. The triangular spaces
outside the oval were to be turfed with a large L-shaped bed and two
smaller oval beds cut out. The L-shaped bed (6 feet wide) would be
filled with a centre row of mixed standard hybrid perpetuals amid
two rows of mixed bushes, also hybrid perpetuals. The ovals were for
mixed bush roses. Also in each triangle were three specimen trees,
which could be conifers or standard weeping Ayrshire roses, or
gigantic bushes of alba roses. Presumably if Hibberd's friends were
really 'half mad' on the subject of roses they might be prepared to go
to the trouble of marking out the scrolls and planting them
intricately with so many different varieties.

The standard roses mentioned were very popular in the formal
mid-Victorian era. This is where the skill comes in. All the books on
gardening explain how to create standard roses and how to bud and
graft roses generally, so although roses were available ready grown
from nurseries, it was thought desirable to create them oneself.

A standard rose bush might have cost two shillings,[9] which was perhaps a little extravagant for the amateur, as they would certainly require half a dozen or so. To create a standard, the common briar stock was first obtained, whereas for a bush rose, it was advised to use the Manetti stock. This was a noisette rose, raised in Italy and brought to Britain by Thomas Rivers. It was used for bush roses and was found to be a fast grower, producing a good abundance of roots. It was therefore suitable for poor soils as it was quick to become established. It also suited the nurserymen because it enabled them to reproduce new roses quickly. The alternative was to grow new roses from cuttings on their own roots. Hibberd recommended this for the amateur, using the 'currant-tree system' for taking cuttings in September or October. He admits that instructions for budding roses on to stocks could be very complicated, even in books written for amateurs, and that the best way to learn the skill was to obtain the help of an expert, as it could then be learnt in five minutes.[10] Of course, this raised the difficulty of finding a willing expert. It was the common practice in the nineteenth century to grow roses on stocks, and it continues to be done by nurserymen today because plants can be produced more readily. Now, improved stocks are used which are less likely to take over so quickly. Although the briar rose was a good tough stock for heavy soil, it proved in the end not to be the best solution for most roses.

Hibberd's book for amateurs, *The Rose Book*, was published in 1864 and subsequently reissued as *The Amateur's Rose Book* in 1874

FIG. 564.—Gloire de Dijon.   FIG. 565.—Marshal Niel.   FIG. 565 a.—Mademoiselle Marie Sisley.

FIG. 566 —Climbing Devoniensis.   FIG. 567.—Moss Rose.   FIG. 568.—Félicité Perpetuelle.

A selection of roses popular in the late nineteenth century: Gloire de Dijon, Maréchal Niel, Mademoiselle Marie Sisley, Climbing Devoniensis, Moss Rose, and Félicité Perpétue. (Engravings from Alfred Smee, *My Garden*, p. 277) (*Author's collection*) and 1894. He said it contained the views of an amateur cultivator, 'not as opposed to, but as differing from, the views taken by the distinguished professional cultivators'.[11] Hibberd gave advice for creating rose gardens in open ground and in towns, as well as in formal layouts, but when writing about his own experiences of growing roses in towns, he does not inspire his readers with much optimism. The soot and pollution found in London meant that the only way he succeeded in growing tea roses was by buying the Paxtonian house referred to in Chapter Five. Before that he did the best he could by growing roses on their own roots and experimenting with different varieties. Even then, he only recommended growing dwarf bushes and protecting them with bell jars if gardening close to the centre of town. At his own house in Stoke Newington, three miles from central London (measured from the Post Office at St Paul's), he had tried over three hundred sorts and recommended about thirty. Of these, the following are available today:

Gloire de Dijon – a deep golden climber

Niphetos – a creamy-white climber of delicate constitution

Madame Bravy – a creamy-white small bush with strong fragrance

Devoniensis – a delicate blush-pink climber

Maiden's Blush – a blush-pink alba rose

Damask (presumably the group generally)

Boule de Nanteuil – a deep pink gallica

Félicité-Perpétue – a pinkish-white small-flowered rambler[12]

Ruga – a soft pink climber or rambler

Boursault Crimson (now known as Amadis) – a deep crimson rambler

Common Moss (now known as Old Pink Moss) – a well-scented pink
  moss rose

Common Cabbage (now known as Centifolia) – a fragrant pink
  globular flower

White Provence – a scented silky-flowered white rose

Crested Moss (now known as Chapeau de Napoléon) – deep pink moss
  rose

Gloire des Mousseux – a strongly scented bright pink moss rose

White Bath (now known as Shailer's White Moss) – fragrant white
  moss rose

Salet – another pink moss rose.

Although pollution took its toll of roses in towns, because too much soot would not only disfigure the appearance of the rose, but also suffocate it, there were compensations. Black spot, a common disease of roses now, was virtually unheard of. It is thought to have taken hold when *Rosa foetida*, the Persian rose used for hybridising yellow roses, became interbred with roses in Europe from the end of the nineteenth century, but the disease is controlled in sulphurous atmospheres, like those of a Victorian town. So as long as coal fires were used for cooking and heating, roses resisted black spot. Unfortunately the atmosphere did not have the same effect on greenfly, and the confined nature of many town gardens, surrounded by walls and with little breeze, probably only helped them to multiply. The *Gardener's Magazine* in 1874 gave a comprehensive guide to dealing with 'the consuming canker' as 'the leader of a host of harpies that war against the welfare of the rose'.[13] The first golden rule they offered was to ignore all pests and build up the health and strength of the roses to encourage their immunity. However, it was admitted that remedies may have to be used and, of the thousands available, all were probably equally effective. They recommended three by name: Fowler's Insecticide, Aphis Wash of the City Soap Company and Pooley's Tobacco Powder, the first two of which should be diluted with 'soft water as hot as the hand will bear'. Tobacco powder was said to be the simplest, but had to be dredged on from a pepper box or flour dredger covered with coarse muslin, when the plants were wet with dew or had been sprayed with a garden engine. Actually, it was remarked that pure water on its own, sprayed regularly, was probably the most effective remedy of all, or better still, diluted sewage, which had the extra benefit of feeding the plants with the drops that trickled to the ground. There were other home-made remedies, such as a decoction of quassia chips. The quassia was a tree, originally from South America, whose bitter bark extract was found to be effective against fever. Here, the bark chips had to be steeped in water for an hour, then a dilution of soft soap was added. The mixture was then brushed on to the underside of the plants and later syringed off with hot water. Another, cheaper, remedy was referred to as *de l'eau trouble* or mud water, and was simply a mixture of mud and water applied, again to the underside of the plants, with a mop, which need not even be washed off. Tobacco smoke was then discussed. Although effective inside the rose house, it was said to be a complete waste of money outside, as however carefully a tent might be erected over the roses, the smoke would always be lost into the atmosphere.

Other enemies of the rose were 'mildew' and 'grub'. Mildew could be dealt with by aphis wash mixed with mud, or flowers of sulphur could be used, or alternatively, dry dust itself. 'Grub' was a collective term for all other insect predators, which were best dealt with by hand-picking them off, or: 'A shower of hot sewage now and then, and a dusting with tobacco-powder, will render the roses unpalatable to these marauders, and by diligently hunting, with the aid of a sharp eye and a quick hand, you will surely manage to mock these vagabonds, whose aim is to rob you of your roses and your peace.'[14]

The best friends of the rose were said to be the birds, both sparrows and flycatchers, to be encouraged to eat the insects, as well as ladybirds, lacewing larvae and the ichneumon fly.

As the formality of mid-nineteenth-century gardening started to go out of fashion, so other ways of growing roses were recommended. Dean Hole, one of the utmost authorities on Victorian roses, described his ideal rose garden as an enclosed area of turf, 'always broad enough for the easy operations of the mowing-machine', with 'rose-clad mounds high enough to obstruct the view'.[15] On the level ground would be the beds and single specimen plants, and at the corners 'bowers and nooks'. He preferred that the rose garden should be approached by obscure and narrow paths between walls of rockwork, so that the roses come as a surprise.

As to Hole's selection of varieties, for climbers, he also favoured Gloire de Dijon as an 'all-rounder' although he admired the beauty

REVD SAMUEL REYNOLDS HOLE, DEAN OF ROCHESTER (1819–1904)

DEAN HOLE is probably the best known of the clergymen–gardeners who had so much influence over amateur gardening in the nineteenth century. He was born at Caunton Manor, near Newark, Nottinghamshire, was later Canon of Lincoln and in 1887 became Dean of Rochester. He contributed to gardening magazines from the 1850s, writing about amateur gardening, and even wrote short stories with a horticultural theme. He became an authority on roses, publishing *A Book about Roses* in 1869. He also wrote *Our Gardens* (1899), and *A Book about the Garden* (1904), which are collections of anecdotes about himself and fellow gardeners and their gardens. The subjects of Hole's anecdotes, however, range from humble cottagers and allotment holders on the one hand to wealthy landowners or their gardeners on the other, and he has much to say on other garden journalists. He gives the impression that he was hard working in his parish and his church, but that his real love was flowers and the growing of them. He was a founder and president of the National Rose Society and he wrote for *The Garden*, *The Gardener* and other magazines.

S. Reynolds Hole (1819–1904). (Engraving from *Gardeners' Chronicle*, 3 September 1904) (*Royal Horticultural Society, Lindley Library*)

of the noisette, Cloth of Gold, although tender. His second climber was Maréchal Niel, another golden noisette, but also one that needed protection. More reliable for him were what he called the Ayrshire and evergreen roses. The Ayrshires were early rambling roses descended from the species *Rosa arvensis* and raised in Ayrshire, Scotland. The evergreens were a group descended from *R. sempervirens*, raised in France. Both groups were hardy and vigorous but not strongly scented. Hole recommended them for covering ugly walls or for use in difficult conditions. The Ayrshire varieties he mentions that can still be found are Dundee Rambler (white tinged with pink), Queen of the Belgians (white) and Ruga; the evergreens are Adelaide d'Orléans (pinkish-white) and Félicité-Perpétue. He then described the Banksian roses, both white and yellow, which although not completely hardy could be kept through most winters with careful mulching, and he said they would grow up again from the roots even if the tops were destroyed. Next the Boursault rose, Amadis, from another forgotten group and almost lost by Hole's time. He mentioned as a more recent introduction, William Allen Richardson (another less than robust golden noisette) and also recommended Captain Christy (a pink climbing hybrid tea).

The next group Hole mentions are pillar roses, which were popular in Victorian times for growing up single poles as specimen plants. They could be small climbers or rangey shrubs that responded to training. He recommended using iron stakes rather than wooden ones, to avoid them rotting away at the base and falling over in strong winds. His best roses for pillars which are still available today are Belle Lyonnaise (creamy yellow), Blairi No. 2 (pink double flower), Coupe d'Hébé (a pink Bourbon shrub), General Jacqueminot (clear red hybrid perpetual), Jaune Desprez (now Desprez à Fleur Jaune) (a tender golden noisette), Juno (blush-pink centifolia), Mrs John Laing (double soft pink), Paul Neyron (rich pink hybrid perpetual), and Paul Ricault (quartered bright pink).

As 'garden roses', Hole suggests a bed of Provence or centifolia roses (which he thinks inappropriate to call 'cabbage' roses) and he loves the miniature or pom-pom Provence roses, which have almost disappeared now. He mentions De Meaux (a double pink) and Spong (rich pink, noisette flowered), which can still be found, as well as several Victorian polyantha roses, the only one of which still exists being Perle d'Or, a buff-yellow China. He also mentions Blanchefleur, a pinkish-white damask, which he calls a Hybrid Provence. Of the moss roses he names, the Common Moss (or Old Pink Moss), Baron de Wassenaer (crimson), Comtesse de Murinais (pink), Crested Moss (Chapeau de Napoléon) (silvery pink), Gloire de Mousseux (bright pink), Laneii (deep pink) (for which he gave half a

guinea in 1846) and Marie de Blois (bright pink) can still be found. For those who do not have room for an extensive garden, he suggests they stick to the common and miniature Provence roses and the Common and Crested Moss. Of the older roses he still recommends the York and Lancaster rose and Rosa Mundi, both gallicas and mixed pink and white, the Sweet Briar or Eglantine (*R. eglanteria* or *R. rubiginosa*), for its delicious scent after a shower, and the Monthly Rose (Old Blush China). Writing near the end of the nineteenth century, Hole is high in praise for the hybrid perpetuals and some Bourbons, which have proved themselves within his rose-growing experience. He lists, as well as those already mentioned, Anna de Diesbach (a tall pink hybrid perpetual), Baron de Bonesetter (dark red), Baronne Prévost (flat-flowered pink), Boule de Neige (white Bourbon), Duke of Edinburgh (crimson), Dupuy Jamain (dark red), John Hopper (pink and lilac), La France (rose pink, the first hybrid tea) and Louise Odier (pink camellia-like Bourbon). Finally, he recommends some more tea roses: Anna Olivier (soft yellow), Homère (soft pink), Madame Lombard (dark rose-salmon), Marie Van Houtte (bright pink), Souvenir d'un Ami (double rose-pink), and the

Pillar roses were popular in the late nineteenth century and provided a good display near a path. (Engraving from *Amateur Gardening*, 18 May 1889) (*Amateur Gardening*)

noisettes, Rêve d'Or (pinkish-buff), Bouquet d'Or (coppery-yellow), Céline Forestier (pale lemon), and Lamarque (pure white and tender).

By the last quarter of the nineteenth century, modern gardeners influenced by William Robinson were coming round to the idea of growing roses in among other flowers in the garden. He reasoned that as newer varieties flowered over a longer season there was no shame in growing them in the same way as other shrubs, mixed with herbaceous perennials and bulbs in the main part of the garden. He believed that rose shows had harmed the rose by concentrating too much on producing large, impressive blooms to the detriment of the plant itself. He abhorred the idea of growing roses on briar or Manetti stocks because after a few years of impressive flowering the rose weakened and died and the stock plant took over. He encouraged gardeners to grow roses on their own roots and to avoid too much mulching and manuring. Instead he suggested covering the ground beneath roses with shallow-rooted alpines and annuals. The roses he liked best were the old climbing roses and the tea roses. He mentions Anna Olivier, Bouquet d'Or and Marie Van Houtte,[16] as well as species roses and the polyanthas.[17]

Robinson was against severe pruning as he preferred his roses to look natural and he did not value them just for their large blooms. *Amateur Gardening*, on the other hand, gave strict instructions for its readers on how to prune different varieties. It gave a list of a dozen hybrid perpetuals for the beginner in rose growing with a small garden on ordinary soil. Several were the same choices that Dean Hole favoured (Boule de Neige, Duke of Edinburgh, Dupuy Jamain, General Jacqueminot and La France), but they also included Baroness Rothschild (soft pink), Prince Camille de Rohan (deep blackish-red), Ulrich Brunner (red) and Fisher Holmes (crimson).[18] It is clear that in spite of what Robinson thought, the deeper, brighter colours were appealing to the 'average' gardener who was ready for the dazzling hybrid teas of the twentieth century.

CHAPTER FOURTEEN

The Water Garden

We are so used to hearing about 'water features' in modern garden designs that perhaps we forget how dramatic a real water feature can be. Paxton's Italian terraces at the rebuilt Crystal Palace gave the public a taste of the dramatic and the classical, and many suburban garden owners then began to feel the need to try to emulate Paxton's creations. In those days there were no handy electric pumps to drive these works of art, and no butyl liners to prevent the water seeping away if the concrete base cracked after freezing. However, amateurs did manage to create ponds and grow water plants outdoors as well as indoors.

One of the wonders of the age was the royal water lily (*Victoria Regia* or *Amazonica*), for which a special glasshouse was built by Paxton at Chatsworth and from the structure of which, it is said, he obtained the idea for the method of construction of the Crystal Palace. *Cassell's Popular Gardening* assured amateurs that they could grow this themselves if they had a tank at least 27 feet in diameter and 4 feet deep. They would also need to maintain a temperature of 85 degrees Fahrenheit, which could be accomplished with one foot of four-inch piping to 12 cubic feet of water. They did say, however,

Good gardeners tell you never to cut flowers except with a sharp knife, the clean cut being better for the plants; but I advise that the knife should be on a steel chain a foot or so long, with a good pair of garden hook-shaped scissors at the other end. Another advantage of knife and scissors together on the chain is that they are more easy to find when mislaid in the warm and bushy heart of some plant.

Mrs C.W. Earle, *Pot-Pourri from a Surrey Garden*, pp. 116–17 that the *Victoria* should be regarded as a luxury and that the ordinary water lilies were much less costly. If such an 'arrangement' as the water lily house at Kew were not possible, then, they were told, 'Paraffin casks cut in two, each part forming a tub, answer well. Before being used, the inside should be charred slightly with a burning wisp of straw, in order to burn out the oil.'[1]

It seems that the Victorians were undaunted by the intricacies of forming indoor water gardens for tropical plants. *Cassell's* goes on to explain how to build a naturalistic setting for the aquatics in a large tank with rockwork forming bays for different plants, and using tender plants, such as aroids, monstera and philodendron above the water. It even explains how to have seeds sent over from the tropics of plants that have been lost to cultivation, or have not yet been introduced. One plant illustrated is the water yam or lattice plant, from Madagascar, the leaves of which consist only of veins. The difficulty with it was that it needed dense shade and pure water, preferably rainwater, as well as heated greenhouse.

As to outdoor aquatics, John Loudon said (through the medium of his wife Jane's book, *The Ladies' Companion to the Flower Garden*):[2]

> Water, as an element of landscape scenery, is exhibited in small gardens either in ponds or basins, of regular geometrical or architectural forms; or in ponds or small lakes of irregular forms, in imitation of the shape seen in natural landscape. In general, all geometrical or architectural basins of water ought to have their margins of masonry, or at least of stones placed so as to imitate a rocky margin . . . Water in imitation of nature should be in ponds or basins of irregular shape; but always so contrived as to display one main feature or breadth of water . . . The general extent and outline of a piece of water being fixed on, the interior of the pond or lake is to be treated entirely as a lawn. If small, it will require no islands; but if so large as to require some, they must be distributed towards the sides, so as to vary the outline and to harmonise the pond with the surrounding scenery, and yet to preserve one broad expanse of water exactly in the same manner as, in varying a lawn with shrubs and flowers, landscape-gardeners preserve one broad expanse of turf. [3]

Shirley Hibberd was not as strict: 'The appearance of water is always pleasing; even if ever so clumsily shaped or planted, still it is water; it reflects the blue sky and the fleecy clouds . . . and it gives a brighter verdure to the adjoining lawn, a sweeter fragrance to the neighbouring flower border.'[4] He was an expert on water in the form of aquariums, having written three books on the subject in 1856,[5] and water held a constant fascination for him. He agreed with Loudon that a formal pond should be surrounded with rockwork,

with a ring of turf outside it. The pond should be puddled with clay
or lined with 'Roman cement'. Here the difficulties for the amateur
begin, although some may have been strangely drawn towards
messing about with wet clay and making cement, just as they were
with brickwork and rustic carpentry. Hibberd's instructions seem
simple enough, but, like his rockwork, the final effect may not have
been convincing. He suggests using the usual combination of stones
and rejected bricks:

> Spoilt bricks from a kiln, which form large blocks of half-a-dozen bricks
> together, are very suitable for edging a small fish-pond. Around this a
> light fence of wire-work should be placed, and on the turf about eight or
> ten standard roses should be planted so as to form a ring. The stones
> should be planted with one or two bushes of juniper, which form very
> handsome masses of a rich green, when they overhang the pool.
> Common and major periwinkle, several varieties of sedum, rock-rose,
> sempervivum, violets, gypsophila, and some showy perennials may be
> set in the crevices, and the pond furnished with a fountain and goldfish.[6]

This was written in 1856, when perhaps Hibberd did not have the
experience of gardening that he later attained, but surely the
combination of major periwinkle, a rampant spreader suited to
shade, with sedum and rock-roses, suited to sunshine, was doomed to
failure, and as for the standard roses forming a ring around some
ornate wirework, it seems totally out of keeping with the rustic
appearance of the pond. However, he assures us that this very pond
exists in 'a well-kept suburban garden of small extent, the hobby of a
respected friend'.

For a less formal appearance, Hibberd suggests siting a pond at
the base of a rockery or sloping bank, well away from the house. It
can be made by digging out a hole of the appropriate size, four feet
deep. Six to twelve inches of puddled clay must be used to line it,
covered with a layer of rich sandy loam, finished with sand and
pebbles, which must be terraced like an amphitheatre, so as to
provide shelves for the plants. He advises against too much detail in
the shape of such a pond, believing that 'persons of taste' would
prefer a circular pool broken only at one part, where it would be
made to flow into a shallow inlet. The inlet would be formed into a
'dimple' running up to a bank of ferns and alpines. This would be
used for what is now usually called a bog garden for 'choice marsh
plants'. Suggestions are yellow irises, flowering rushes, water forget-
me-nots, water violets and the buck bean. In this situation any water
feature must be in keeping: 'The fountain should be of a rustic
design; tritons and dolphins, and even old Neptune himself, and all

the water-gods, had better seek more congenial scenes. A fountain flowing easily down the face of a pile of rock-work, gently splashing and gurgling, will be more appropriate than a jet of water of any kind, for the mixture of incongruities betrays a want of taste, which no perfection of individual details will atone for.'[7]

Generally Hibberd advises that water should always be sited below the level of a house because putting it on a higher level will make people think that that house is 'irredeemably damp, though it may in fact be one of the driest and healthiest in the world'. He also has plenty of advice as to where to go for fountains, which can be equally well made of iron as of stone, or one of the patent artificial stones then available. He gives the names of suppliers and recommends, as ever, one of Mr Ransome's designs which, exclusive of rockwork, costs £8 18s 6d.

A way of creating a natural setting in a pond with a mud base, without using stone, was to create islands by driving tree stems into the mud and piling up the soil inside. It was something like the rootery or stumpery, but under water. Water iris and gunnera could be planted in the soil and peat could be used to keep the area damp. However, a constant supply of water would have to be piped in when the weather was dry. A bog garden could be formed from a natural stream, dammed at intervals, thus providing a series of wet beds and pools for different plants.[8]

Alfred Smee was lucky enough to have a trout stream running through his garden, and *My Garden* features several views of it, crossed by rustic bridges and with strategic planting on the banks, but it was hard for amateurs of more modest means to achieve anything like natural scenery, even if they had the space. David Thomson (1823–1909), in *Handy Book of the Flower Garden*, does not hold out much hope of success:

There are few gardens where there is not a piece of water, however small; but in many instances, instead of being either useful or ornamental, this is allowed to become a cesspool of malaria and rottenness. The great mistake committed in introducing small pieces of water into small gardens, is the formation of them in places where they are exposed to the full sun all day long. This is sure to produce scum and rottenness, unless the supply of fresh water be constant and in considerable quantity. If, instead of forming such ponds in fully exposed situations, they were situated in partial shade, and a supply of water, however small, constantly kept up from even a tap, they would always be fresh and beautiful; and when planted with suitable plants, and stocked with some gold and silver fish, they form one of the most interesting features of a garden.[9]

He gave a list of flowering aquatic plants, but first cautioned, 'In no section of ornamental plants do we see more worthless weeds included than in this. Looked at from a horticultural point of view, there are not a great many that are worth cultivating.'[10]

There seemed to be more hope later in the century, when it became more common for amateurs to accept that ambitious plans were doomed to failure, but something on a small scale could still provide pleasure and interest. In *Amateur Gardening* in 1884 the water hawthorn, or Cape pondweed, was suggested as suitable for small pools:

Very few, comparatively speaking, have water at their command for the cultivation of aquatics, and, therefore, any remarks made upon them would only be useful to a few. The Cape Pond Weed, *Aponogeton distachyon*, is an exception; for although an aquatic, it can be successfully grown by all, and is one of those plants which should be found in every garden throughout the length and breadth of the land. It is admirably adapted either for the stove or cool greenhouse, and is hardy enough to withstand our winters, providing the roots are sufficiently deep to be beyond the reach of the frost. It can be grown in any ordinary large-sized flower pot, tub, or earthenware pan, about eighteen inches in depth, and filled to within a few inches of the top with water.[11]

Cape pond weed grown in 'a common earthen pan', which might be the best water garden an amateur could hope for. (Engraving from *Amateur Gardening*, 19 July 1884, p. 135) (*Amateur Gardening*)

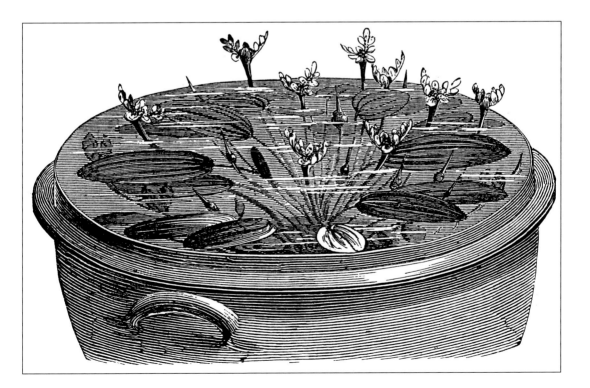

A year later the magazine suggested something a bit more exciting, although it continued to stress that many water plants were not worth cultivating in an amateur's garden: 'When all the hypothetically worthless plants are put out of court, there will remain a number of fine subjects that an amateur may take in hand with a reasonable prospect of adding to the number of his garden pleasures.' It was not necessary to puddle clay or construct rockwork because this water garden was made of wood, 'well caulked and pitched inside and painted outside'. Actually, instructions were not given for making these 'rustic aquariums', other than to say that inch-and-a-half deal was used and that they were 19 inches deep and similar to roadside horse troughs. They could be any length required and were designed to hold plants in pots. Despite these basic instructions, two illustrations were supplied, showing intricately decorated raised ponds with a variety of vegetation growing inside. Crinums, water-violets and flowering rushes were some of the suitable plants listed.

A rustic aquarium made of preserved and decorated wood, allowing a selection of plants to be grown. (Engraving from _Amateur Gardening_, 27 June 1885, p. 103) (_Amateur Gardening_)

CHAPTER FIFTEEN

The Exotic Garden

Exotic plants could be status symbols and they also appealed to the Victorians' interest in the unusual and sometimes even the unnatural. Plants that were rare in the 1840s were everywhere in the 1880s. Nowhere is this more true than of orchids. By the 1880s all the gardening magazines featured orchids along with florists' flowers and kitchen gardens as one of the usual sub-sections, and advertisements for gardeners frequently required that they have experience with orchids as much as with pineapples. Growing orchids in a modest suburban home became possible because glasshouses and conservatories had become affordable, and nurseries were selling orchids at reasonable prices. However, not all orchids could be grown in an amateur's general-purpose greenhouse: tropical orchids needed the conditions of a 'stove' and would probably require the skills of a professional gardener as well.[1]

In *My Garden* Alfred Smee claimed:

> I do not pretend to grow exotic orchids, but I never refuse a spare bulb from a friend. They grow with me like weeds, and so by the gifts of many kind friends I have now more plants growing, in good health, than existed in the country when I was born. The secret of my success is to supply water by giving moisture to the air, and not to soak the roots of the plants. The greater part of my orchids are grown in the fernery, and the highest temperature which any of my plants get is that which is necessary for the growth of cucumbers . . . All the epiphytic orchids shun the direct rays of the sun, but rejoice in light. They never do well in a large house, probably because the hygrometric state continually varies. The part of my fernery in which the orchids grow has some light admitted from the south; but rows of trees are planted before the glass, effectively to intercept the direct rays of the sun in summer, though some of the rays in winter are beneficially admitted.[2]

He then went on to write eight pages about the orchids he claimed not to grow, including the vanilla plant with roots six to eight feet long hanging from the roof of the glasshouse to the ground.

Beeton's All about Gardening recommended Messrs Veitch of Chelsea and Mr Williams of Holloway as the best suppliers of orchids.[3] Amateurs could grow some orchids even without stove heat:

> The orchids and Pitcher Plants adapted for greenhouse culture are not sufficiently appreciated owing, no doubt, to the prevalent belief that all such plants require steaming stoves, and are utterly beyond the reach of amateurs, whose short purses compel them to the observance of limited liability. It so happens, however, that a very choice selection may be made of plants equally to be desired for their curious structure, interesting history, and high floral beauty, and that such a selection may be grown to perfection in any greenhouse with the aid of a little more care than such things as bedding plants require.[4]

Epiphytic orchids (the kind that grow on tree branches) were recommended to be grown on blocks of wood suspended from the

Masdevallia orchids could be grown in a cool house and were therefore suitable for amateurs without specialised orchid houses. (Engraving from *Amateur Gardening*, 10 January 1885, p. 436) (*Amateur Gardening*)

roof or in pots or baskets, but no orchids should be watered too
freely. One of the most useful orchids was the lady's slipper
(*Cypripedium insigne*), which would flower all winter in a stove house,
and would also thrive in a 'snug greenhouse' or even a 'fern case in
the parlour' in skilful hands. One of the joys of growing orchids, or
any other exotic indoor plant, was the pleasure for a gentleman of
putting one in his buttonhole to show the world what he was
capable of growing, or could afford to grow. Special tubes were sold
in which to place a choice bloom in a small amount of water, so that
the flower would remain fresh all day or evening. Many florists liked
to wear their own flowers as a self-advertisement, and many
gentlemen wore flowers as a form of decoration. It could be a
talking point when one met a fellow enthusiast, and was another
way of bringing people together on the subject of horticulture.
Joseph Chamberlain, the politician, was a wealthy man with an
interest in orchids. His garden, Highbury, in Birmingham, had
thirteen orchid houses and when he was in London he had the
flowers sent down to him every day so that he could always wear
one. He contributed to the building of the Temperate House at Kew
and he also campaigned for allotments.[5]
  Mrs Earle was a convert to orchids:

For anyone with a small stove I can thoroughly advise growing some of
the more easily cultivated orchids. For many years all orchids seemed
to me to smell of money, and to represent great expenditure; but this is
not the case at all. They only want the treatment suited to them, and
the same care and attention required by other plants that are grown in
heat. Cyprepediums come in most usefully at this time of year; they
last well in water, and continue to flower at times all through the
winter. There are endless varieties of them to be bought, and some of
the least expensive plants are often as good as the costly ones; it is only
the new varieties that are dear.[6]

  Pitcher plants (insectivorous plants with hanging conical pouches
into which creatures fell) were appropriate to grow with orchids
because they required the same conditions and provided interest
when the orchids were not flowering. Again, not all were viable in an
amateur's cool greenhouse, but plenty were. Shirley Hibberd goes
into some detail in describing pitcher plants and how they grow,
perhaps because they were not as well known as orchids, although
they seem to have been something of a craze in the late Victorian era,
providing some home entertainment in watching insects go to their
destruction. In his description of pitcher plants and how they work,
he takes the opportunity to include some ancillary lessons in life:

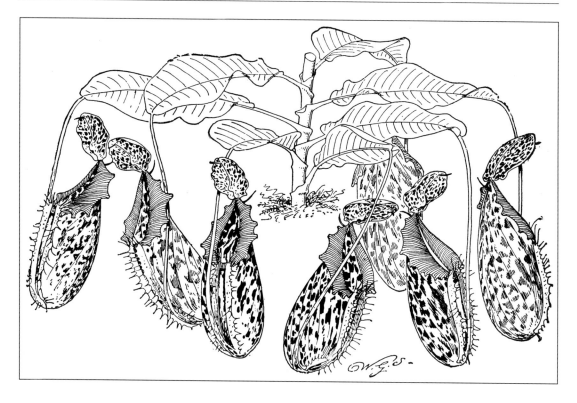

It will be observed that the young pitchers have a lid fitting down quite close; but as the pitchers increase in size the lid gradually rises, and then we may suppose it possible that water can find its way into the pitcher by means of condensed dew or the fall of rain. Not that water does find its way in; no! But water is almost always found there; *it is secreted by the plant* . . . Inside the pitcher are numerous hairs, which project downward; and it is found that when an insect enters, its downward course is easy, but escape is almost impossible; hence we not only find water, but also flies, wood-lice, and even beetles. Ah! The way to ruin is smooth and sometimes pleasant, and to go down is easier than to go up; so perhaps the flies find it in the pitchers, as we do also in the conduct of life . . . What, then, is the wonder that flies, finding the pitchers open, and smelling the moisture, should be tempted to their destruction? An English naturalist once supposed that the ichneumon fly would drag other flies, and hurl them over the edge of the pitcher to destruction, as a human murderer might throw a victim over a bridge. There is no mystery about the flies being there. Watch long enough, and you will see them go down, but however long you watch you will never see them return. The moral is too obvious.[7]

Pitcher plants were popular companions to orchids, as they thrived in the same conditions and appealed to the Victorians' liking for curiosities. (Engraving from *Thompson's Gardener's Assistant*, vol. 3, p. 478) (*Author's collection*)

All exoticism is not orchids, however, nor even pitcher plants. Other plants which became popular with the rise of the conservatory were the tender foliage plants that we grow as house plants today. These often survive under less than ideal conditions for long enough for people to feel they have had their money's worth, but are not ideally situated for most indoor conditions. The Victorians did not have the typical conditions of modern centrally heated homes, which usually create an atmosphere that is too dry for plants that come from warm, humid climates, but they had other problems such as gas lights with poisonous fumes, coal fires producing soot, and fog. As now, plants left all night on a window sill with the curtains closed would get chilled and not grow well.

Writers in the magazines had to try to help readers choose the right plants for their small-scale glasshouses. 'Palms for Small Plant-Houses' was written by 'A Practical Hand at the Royal Gardens, Kew' and appeared in the *Floral World* in 1868:

> If I were only going to grow three palms, I should select *Latania rubra*, a *Calamus*, and a *Chamaedorea*. This Latania is a magnificent plant, with fan-shaped leaves, the petioles and ribs of leaves of a crimson or deep rosy colour. It must be kept in mind that they vary a good deal in this colouring, and if I were buying a plant I should take care and go to the nursery and select the plant which pleased me best. *Latania aurea* is in the same way, but yellow instead of red. I have never yet seen a specimen of either of these species with a stem; there is, therefore, not much fear of its becoming too large very soon. Besides if it should ever grow too large for the space at your command, any nurseryman would take it, and give you in exchange something which would suit you better. I should say that any person might buy a young plant, and after having had the pleasure of growing it for eight or ten years, find that it would be worth something good in the way of exchange.[8]

The *Calamus* and *Chamaedorea* were also recommended for their small size, but all three palms mentioned required 'stove heat', which meant high temperatures throughout the year. The writer went on to say that there were palms such as *Chamaerops humilis* which could be grown in a conservatory with camellias and oranges, and therefore only needing mild heat. If even this could not be managed, he mentioned that there was 'a fine plant of *C. Fortunei*, [which] has been growing in the open ground for five years past in the garden of the Royal Botanic Society, Regent's Park; and at Osborne this glorious palm is as hardy as a weed'.[9]

Which was better, a greenhouse or a conservatory? No doubt for most amateurs it was a matter of what they had at their disposal when they took on the house. Shirley Hibberd was adamant about the different uses for greenhouses and conservatories:

The first step towards a proper recognition of the kind of embellishment required is to remember that a conservatory is not a stove, or a greenhouse, or a pit, or a hand-light, consequently it should not be used as any one of these things, or as all these things combined. We employ the several structures enumerated, the conservatory alone excepted, for production simply; and, therefore, although a tasteful arrangement of plants is everywhere or every how to be desired, yet where *production* is the primary proposal, mere display is of secondary importance . . . The glass structures that are devoted to horticultural production are related to manufactures; the conservatory is related to the drawing-room, and, in the broad scheme of horticultural work, it is not a workshop or a museum, but a *garden under glass* . . . In a word, a conservatory is the proper place to display the beauties of the plants previously grown to perfection in the greenhouse.[10]

If a conservatory was what one had available, how to fill it?

Every season should supply new flowers to the conservatory. In the spring, potted bulbs will make a gay beginning, and if orchids are grown in the stove the bulbs will be followed closely by some of the most resplendent of the family. As the season advances the greenhouse will supply pelargoniums, heaths, herbaceous calceolarias, and specimen petunias, and in autumn the pits will prove their usefulness by providing a glorious display of chrysanthemums. As a rule, however, the less we see of bedding plants in the conservatory the better, for we see enough of them in the open garden during the summer, and it is simply a tax on one's patience – that is, on the patience of one who believes in eclectic horticulture – to pass from a blaze of geraniums in the parterre to another blaze of geraniums in the conservatory. It is neither our business or our pleasure to denounce people who, in their horticultural enterprises, are content with some half dozen genera of plants; but we are bound to say, in defence of plants in general, that there are many fine things adapted to the conservatory which many who profess to love plants have hitherto not made acquaintance with. A rabbit cooked a hundred different ways is tiresome, and the cooking must be very tiresome to the rabbit.[11]

Another suitable group of plants for the amateurs to try was cacti and succulents. Those who had been to Kew Gardens may have seen some very impressive specimens. The *Pictorial Times* of 15 March 1845 reported on the arrival of a 'monster cactus' from Mexico which had arrived packed in fifteen mats 'each as large and thick as an ordinary doormat', which had kept it perfectly green and uninjured 'as if it were that morning removed from its native rocks'. It weighed over 700 pounds and was four and a half feet high. Shirley Hibberd thought cacti well suited to modest conservatories:

The capability of bearing any amount of sunlight renders these plants admirably adapted for the possessors of those little glass boxes which, in town houses, are called 'conservatories' for, unfit as these structures usually are for plant growing, they answer admirably for sheltering succulent and hard leaved plants of small size on account of their dryness and strong light. The wonderful variety, both of form and colour, that may be ensured in a collection of succulents costing almost nothing in the first instance, and the very small space occupied by them if judiciously selected, are additional reasons in favour of their adoption by amateurs who value a bit of glass more highly than to waste it on ephemeral plants that can only be properly grown in comparatively large and well appointed plant houses.[12]

A collection of cacti was an original choice for an amateur's glasshouse, and easier to look after than orchids or palms. (Engraving from *Cassell's Popular Gardening*, vol. III, p. 225) (*Author's collection*)

The 'hard-leaved' plants referred to above included agaves and aloes, cycads, palms, aspidistras, phormiums and yuccas. Many of these have become popular at the beginning of the twenty-first century, probably because of their statuesque or architectural appearance in minimalist gardens, and also because they are resilient plants that will survive a lot of neglect. Hibberd says that in the nineteenth century they had been steadily rising in popularity, 'but as yet are not sufficiently understood as to their management, or appreciated as to their beauties. Being for the most part quiet in colour and slow in growth, they do not readily obtain a hold on the affections of amateurs, and only such as are amateurs indeed, and influenced by peculiar tastes, will ever become permanently interested in them.'[13]

Not all exotica lived inside. The fashion for subtropical bedding in the 1860s led many people to try planting out bananas, palms and other tender herbaceous plants and shrubs. In the great gardens, the staff were numerous enough and well informed enough to bring them into the glasshouse at the end of the summer. In more modest gardens this may not have been possible, and amateurs could be disappointed at the results. Shirley Hibberd counselled against attempting such planting unless one had the necessary resources:

> The 'subtropical garden', as at present understood in this country, is an importation from Paris, of limited, and indeed almost questionable value. Considered in close accordance with its designation, it requires us to expose to the common atmosphere, and to all possible changes of weather, any and every kind of stove plant that, owing to its distinctive outlines, or brilliant colours, may be considered suitable for purposes of outdoor embellishment. We may set apart a plot of ground for the purpose, and having crowded it with cannas, palms, tree-ferns, caladiums, begonias, and other elegant and valuable stove and greenhouse plants, pronounce the affair a subtropical garden. It may be a good or bad example, as taste and judgment have or have not been employed in its production, and we may premise that, unless taste and judgment are employed, the subtropical garden is likely to prove the most ludicrous of all possible garden failures.[14]

However, although he reflects that Britain is a 'sub-arctic clime', he does go on to explain how a subtropical garden can be created if certain conditions are satisfied. First, the ground must be prepared properly to retain heat for the plants' roots, and shelter must be provided in the way of surrounding trees to minimise the cold winds. Next, it is important to know that many hardy, or at least less tender, plants can be grown which, when associated with genuine subtropical plants, create an exotic effect. Once this is done, however, why pretend and call it subtropical? He maintains that the correct description is 'the Picturesque Flower Garden'. David Thomson in *Handy Book of the Flower Garden* uses the same designation. He contrasts the effect produced in flower gardens of masses of colour with the careful planting of these plants with 'peculiar beauty and grace of outline, which can only be enjoyed when they stand in bold relief to plants of different habits and stature from themselves'.[15]

Thomson's plan was to grow exotics in a bed he termed 'a hollow square', with small circular beds at each corner. He is not writing for the small amateur, but more the wealthy country garden owner with a professional staff. However, his advice can be followed by anyone. The bed is raised above ground level, which means that the soil can

be specially prepared and the plants will stand out in an elevated position. The circular beds are also raised conically. A palm tree, *Chamaerops fortunii*, is placed in the middle of the large bed, and yuccas in each of the smaller beds. Surrounding the palm is *Sedum spectabilis* and round the yuccas, *Echeveria metallica* and golden feather pyrethrum. Medium-sized New Zealand flax (phormium) and india rubber plants are used in the larger bed, half-way along the sides, with iresines, centaurea and more pyrethrum filling the spaces between. Most of these can bear some frost and would therefore not be too risky in any garden. He then goes on to suggest more plants, such as yuccas and aloes as well as bananas and dracaenas, which can be used in sheltered situations. Thomson also recommends beds of 'succulent and curious-looking plants', which he thought of a distinct character and not suitable for mixing with ordinary bedding plants. These included agaves, sempervivums and sedums, as well as echeverias and a dark-chocolate coloured oxalis: 'All capable of being wintered and grown in a cool greenhouse, and consequently more suited to the masses than stove succulents, many of which, however, can be plunged out-doors for the summer months with impunity.'[16]

A bed of succulents and aloes would thrive outside in the summer and was more restful on the eyes than many dazzling colourful displays. (Engraving from David Thomson, *Handy Book of the Flower Garden*, p. 217) (*Author's collection*)

CHAPTER SIXTEEN

The Indoor Garden

Window gardening was popular even among the poorest people in towns without gardens, but there was more to window gardening than just growing things in window boxes or pots on window sills. The Victorian cult of the invalid meant that indoor gardening was always popular as amusement for those who were confined to the home. Those who had the space and the means could make their bay windows into miniature conservatories with a little structural improvement:

My bay window is fitted in a very simple manner. It consists, in the first instance, of a series of zinc trays eighteen inches wide, and the same in length, the depth being one foot. These fit closely together, and are completely hidden by an ornamental skirting of rosewood, which can be removed in one piece, as it is attached to a front of deal. The zinc trays are all freely pierced for drainage, and they rest on thin slips of wood on a slab of slate, which in its turn rests on the sill and the central support. The furnishing consists of a combination of pot plants with plants which are naturally rooted in the zinc boxes. Thus in two of the side-boxes small-leaved ivies have long been established, and form a most elegant tracery on iron wires, the two main supports to the trellis being fitted with glass trumpets removed from a table decoration, and

A window conservatory was used in a similar way to a Wardian case and helped screen the inside of the house. (Engraving from *Amateur Gardening*, 14 March 1885, p. 547) (*Amateur Gardening*)

fitted into a socket, so as to be movable when required. In these I generally plant fine-leaved ferns, and as soon as they begin to decline in beauty, I take them out, plant them in the fernery, and refurnish the trumpets with fresh plants.[1]

Women were particularly keen on window or indoor gardening, and could be quite inventive in what they used. Miss I.L. Hope Johnstone even took her ideas abroad, but was not totally prepared for what transpired:

Finding myself again in a part of the Continent where, owing to the usual severity of the climate in winter, all sitting-rooms must be closely shut, and the air in them consequently becoming very hot and dry, I thought it a good opportunity for making another attempt at invalid gardening without appliances. I again commenced with the brown basin mentioned in a former paper . . . it is just the size of a common wash-hand basin, and of the rich deep chocolate brown ware so much employed on the Continent for cooking purposes.

I filled this basin with good-sized lumps of charcoal, some stones, and good leaf-loam, to which I had previously added a little grit, not having any silver-sand by me at the time . . . This done, and the mould and charcoal settled, a little bushy Ivy, some dwarf reedy grass, a few plants of wild Ribbon grass and Moneywort were planted to make an edge. Then came planted at intervals inside these early Van Thol Tulips. Then inside these again, Rex Rubrorum Tulips and Hyacinths, with a fine large bulb of Narcissus in the centre of all. So far, all went well. Now I stood the basin in the centre of a flower-stand, lent me for the purpose by a friend. All round the edge of the stand I placed small phials (large mouthed are best) containing a little charcoal and some water for preserving single flowers or stems, and in between these again were saucers for plants in pots. This also promised well, but now I made my grand mistake. I obtained a long, graceful, feathery moss I had admired in the woods, and *thought* I had dried it, but to my dismay discovered it to be teeming with animal life. However, as it was too late in the season to replace them in kind, there was nothing for it but to have recourse to the woods, and fill the spaces as well as circumstances will allow by hardy subjects, hoping for better times rather later in the year.[2]

Miss Johnstone's real reason for writing this piece in the *Floral World* was to raise the question of *dust*, her plants being 'white and dry with it'. She knew it was caused by the closed burning stove and lack of ventilation and that the usual remedy was wiping with water or covering with a wet cloth at night, but she felt this was not appropriate for invalids: 'it is troublesome; water is not always at hand: some rheumatic patients may not even touch damp things, and, in fact, very few persons care to do it'. Then one day, while flipping through *Enquire Within*, she found the answer. She read that maps and important documents were sometimes covered with a thin film of gutta-percha to protect them and keep them waterproofed. She also read that tartalan (a kind of muslin) brushed over with boiled oil was effective in keeping out dust: 'Why not make a sort of dome the size of the flower-stand, and about three inches taller than the plants, like the skeleton of a dish cover, and strain tartalan or the parchment-like foreign post paper – I think called 'vellum made' – over it, and cover all inside and out with a slight glaze of gutta percha?'³ Why not indeed? Possibly because if the woman were an invalid, boiling oil and painting muslin with gutta-percha might possibly be a bit more messy than using a damp cloth (especially if 'water is not always at hand' to clear up with). Anyway, undeterred, she even added that 'Before covering, a handle might be made at the top, of cord, overcast button-hole fashion, to make it firm.'

Household objects were also recommended by the flower arranger Annie Hassard in 'Floral Decorations on a Small Scale' in the *Floral World*:

> The two stands in which my friend's flowers were arranged were to all appearances those elegant little glass tazzas with a trumpet rising out

FRANCES JANE HOPE (d. 1880)

FRANCES JANE HOPE was the niece of the professor of chemistry and pharmacy at the University of Edinburgh, which owned the house, Wardie Lodge, where she lived and gardened. She was one of the few women to contribute to gardening magazines as early as the 1860s. Her articles appeared in both the *Gardeners' Chronicle* and the *Cottage Gardener*, and some were collected after her death in *Notes and Thoughts on Garden and Woodland Written Chiefly for the Amateur* (1881). The garden was a grand one, having at least one border 86ft long and 5ft wide. Miss Hope felt that flowers should be looked at for their own qualities, not merely as parts of a flower bed, and used not only flowers and foliage for effect in the garden, but vegetables too. Much of the floral produce of her garden was made up into baskets given to the poor and sick in the neighbourhood, as she believed that it brightened up their lives. These gifts became known as her Flower Missions, and Canon Ellacombe said that they always contained aromatic plants to give the invalids memories of home.

of the centre of each, which are so well adapted for standing on console tables, etc., in the drawing room.

I remarked, 'I see you have been investing in new stands, and a very pretty pair they are, too. Where did you get them?' The answer was, 'Well, I don't mind letting you into a secret,' and thereupon my friend raised one of the fern-fronds, which were drooped thickly round the edge, and expose to view the edge of a *common china saucer*, which same saucer formed the tazza, and the trumpet was formed by a well-shaped specimen glass being placed in the centre of the saucer. This little plan is worth knowing, as every one who attempts floral arrangements of any description possesses a few specimen glasses and, need I add, are likely to have saucers for their teacups.[4]

Amateur Gardening in 1888 gave instructions for making a home-made window case attached to a sash window. Although the instructions were specifically for amateurs, the amateur was expected to be fairly skilled at glazing with putty and creating tenon and mortise joints, not to mention understanding the mixing of white and red lead, boiled oil and joiners' glue. It was also explained that the window case could be heated with a hot-water boiler (called 'The Louise') inside the room, heated by a gas jet or oil lamp, applied to the window case by means of a small lead pipe.[5]

It was mentioned in this article that the window case lent an air of elegance to a property, and was also effective as a window screen. This idea should not be underestimated. The Victorian era had brought a lot of people together into small spaces when housing was so quickly developed in towns and suburbs. The tall sash windows which gave an air of stateliness to terraced houses also put the whole living area of a house on display. Many of these windows were fitted with inside shutters which folded away into the window frame during the day, but it was common to have wooden venetian blinds fitted for use in daytime to keep the light off the furnishing fabrics and for privacy.[6] However, this would make a room dark and gloomy, so a green translucent screen of plants would often be a good compromise. It would prevent a direct view into the house by passers-by, but allowed light through and looked attractive and interesting as well. It had the added bonus of screening unsightly views of ugly buildings or industrial landscapes from inside the house.

The best-known form of indoor gardening in Victorian times was the Wardian case. It may be thought that these were adapted from the carrying cases used to bring plants back from abroad on sea voyages to protect the plants in houses from dust and soot. This is one reason why they became popular, but there may have been other

Window cases could be built by a keen do-it-yourselfer and provided a poor man's greenhouse. (*Museum of Garden History*)

reasons too. The nineteenth century was the peak of the era of natural-history collecting. Lepidopterists caught and chloroformed millions of butterflies and moths to pin on boards and keep classified in their cabinets; humming-birds were mercilessly killed and stuffed to provide luminescent displays in people's halls, and of course game animals were pursued to extinction to be exhibited on the walls of stately homes and gentlemen's clubs. The Wardian case was just another manifestation of the collecting mania, and it was no coincidence that ferns were one of the most popular subjects for both Wardian cases and collecting. Ferns had the added interest that the collection was still alive, or at least it was when it first went into the case. The principle of the Wardian case was said to be that it was a closed case with a self-supporting ecosystem (although they did not call it that then) in which the plants flourished once the balance of moisture and air was right.

Shirley Hibberd thought otherwise. He conducted experiments to discover why people found it so difficult to keep their plants alive and healthy (and put up with the glass constantly being misted up), and pronounced it 'a delusion and a snare'. He knew that ferns seemed better adapted to life in a Wardian case, but stated simply that 'In a close case some kinds of ferns will maintain their beauty for a length of time, and *then* perish.'[7] In other words, they just took longer to die than other plants. Hibberd therefore concluded that the only way to succeed with a Wardian case was to treat it like a miniature greenhouse and give it adequate ventilation. Then you could grow anything. He encouraged people to grow wild flowers in them to make their friends look at the flowers anew, and realise they were just as interesting and attractive as more exotic plants. He also suggested using small glass bottles known as Florence flasks, in which olive oil was imported, which could be hung in a row from a brass rod.[8] Wardian cases could be anything from a simple greenhouse structure, a glass dome, or the ornate gothic 'cathedrals' on their own decorative stands. He recommends filling them with ivies as well as ferns because ivy is even less destructible. He mentions glass cases at the windows of a house in Finsbury Square, London: 'These windows were fitted with cases projecting outwards, and forming a narrow glass box, with a trough at the bottom in which the ivies were planted. And a few copper wires served for training them over the outermost sheet of glass. The result was a cheerful, leafy screen, agreeable in appearance as seen from without, but decidedly beautiful as seen from within against the light, every leaf then showing its elegant veining, sharp and clear, upon a semi-transparent ground of the richest green.'[9]

The Waltonian case was a heated version of the Wardian case. It was invented by a Mr Walton of Surbiton, Surrey, who used it for growing cuttings as we would use a heated propagating frame. It was originally heated with an oil lamp, and in *Rustic Adornments*, in 1857, Hibberd explained how easy the maintenance was: 'The lamp in front is a common tin one, burning colza oil [rape-seed oil], and the cost of working is barely a shilling a week. The lamp is understood to burn eight hours, but I find that I can, if necessary, so trim it that it will burn twelve, or even fourteen; so that five minutes twice a day is all the attention the case ordinarily requires.'[10] However, he later discovered that it could be made more convenient:

A very slight variation in the method of trimming, which may occur if one is in a hurry, may cause it to smoke terribly or go out in an hour or two . . . if ever so well managed the lamp is a dirty affair, and there are few who would venture to use the apparatus in a decent room or even in a well kept greenhouse. I stated this case to Mr G. Wilson, the talented director of Price's Patent Candle Co, and he at once turned his attention to the providing of a remedy. This is now at our command in the form of a candle, which burns twelve hours in a lamp which stands eight inches high. The Waltonian case may now be placed beside the bed of an invalid to relieve the monotony of a sick chamber, and the most delicate hands may manage it without fear of contamination by oil or soot, and the source of heat is certain. It has proved the best of contrivances for propagation on a small scale, it will now prove the cleanest.[11]

As well as growing plants indoors, Victorians also brought cut flowers into the home. Mrs Earle described her London living room in January as an example of the comprehensive variety of floral life available even at the dullest time of the year:

On the side ledge of two large windows I have pots of the common Ivy of our hedges. We dig it up any time in the spring, and put it into the pots, which are then sunk into the ground under the shade of some wall, and kept well watered. Before bringing it into the room in winter, it is trained up on an iron stake or Bamboo-cane, singly or in bunches, to give variety to its shapes. If kept tolerably clean and watered, this Ivy is practically unkillable, even in London.

Then there are some pots of the long-suffering Aspidistras, the two kinds – variegated and dark green. These also want nothing but plenty of water, and sponging the dust off the leaves twice a week. They make pretty pot-plants if attended to during the summer in the country. They should be well thinned out and every injured leaf cut off, tied together towards the middle, kept growing all the summer in the greenhouse, and encouraged to grow tall; they are then more graceful and satisfactory. They seldom want dividing or re-potting. I have two sorts of India-rubber plants – the large-leaved, straight-growing common *Ficus elastica*, and the *Ficus elastica indica*, which is a little more delicate, and the better for more heat in summer; but it has a smaller leaf, and grows in a much more charming way than the other.[12]

Ivy was often trained for indoor or balcony decoration into an umbrella shape or screen. Shirley Hibberd explained how to do it in *The Ivy*: 'Pot young plants liberally, and set them growing; train out on wire, and when the outline of the design is covered, pinch in all side-shoots, so as to form the head into a dense mass of verdure. Do not entirely remove the side-shoots from the stem until a good head has been obtained, as they help to swell the stem, but keep them pinched back, and when they may be dispensed with remove a few at a time, commencing at the bottom.'[13]

There were other forms of winter decoration. Mrs Earle described the use of sprouting seeds:

> You know, I daresay, the old nursery secret of growing either wheat or canary-seed on wet moss. You fill some shallow pan or small basin with moss, and keep it quite wet. Sow your seed quickly on the moss, and put the pan away in a dark cupboard for nine or ten days. When about two inches high, bring it out and put it in a sunny window, turning it round, so as to make it grow straight. Wheat is white at the base with brave little sword-blades of green, on which often hangs a drop of clear water. Canary-seed is red, like Rhubarb, at the bottom and green at the top. I know nothing more charming to grow in dull town rooms or sick rooms than these two seeds. They come to perfection in about three weeks, and last for another five or six. Grown in small saucers, they make a pretty dinner table winter decoration.[14]

Moss was used as a useful filler between plants on display and in which to germinate seeds. As with many commodities used in the garden, the nineteenth-century gardener did not have to buy it, he simply went out and gathered it from the wild. This was done so often that it is likely some species died out in Britain, as many ferns did. Keen collectors even had specially adapted sticks and umbrellas with which to cut it.

The *Floral World* gave hints on choosing decorations which would look good by gaslight at Christmas: 'Elaborate colouring is less needful than broad and bold effects. Half-tints, as a rule, are quite washy by gaslight, though some neutrals, such as lilac, dove colour, and fawn, are valuable, as they afford by gaslight various chaste shades of grey, and are more pleasing than white. These colours will generally be preferable to red, or any of the primary colours, for ribbons to tie garlands, and in artificial flowers to brighten the effects of the stronger colours. The two predominating colours in Christmas decorations should be RED and GREEN.'[15]

It was advised to choose artificial flowers consistent with the season, such as chrysanthemums and camellias, and to use other shrubs in addition to holly, such as hawthorn, cotoneaster and euonymus. Flowers could be pinned on to ivy wreaths, but there was the ever-present problem of soot when gathering foliage from outside: 'a little purification of the leaves should be attempted' by wiping with a dry cloth. For table decorations Berlin wool of the colour of green grass was suggested to represent moss (and thus avoid

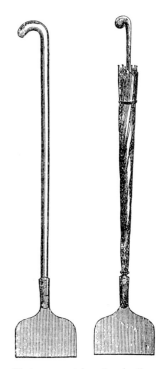

Blades on a stick and umbrella for gathering moss while out walking. (Engraving from *Floral World*, 1874, p. 339) (*Hackney Archives*)

the problems of unseen animal life) placed in a pot: 'the ladies of the household will soon find something clean and dry to serve'.[16]

There were various ways of using cut flowers in Victorian homes, apart from just putting them in a vase, which would of course expose them to the ever-present soot and dust. Some of the methods were described in *Rustic Adornments for Homes of Taste*: 'In spring time you may delight yourself by culling a few violets . . . and placing them in a glass dish, in which there is a little wet silver-sand. The short stems stuck into the sand get sufficient moisture, and a glass over the whole confines the fragrance, so that whenever you are inclined to inhale a full breath of unadulterated violet perfume, you have but to lift off the glass, and enjoy it to your heart's content.'[17]

A more sophisticated version of the flower shade was a vase with a groove round the upper edge to hold the cover, so constructed that once the flowers were inside, arranged in damp sand, water was poured into the groove to make a seal and thus render it airtight. This kept the flowers fresh for a longer period and preserved the fragrance, which could be enjoyed when the shade was taken off. A further method of displaying flowers was the 'Pyramidal Boquet Stand' supplied by Henderson's Nursery and used at flower shows. It consisted of metal cylinder pierced with holes, within which was another cylinder with just enough space between the two to hold the stalks of flowers, which would take up water from inside the cylinder by capillary action. It was said to be ideal to display flowers, but Hibberd was not happy with its overall design: 'I must, however, not quit the subject without a protest. They are not made as elegantly as they might be. Mine is mounted on a turned mahogany stand, which is destitute of design, and *pimping* in dimensions, and I shall not be happy till I have it mounted on a more elegant and substantial basis – that, however, is a matter of taste, easily rectified, and does not affect the *principle* of the invention.'[18] Other patent methods could be employed for arranging flowers, such as the 'Cazenove Flower Rack', illustrated in *Thompson's Gardener's Assistant*, which allowed the flowers to look loosely informal, but to be kept in place.[19]

When fresh flowers were not available, homes could still be decorated with dried foliage. An advertisement for 'African grasses for vases' featured portraits of Africans to give an exotic appearance, stating that the 'tall, graceful, silky, stately and imposing' grasses of 'delicate natural tints' would not drop off and would last for years. The same supplier could also provide natural silver leaves 'for painting on', seaweed 'for table decoration' and ostrich egg shells for painting on, or for natural-history collections.[20] The woman desperate to have some form of floral decoration could even make her own artificial flowers. *Wax-Flower Modelling Made Easy* by

The 'Cazenove Flower Rack' was used inside vases to create floral decorations before 'oasis' came into use. It could be adjusted to fit the size of the vase. (Engraving from *Thompson's Gardener's Assistant*, vol. 3, p. 651) (*Author's collection*)

Annie M. Williams was recommended in the *Floral World* in 1871, said to supply 'a much felt want in an admirable manner'.[21]

Finally, there was no need to waste anything left over after using the best specimens: 'As you will now be making up your herbarium, and recalling on rainy days and long evenings the delightful rambles your dried specimens remind you of, a hint as to the uses of herbarium waste may be useful. Save carefully all the spare tormentils and small grasses, and whatever else appears to be fit for embroidery to be worn by fairies. Mount these delicate scraps with gum on note papers as floral vignettes, and give them freely to those who love you.'[22]

Epilogue: What the Victorian Gardeners Did for Us

The detailed exploration of how the Victorians gardened, what they grew and how they learned to do so brings home to us their pleasure in gardening, their sense of invention and their determination in not being daunted by bringing questionable substances into their homes or indulging in heavier exercise than they previously thought possible. But the horticultural world of which they became so proud was a microcosm of the real world from which their beloved plants were plundered. The British Empire in Victorian times is not very attractive to us now because we see the exploitation and prejudices on which it was founded, but it is to that empire that we owe the discovery of many plant species, now common in English gardens, and the foundations of the growth of gardening 'for the millions'.

Between the 1850s and the 1890s the middle classes took over gardening, but the so-called 'working people' were not far behind. They built on what the villa gardeners had done beforehand. It is hard to estimate the number of people who enjoyed gardening by the end of the nineteenth century. Circulation figures of magazines are not generally reliable because they are always exaggerated to increase advertising. When the *Gardening World* claimed in 1884 that there were a million people in the United Kingdom who loved gardening (see Chapter Three), it gave no evidence to show what this figure was based on. In 1872 *The Leisure Hour* stated that there were between 800 and 1,000 gardens around Coventry (whose population was then about 40,000) from an eighth of an acre to an acre or more, which were much sought after and prized by their occupiers, and it also claimed that the death rate in the town had fallen as a result.[1] In 1891 *Amateur Gardening* praised the allotment system as providing healthy and profitable exercise for all men: 'It is a most interesting sight, on any evening during the spring and summer months, to take a walk round and note the pleasure with which men devote their time to their allotments after a hard day's work. They all seem to be extremely anxious to get as much out of their land as possible.'[2]

But figures do not illustrate the story of amateur gardening: we see it all around us now. By the early twentieth century there was nothing to stop anyone from creating their own garden, and crucially they were able to go out and buy what they needed and read books and magazines that were written specifically for them. The amateur gardener had become a concept and a retail market in itself. When we see people today in a garden centre, filling up their cars with multi-purpose compost, potted shrubs, strips of seedlings, tools and fertilisers, we should remember the struggle that went into gardening before the days when all this was available for anyone's 'ready money' or, indeed, credit.

The people who made amateur gardening possible were pioneers, but their intentions were the same as ours are today: to add an extra dimension to our everyday lives and lose ourselves in a different world, transcending the one in which we are forced to spend most of our time. Anyone who takes on a garden and embarks on the process of making it their own still shares the enthusiasm of these pioneers and gains the same satisfaction from the practice of gardening now as then:

> May your hours of rustic recreation profit you in body and soul. May your flowers flourish, your bees prosper, your birds love you, and your pet fishes live for ever. May the blight never visit the tendrils that make your arbours and porches leafy, your borders gay, or your fern-banks verdurous; and may you find in every little thing that lives and grows a pleasure for the present hour, and a suggestion of things higher and brighter for contemplation in the future. I herein reach my hand towards you with an affectionate FAREWELL![3]

APPENDIX 1

Victorian Gardening Magazines

This is by no means an exhaustive list of periodicals and does not include botanical magazines, but it supplies more information than is found in the text and allows comparison of similar names. Information was originally obtained from Ray Desmond's 'Victorian Gardening Magazines' and Brent Elliott's 'Gardening Times'. Further details were found in the catalogues of the British Library, the Lindley Library and the Colindale Newspaper Library. Biographical information came from Ray Desmond's *Dictionary of British and Irish Botanists and Horticulturalists*. Where discrepancies were found in dates of publication, a decision was made based on personal research, and any mistakes are my own responsibility. Most publications are available at the Lindley Library, the Royal Horticultural Society, 80 Vincent Square, London SW1P 2PE. The following are exceptions and can be found at the stated places (and possibly others):

Amateur Gardening (nineteenth-century editions)	Colindale Newspaper Library
Country Life (nineteenth-century editions)	Westminster Public Library
Garden and Horticultural Sales and Wants Advertiser	Colindale Newspaper Library
Gardeners' Hive	Colindale Newspaper Library
Gardener's Magazine, 1862–73	British Library
Glenny's Gardener's Gazette	Colindale Newspaper Library
United Gardeners' and Land Stewards' Journal	Colindale Newspaper Library

Amateur Gardening (1884–present)
Weekly, aimed at amateurs, price originally one penny. Edited by Shirley Hibberd until 1887, then T. Sanders until after 1900.

Birmingham and Midland Gardeners' Magazine (1852–3)
Edited by C.J. Perry and J. Cole. Intended to supply information to northern gardeners.

British Gardening for Amateurs and Professionals: see **Gardening and Horticultural Sales and Wants Advertiser**

Cottage Gardener (and Country Gentleman's Companion) (1848–61), continuing as **Journal of Horticulture** (1861–1915)
Weekly paper started to promote 'spade cultivation' by George W. Johnson and published by Orr & Co. Newspaper format; price threepence. Robert Hogg joint editor from 1858. At various times it incorporated the *Poultry Chronicle*, and *Beekeeper's Chronicle*, later the *Poultry, Bee and Household Chronicle*. Hogg bought the paper and set up the Journal of Horticulture publishing company, which later took over the **Florist** and published booklets called 'Manuals for the Many'.

Cottage Gardening (1892–8)
Weekly published by William Robinson; price halfpenny. Incorporated into the **Gardener** in 1899.

Country Gentleman ('a Cottage, Villa, Farm and Garden Newspaper') (1850)
Price sixpence. George Glenny was horticultural editor.

Country Life (Illustrated) (1897–present)
Glossy, photographically illustrated weekly, including gardening with country pursuits. Started by Edward Hudson; price sixpence. Originated as *Racing Illustrated*; gradually incorporated information on gardens and a gardening column, 'In the Garden'.

Floral Magazine (1861–81)
Monthly magazine specialising in new flowers, with many coloured illustrations, similar to the earlier botanical magazines. Started by Lovell, Reeve, who published *Curtis's Botanical Magazine*. Editors were Thomas Moore and Revd H.H. D'Ombrain. Artists were W.H. Fitch, James Andrews, W.G. Smith, F.W. Burbidge and R. Dean. It was too botanical to appeal to florists.

The Floral World and Garden Guide (1858–80)
Monthly paper published by Groombridge and Sons, small format, price fourpence. Editor Shirley Hibberd until 1876. Aimed primarily at amateurs 'with moderate means'. Wood engravings by Benjamin Fawcett.

Floricultural Cabinet and Florist's Magazine (1833–59)
Monthly paper in book format, price sixpence with two colour plates. Published by Whittaker, Treacher in London and G. Ridge in Sheffield. Started by Joseph Harrison for floriculturalists and carried on after his death in 1855 by his sons, J.J. and E. Harrison. Claimed circulation of 50,000 in first year, and in 1840 still claimed 10,000. Replaced by *Gardener's Weekly Magazine* in direct succession.

Floricultural Magazine and Miscellany for Gardeners (1836–42)
Editor Robert Marnock; sixpence per issue.

Florist (1848), *Florist and Garden Miscellany* (1849–50), *Florist, Fruitist and Garden Miscellany* (1851–61), *Florist and Pomologist* (1862–84)
Monthly paper of thirty-two book-sized pages and one colour plate, started by Edward Beck, Henry Groom, John Edwards, Charles Fox, Charles Turner and Thomas Rivers. Beck was the first editor, but in 1851 Turner took over, assisted by John Spencer. Sold 900 copies in 1848. In 1853, Robert Hogg became editor and later assumed ownership. Spencer was joint editor in 1862, and was succeeded by Thomas Moore (and possibly William Paul). Moore was sole editor from 1875.

Florist's Journal (1840–5), *Florist's Journal and Gardener's Record* (1846–8)
Monthly published by Groombridge and Sons, with one colour plate, successor to the *Horticultural Journal* and intended as a better-quality paper for florists. Editor George Glenny.

Florist's Magazine: see *Floricultural Cabinet*

Florists' Magazine ('a Register of the Newest and Most Beautiful Varieties of Florists' Flowers') (1835–56)
Edited by Frederick W. Smith; four shillings a copy.

Florists' Register: see *Horticultural Journal*

Garden ('An Illustrated Weekly Journal of Gardening in All Its Branches') (1871–1927)
Weekly paper, twenty-two pages, price fourpence, 'conducted' by William Robinson and launched as a rival to Shirley Hibberd's *Gardener's Magazine*. First weekly to include colour plates. Taken over by Edward Hudson (of *Country Life*) in 1900. Became absorbed into *Homes and Gardens*.

Garden and Horticultural Sales and Wants Advertiser (1888), *Garden and Horticultural Gazette* (1889), *Northern Gardener* (1889–92), *British Gardening for Amateurs and Professionals* (1892–3)
Published in Manchester, at first bi-weekly, then weekly; one penny per issue.

Garden Oracle ('and Economic Year Book') (1859–beyond 1900)
Annual publication under editorship of Shirley Hibberd, originally connected with the *Floral World*.

Gardener ('a Magazine of Horticulture and Floriculture') (1867–82)
Monthly paper, forty-eight pages, published in Edinburgh and later London as well. Aimed at amateurs, florists and professionals. Edited by William Thomson and later David Thomson; contributors included S. Reynolds Hole. Revived in 1899 as *Popular Gardening*.

Gardener (1899–1919)
Price one penny; weekly. Took over *Cottage Gardening* and amalgamated with *Popular Gardening* in 1919.

Gardener and Practical Florist (1843–4)
Published by Groombridge and Sons. Included George Glenny as writer.

Gardeners' and Farmers' Journal (1847–53)
Successor to the *United Gardeners' and Land Stewards' Journal*. Included with *Mark Lane Express and Agricultural Journal* (1854–80)

Gardener's and Forester's Record (1833–6)
Launched by Joseph Harrison; sixpence per issue.

Gardeners' Chronicle (and Agricultural Gazette) (1841–1969)
Weekly paper founded by John Lindley (editor of the horticultural part) and Joseph Paxton to provide a rational alternative to papers of George Glenny and John Loudon. Originally sixteen pages including general news, published on Saturday and costing sixpence. The *Agricultural Gazette* was included 1844–73. Lindley and Paxton both died in 1865 and Maxwell T. Masters took over editorship. Amalgamated with the *Horticultural Trade Journal* in 1969.

Gardener's Gazette (1837–44), *Amateur and Working Gardeners' Gazette* (1844–5), *Amateur Gardeners' Gazette* (1845–6), *Gardeners' Gazette Edition of United Gardeners' and Land Stewards' Journal* (1845–7), *Glenny's Gardener's Gazette* (1859–63), *Glenny's Gazette and Midland Florist* (1863–4), *Gardeners' and Farmers' Journal* (1847–80)
First weekly gardening paper, founded by George Glenny, who was editor 1837–40. John Loudon editor 1840–1; James Main 1841; then Glenny reinstated until 1843. Other papers were different versions of Glenny's paper as his fortunes waxed and waned.

Gardeners' Hive (1850)
Editor J.T. Neville. Weekly aimed at florists and amateurs; price twopence.

Gardener's Magazine ('and Register of Rural and Domestic Improvement') (1826–43)
Conductor John Loudon; published by Orr and Co. Started with circulation of four thousand copies. Originally quarterly (price five shillings), then bi-monthly (price three shillings and sixpence), finally monthly (price two shillings and sixpence, reduced to one shilling and sixpence in 1834). Reputedly brought in an income of £750 a year for Loudon.

Gardener's Magazine (1862–82); *Gardeners' Magazine* (1882–1916)
Successor to *Gardener's Weekly Magazine*. Shirley Hibberd editor. Launched in new, larger format in 1865 and became the best-selling gardening magazine of the 1860s, when published by Collingridges. Price twopence ha'penny. After Hibberd's death in 1890, editor George Gordon.

Gardener's Record and Amateur Florist's Companion (1852–4)
Editor J.T. Neville.

Gardener's Weekly Magazine (1860–2)
Successor to *Floricultural Cabinet*, conducted by J.J. and E. Harrison. Price penny ha'penny, small-size newspaper format. Succeeded by *Gardener's Magazine*.

Gardening Illustrated (1879–1956)
Weekly paper produced by William Robinson. Price one penny. Absorbed into *Gardeners' Chronicle*. Claimed one and a half million copies issued in six months by 1881.

Gardening World (Illustrated) (1884–1909)
Weekly, fourteen pages, price one penny. Mainly aimed at professional gardeners. Incorporated into *Garden Work* (started in 1901).

Garden-Work for Villa, Suburban, Town and Cottage Gardens (1884–96)

Glenny's Gardener's Gazette: see *Gardener's Gazette*

Glenny's Quarterly Review of Horticulture, Literature, the Arts and General Science (1853–5). Incorporated *Horticultural Journal*.

Gossip of the Garden (1856–63)
Monthly, small size, thirty-six pages, price threepence. For florists and suburban horticulturalists, originally published in Derby and London; from 1857 London only. Founder editors: E.S. Dodwell and John Edwards. Later edited by William Dean, John Sladden and someone referred to as 'A.S.H.'. Originally issued a thousand copies and said it needed five thousand subscribers to survive.

Horticultural Journal and Florists' Register ('of Useful Information Connected with Floriculture') (*and Royal Lady's Magazine* (1831–3)) (1833–9)
Started by George Glenny to promote florists' flowers and his own society, the Metropolitan Society of Florists and Amateurs. *Horticultural Journal* was revived in 1854 and incorporated with *Glenny's Quarterly Review of Horticulture*.

Horticultural Register (and General Magazine) (1831–6)
Founded by Joseph Paxton and Joseph Harrison (who left in 1833 to set up the *Floricultural Cabinet*). James Main was editor from 1835. Cheap alternative to botanical magazines.

Journal of Horticulture: see *Cottage Gardener*

Ladies' Magazine of Gardening (1842)
Edited by Jane Loudon, but discontinued after eleven issues due to her husband's illness.

Midland Florist (and Suburban Horticulturalist) (1847–63), *Glenny's Gazette and Midland Florist* (1863–4)
Conductor John Frederick Wood of The Coppice, Nottingham. Monthly, forty-six pages, very small size. Alfred G. Sutton editor from 1857.

Northern Gardener: see *Horticultural Sales and Wants Advertiser*

Popular Gardening: see the *Gardener* (1867–82)

United Gardeners' and Land Stewards' Journal (1845–7)
Started as a rival to *Glenny's Gardener's Gazette*. Editor Robert Marnock; John Dickson brought in as floricultural editor. Took over *Gardener's Gazette* in 1847 and later that year became *Gardeners' and Farmers' Journal*.

Villa Gardener (1870–5)
Monthly paper with forty-eight pages, aimed at suburban London gardeners. From 1874 edited by D.T. Fish.

Woods and Forests (1883–5)
William Robinson's paper aimed at foresters. Price twopence. Absorbed into the *Garden*.

Suppliers and Places to Visit

To be truly authentic, a Victorian garden should only contain varieties of plants that were grown before 1901, and this is sometimes hard to verify, but a Victorian-style garden can be created by growing the right sorts of plants, which are easily obtainable from specialist suppliers. The suppliers mentioned have good selections and can give historical as well as horticultural guidance. However, the author cannot guarantee their performance.

Suppliers

ALPINES

Darcy & Everest, PO Box 78, St Ives, Cambs PE27 6ZA. Tel. 01480 497672. www.darcyeverest.co.uk
Potterton's Nursery, Moortown Road, Nettleton, Caistor, Lincs LN7 6HX. 01472 851714. www.pottertons.co.uk

AURICULAS

W. & S. Lockyer, 39 Mitchley Avenue, Riddlesdown, Purley, Surrey CR8 1BZ. Tel. 020-8660 1336
Woottens Mail Order, Tel. 01502 478258. www.woottensplants.co.uk

CACTI AND SUCCULENTS

Craig House Cacti, 42 Brentwood Court, Morley Road, Southport, Lancs PR9 9JW. george mcleod@amserve.com
The Plant Lovers, Candlesby House, Candlesby, Spilsby, Lincs PE23 5RU. Tel. 01754 890256
Southfield Nurseries, Bourne Road, Morton, Bourne, Lincs PE10 0RH. Tel. 01778 570168

CARNATIONS AND PINKS

Allwood Bros, Allwoods, London Road, Hassocks, West Sussex BN6 9NB. Tel. 01273 844229. Info@allwoodbros.co.uk
Hayward's Carnations, The Chace Gardens, 141 Stakes Road, Waterlooville, Hants PO7 5PL
Southview Nurseries, Dept G, Eversley Cross, Hants RG27 0NT. Tel. 01189 732206. www.southviewnurseries.co.uk
Steven Bailey Ltd, Silver Street, Sway, Lymington, Hants SO41 6ZA. Tel. 01590 682227

CARNIVOROUS PLANTS

Hampshire Carnivorous Plants, Ya-Mayla, Allington Lane, West End, Southampton, Hants SO30 3HQ. Tel. 023-8047 3314. www.hampshire-carnivorous-plants.co.uk (also exotic plants and ferns)
South West Carnivorous Plants, 2 Rose Cottages, Culmstock, Cullompton, Devon EX15 3JJ. Tel. 01884 841549. www.littleshopofhorrors.co.uk

CHRYSANTHEMUMS

Philip Tivey & Sons, 28 Wanlip Road, Syston, Leicester LE7 1PA. Tel. 0116-269 2968. chris.tivey@ntlworld.com

COTTAGE GARDEN PLANTS

Choice Plants Hardy Plant Nursery, 83 Halton Road, Spilsby, Lincs PE23 5LD. Tel. 01790 752361. www.choiceplants.net
Glebe Cottage Plants, Pixie Lane, Warkleigh, Umberleigh, Devon EX37 9DH. Tel. 01769 540554. www.glebecottageplants.co.uk

DAFFODILS

Walkers Bulbs, Washway House Farm, Washway Road, Holbeach, Spalding, Lincs PE12 7PP. Tel. 01406 426216. walkers@taylors-bulbs.com

DAHLIAS

Avon Bulbs Ltd, Burnt House Farm, Mid Lambrook, South Petherton, Somerset TA13 5HE. Tel. 01460 242177. www.avonbulbs.co.uk

EXOTICS

Anmore Exotics, 8 Bronte Rise, Greenham, Newbury RG14 7UG. Tel. 01635 841541

FERNS

Fernatix, Ivy Cottage, Ixworth Road, Honington, Suffolk IP31 1QY. Tel. 01359 269373. www.fernatix.co.uk
Fibrex Nurseries, Honeybourne Road, Pebworth, Warks CV37 8XP. Tel. 01789 720788. www.fibrex.co.uk
Gilbey's Plants, 42 Park Street, Masham, Ripon, North Yorks HG4 4HN. Tel. 01765 68992. gilbeysplants@aol.com
Reginald Kaye Ltd, Waithman Nurseries, Lindeth Road, Silverdale, Carnforth, Lancs LA5 0TY. Tel. 01524 701252.
Rickards Hardy Ferns Ltd, Carreg-y-Fedwen, Sling, Tregarth, Gwynedd LL57 4RP. Tel. 01248 602944

FRUIT

Deacon's Nursery, Godshill, Isle of Wight PO38 3HW. Tel. 01983 840750
Ken Muir Ltd, Honeypot Farm, Rectory Road, Weeley Heath, Clacton on Sea, Essex CO16 9BJ. Tel. 0870-747 9111. www.kenmuir.co.uk
KORE Wild Fruit Nursery, Warren Fields Farm, Trellach, Monmouth, Gwent NP25 4PQ. www.korewildfruitnursery.co.uk

HERBS AND AROMATICS

Cheshire Herbs, Forest Road, Tarporley, Cheshire CW6 9ES. Tel. 01829 760578. www.cheshireherbs.com
Jekka's Herb Farm, Rose Cottage, Shellards Lane, Alveston, Bristol BS35 3SY. Tel. 01454 418878. www.jekkasherbfarm.com
Stonecrop Herbs, East Lound, Haxey, Doncaster, South Yorks DN9 2LR. Tel. 01427 753355 (also fruit)

IVIES

Fibrex Nurseries – see under 'Ferns'

LILIES

Wilford Bulb Co. Ltd, Lennox House, Station Road, East Leake, Loughborough, Leics LE12 6LQ. Tel. 01509 852905

ORCHIDS

Burnham Nurseries Ltd, Forches Cross, Newton Abbot, Devon TQ12 6PZ. Tel. 01626 352233. www.orchids.uk.com
Deva Orchids, Little Brook Farm, Stryt Isa, Pen-y-Ffordd, Chester CH4 0JY. Tel. 01978 762454. www.devaorchids.co.uk
McBeans Ltd, Cooksbridge, Lewes, East Sussex BN8 4PR. Tel. 01273 400228. www.mcbeansorchids.co.uk

PALMS

Amulree Exotics, The Turnpike, Norwich Road, Fundenhall, Norwich, Norfolk NR16 1EL. Tel. 01508 488101. www.turn-it-tropical.co.uk
The Palm Farm, Station Road, Thornton Curtis, Ulceby, South Humberside DN39 6XF. Tel. 01469 531232

PELARGONIUMS

Fibrex Nurseries – see under 'Ferns'
Labourers Cottage Pelargonium Nursery, Blankney Barff, near Metheringham, Lincoln LN4 3BJ. Tel. 01526 378669
Vernon Geranium Nursery, Cuddington Way, Cheam, Sutton, Surrey SM2 7JB. Tel. 0208 393 7616. www.geraniumsUK.com

ROSES

Acton Beauchamp Roses, Worcester WR6 5AE. Tel. 01531 640433. www.actonbeaurose.co.uk
David Austin Roses, Bowling Green Lane, Albrighton, Wolverhampton WV7 3HB. Tel. 01902 376300. www.davidaustinroses.com
Peter Beales Roses, London Road, Attleborough, Norfolk NR17 1AY. Tel. 01953 454707. www.classicroses.co.uk

SEEDS

Suttons, Woodview Road, Paignton, Devon TQ4 7NG. Tel. 0870-220 0606. www.suttons-seeds.co.uk
Thompson and Morgan (UK) Ltd, Poplar Lane, Ipswich, Suffolk IP8 3BU. Tel. 01473 695200. www.thompson-morgan.com

TULIPS

Avon Bulbs – see under 'Dahlias'
Heritage Bulb Club, Tullynally Castle, Castle Pollard, Co. Westmeath, Ireland. Tel. (UK) 0845-300 4257. www.heritagebulbs.com

VEGETABLES

Medwyns of Anglesey, Llanor, Old School Lane, Llanfairpwl, Anglesey LL61 5RZ. Tel. 01248 714851. www.medwyns-prize-show-vegetables.com

VIOLAS AND PANSIES

A.B. Longden, 9 Middleton Road, Clifton, Rotherham, South Yorks S65 2AY. Tel. 01709 382571
Bouts Cottage Nurseries, Bouts Lane, Inkberrow, Worcs WR7 4HP. Tel. 01386 792923. www.boutsviolas.co.uk

Places to Visit

When planning any historic garden, the best inspiration comes from visiting real gardens established in the right period. Many of the following are far grander than the amateurs' gardens sought for, but they give ideas and create a historic atmosphere.
Details of all National Trust properties (marked **NT**) can be found on the National Trust website: www.nationaltrust.org.uk. Similarly, details of English Heritage properties (marked **EH**) can be found on their website: www.english-heritage.org.uk

Alton Towers, Alton, Staffs ST10 4OB. Tel. 08705 204060. www.altontowers.com
The original Victorian garden still exists, beside the theme park.

Biddulph Grange, Biddulph, Stoke-on-Trent, Staffs ST8 7SD. **NT**. Tel. 01782 517999
James Bateman's unique fantasy recreating different areas of the world to house his plant collection.

Brodsworth Hall, nr Doncaster, South Yorks. **EH**. Tel. 01302 734309
House built in 1860s with contemporary garden, especially featuring a rock garden and fern dell.

Carlyle's House, 24 Cheyne Row, Chelsea SW3 5HL. **EH**. Tel. 0207-352 7087
Restored Victorian walled garden behind Thomas Carlyle's town house.

Clumber Park, Worksop S80 3AZ. **NT**. Tel. 01909 476592
Though the home of the Dukes of Newcastle was demolished, the walled kitchen garden with vast glasshouses remains.

Cragside House, Rothbury, Morpeth NE65 7PX. **NT**. Tel. 01669 620333/620150
Victorian mansion with extensive pleasure gardens, including huge rock garden and early orchard house.

Dinefwr Park, Llandeilo SA19 6RT. **NT**. Tel. 01558 823902
Restored Victorian garden overlooking deer park.

Down House, Luxted Road, Downe, Kent BR6 7JT. **EH**. Tel. 01689 859119
House of Charles Darwin, with restored garden, much of which was designed by his wife.

Dunham Massey, Altrincham WA14 4SJ. **NT**. Tel. 01619 411025/284351
Georgian house with garden including a Victorian bark house.

Gravetye Manor, near East Grinstead, W. Sussex RH19 4LJ. Tel. 01342 810567. Info@gravetyemanor.co.uk
William Robinson's house, now a hotel, where he experimented with his ideas in wild gardening.

Heligan Gardens, Pentewan, St Austell, Cornwall PL26 6EN. Tel. 01726 845100. www.heligan.com
Kitchen gardens run on authentic Victorian principles.

Hestercombe, Cheddon Fitzpaine, Taunton, Somerset TA2 8LG. 01823 413923. www.hestercombegardens.com
Formal garden designed by Gertrude Jekyll, with an eighteenth-century landscaped garden, including a root house.

Hill Top, near Sawrey, Ambleside LA22 0LF. **NT**. Tel. 015394 36269
Beatrix Potter's cottage with cottage garden.

Hughenden Manor, High Wycombe HP14 4LA. **NT**. Tel. 01494 755573
Benjamin Disraeli's house (1848–81) with a garden based on that designed by his wife.

Killerton, Broadclyst, Exeter EX5 3LE. **NT**. Tel. 01392 881345
Georgian house with many Victorian additions. Garden includes a rustic summerhouse and house includes a costume collection and Victorian laundry.

Knightshayes Court, Bolham, Tiverton EX16 7RQ. **NT**. Tel. 01884 254665
Country house built in the 1870s with contemporary garden.

Lacock Abbey, nr Chippenham SN15 2LG. **NT**. Tel. 01249 730227
Medieval house with later gardens, including Victorian rose garden. Also houses the Fox-Talbot Museum of Photography.

Lanhydrock, Bodmin PL30 5AD. **NT**. Tel. 01208 73320
House built in 1881 with display of servants' quarters. Garden features rhododendrons, azaleas and magnolias, as well as roses.

Mrs Smith's Cottage, Navenby, nr Lincoln. Tel. 01529 414294 www.oden.co.uk/mrssmith
Restored Victorian cottage and garden.

Normanby Hall, nr Scunthorpe DN15 9HU. Tel. 01724 720588. www.northlincs.gov.uk/normanby
Walled kitchen garden with glasshouses including exotics and ferns. Restored range of garden buildings with historic displays.

Osborne House, Cowes, Isle of Wight. **EH**. Tel. 01983 2000022
Queen Victoria's house with pleasure garden, partly designed by Prince Albert, including a 'Swiss Cottage' and a summerhouse.

Peckover House, North Brink, Wisbech, Cambs PE13 1JR. **NT**. Tel. 01945 583463
Victorian town garden, including orangery, rose gardens, rustic summerhouse and formal planting.

The People's Park, Welholme Road, Grimsby. Tel. 01472 323436
Classic Victorian park with Floral Hall including displays throughout the year.

Standen, West Hoathly Road, East Grinstead RH19 4NE. **NT**. Tel. 01342 323029
Arts and Crafts house of 1890s with Victorian garden, including ferns, a croquet lawn and conservatory.

Sunnycroft, 200 Holyhead Road, Wellington, Telford TF1 2DR. **NT**. Tel. 01952 242884
Late Victorian suburban villa and garden, including a Wellingtonia avenue.

Tatton Park, Knutsford WA16 6QN. **NT**. Tel 01625 534400
Early nineteenth-century house with grand Victorian garden, including fernery, orangery and rose garden.

Trevarno Gardens and National Museum of Gardening, Trevarno Manor, Crowntown, Helston, Cornwall TR13 0RU. Tel. 01326 574274
Garden has some Victorian features, and museum includes tools and horticultural ephemera.

Tyntesfield, Wraxall, Bristol BS48 1NT. **NT**. Tel. 0870 4584500
Home of the Gibbs family who first imported guano to Britain. Pre-booked groups of visitors only while restoration takes place.

Waddesdon Manor, nr Aylesbury, Bucks HP18 0JH. **NT**. Tel. 01296 651211
One of the finest Victorian gardens in Britain with intricate bedding displays and subtropical planting, as well as a Pulhamite rockery.

West Dean Gardens, Chichester, W. Sussex PO18 0QZ. Tel. 01243 818210/811301. www.westdean.org.uk
Victorian garden and arboretum in the grounds of a college.

Wightwick Manor, Wightwick Bank, Wolverhampton WV6. **NT**. Tel. 01902 761400
Arts and Crafts house with garden to match.

Notes

Introduction

1. Shirley Hibberd, *Floral World*, 1859, p. 197.

Chapter One

1. Shirley Hibberd, *Rustic Adornments for Homes of Taste* (Groombridge and Sons, 1856, 2nd edn 1857; repr. Century and The National Trust, 1987), p. 3.
2. See e.g. John Burnett, *A Social History of Housing* (Methuen, 1980); H.J. Dyos, *Victorian Suburb* (Leicester University Press, 1961); Stefan Muthesius, *The English Terraced House* (Yale University Press, 1982); and Isobel Watson, *Gentlemen in the Building Line* (Padfield Publications, 1989).
3. The *Gardeners' Chronicle* began in 1841 and continued throughout the century. As it has always been conveniently laid out on the open shelves of the Lindley Library at the Royal Horticultural Society, researchers are often tempted to use it as a first reference point for research, and, if time is limited, to look no further. Since the new library opened in 2001, several other magazines have become available on the open shelves, but many more are shut away and require to be ordered. In the old library they were housed in glass-fronted cabinets, and it was possible to see what was available and simply ask for the cabinet to be unlocked. Now it is necessary to look through the catalogue before the existence of a particular title is discovered, which limits random curiosity and may inhibit detailed research.
4. Asa Briggs, *Victorian Things* (Penguin Books, 1990), p. 23.
5. See Harold Perkin, *Origins of Modern English Society* (Routledge, 1969; 2nd edn 1994); J.M. Golby and A.W. Purdue, *The Civilisation of the Crowd: Popular Culture in England 1750–1900* (Sutton Publishing, 1999).
6. Most gardens referred to in this book are English, rather than Scottish, Welsh or Irish, as most of the publications used refer to English gardens. However, many of the professional gardeners who were so influential and important in Victorian gardening were Scottish, and one very important one Irish.
7. John Claudius Loudon, *The Suburban Gardener and Villa Companion* (Longman, 1838).
8. For the history of public parks, see Hazel Conway, *People's Parks: The Design and Development of Victorian Parks in Britain* (Cambridge University Press, 1991).
9. *Gardener's Magazine*, July 1838, p. 322.
10. Jane Wells Loudon, *Gardening for Ladies* (John Murray, 1840), pp. 8, 9.
11. Elizabeth Watts, *Modern Practical Gardening, Vegetables, Flowers and Fruit: How to Grow Them* (Frederick Warne and Co, *c.* 1865, originally published as three separate books).
12. See *Gardeners' Chronicle*, 27 March 1858, p. 241, followed up on 3 April, p. 266.
13. Mrs C.W. Earle (1836–1925), Ellen Wilmott (1858–1934) and Gertrude Jekyll (1843–1932).
14. See Flora Thompson, *Lark Rise to Candleford* (Penguin, 1973), pp. 62–3.
15. Jeremy Burchardt, *The Allotment Movement in England 1793–1873* (The Royal Historical Society and The Boydell Press, 2002); see particularly pp. 143–4, 165–6, 172.
16. A guinea was one pound and one shilling, equivalent to £1.05.
17. *Amateur Gardening*, 23 June 1888, p. 85.

Chapter Two

1. The book was said to be written by Thomas Mawe, gardener to the Duke of Leeds, but was really written by John Abercrombie (1726–1806), who went on to write several other gardening books.

2. 'Florist' has a very specific meaning: see Chapter Four.
3. *Gardeners' Chronicle*, 14 April 1855, p. 239. The phrases are all classical references, but 'Asderas' is a mis-spelling. Hibberd wrote 'Abderas', which referred to a Greek city overrun with rats. Tantalian refers to the legend of Tantalas, who was condemned to live in a river, but could not drink. Stagyria was the retreat of the philosopher Aristotle.
4. See *Gardeners' Chronicle*, 7 March 1857, pp. 149, 150.
5. *Florist*, February 1861, pp. 36–8.
6. John Claudius Loudon, *The Suburban Horticulturalist* (William Smith, 1842).
7. *Ibid.*, introduction, p. 1.
8. A perch is thirty and a quarter square yards, or 25.288 sq. m.
9. Loudon, *Suburban Horticulturalist*, p. 401.
10. *Ibid.*, p. 189.
11. *Ibid.*, p. 407.
12. *Gardeners' Chronicle*, 3 April 1858, p. 266.
13. *Floral World*, April 1858, p. 92.
14. Shirley Hibberd, *The Amateur's Flower Garden* (1871; repr. Croom Helm, 1986), p. 102.
15. Nathaniel Paterson, *The Manse Garden* (James Blackwood & Co., *c.* 1837), pp. 220–1, which are part of Appendix 1, the whole of which describes training the boy.
16. Shirley Hibberd, *The Town Garden* (Groombridge and Sons, 1855), introduction, pp. 6, 7.
17. *Gardening for Ladies*, introduction, p. v.
18. *Handbook of Town Gardening by a Lady* (Orr & Co., 1847), introduction.
19. Shirley Hibberd, *Town Garden*, preface, pp. 3–5.
20. William Paul, *The Hand-Book of Villa Gardening, in a Series of Letters to a Friend* (Piper, Stephenson and Spence, 1855).
21. *Ibid.*, p. 3.
22. *Gardeners' Chronicle*, 27 March 1858, p. 240.
23. *Ibid.*, 8 May 1858, p. 382.
24. *Ibid.*, p. 400.
25. See the *Gardener's Magazine*, May 1834. He recommended, for those who could hardly read, Charles Lawrence's *Practical Directions* (price sixpence), and, for 'those who can read and think', Denson's *Peasant's Voice* and his own *Cottage Manual*. (No publishers are given.)
26. *Gardener's Magazine*, January 1827, pp. 19, 271.
27. *Ibid.*, January 1830, p. 139.
28. This may not have been for personal smoking, but for use as an insecticide: see Chapter Nine.
29. *Amateur Gardening*, 9 June 1888, p. 62.
30. *Gardening Illustrated*, 31 December 1892, p. 623.
31. See the advertisement in the *Cottage Gardener*, 3 March 1857, p. 388.

Chapter Three

1. The earliest editions were written under the name Thomas Mawe, as it was considered ungentlemanly to write for a living.
2. William Cobbett, *The English Gardener* (1829; repr. Bloomsbury Gardening Classics, 1996), p. 4.
3. In 1995 the name *Curtis's Botanical Magazine* was revived and used for the *Kew Magazine*, first published in 1984. It continues at the time of writing.
4. In pre-decimal currency, twelve old pence (*d*) made one shilling (*s*) and twenty shillings made one pound (£). At the time of decimalisation, one new penny was worth two and a half old pence.
5. *Gardener's Magazine*, January 1826, p. 2.
6. *Horticultural Register*, 1 July 1831, introduction.
7. *Ibid.*, 9 June 1831.
8. See Elisabeth B. MacDougall, ed., *John Claudius Loudon and the Early Nineteenth Century in Great Britain* (Dumbarton Oaks, Trustees for Harvard University, 1980).
9. *Floricultural Cabinet*, 28 November 1833, introduction. Ray Desmond, in 'Victorian Gardening Magazines', *Garden History*, Winter 1977, p. 47, gives a figure of 10,000 copies per issue by 1840.
10. Will Tjaden, 'George Glenny, Horticultural Hornet', *The Garden*, 1986, p. 318. Most of the biographical information comes from this article.
11. *Horticultural Journal*, 1833, p. 31.
12. See *ibid.*, vol. III, 1835.
13. Loudon's financial difficulties were mainly a result of publishing his books and magazines himself and having to pay illustrators in advance. Once the papers went on sale, they never produced enough to pay off the debts. However, Loudon did reduce his debt quite considerably before he died, by going back to designing gardens and with the help of his wife and sister working for him for nothing.
14. *Gardeners' Chronicle*, 2 January 1841, p. 1.
15. *Midland Florist and Suburban Horticulturalist*, January 1847, p. 4.
16. *Ibid.*, 1857, vol. i, p. viii.
17. *Florist*, January 1848, introduction, pp. 1, 2.
18. *Cottage Gardener*, 1848, introduction, p. 1.
19. *Ibid.*, 2 January 1855, p. 266.
20. *Birmingham and Midland Gardeners' Magazine*, 1852, p. 2.
21. The word 'cheap' in Victorian literature never seems to be used in a derogatory sense, but is used rather as twentieth-century writers would use euphemisms such as 'reasonable' or 'good value'.
22. *Gardener's Weekly Magazine*, 2 January 1860, p. 1.

23. S. Reynolds Hole, *The Memories of Dean Hole* (Edward Arnold, 1892), p. 240.
24. *Floral World*, January 1872, p. 17.
25. *Amateur Gardening*, 31 May 1885.

Chapter Four

1. Florists are grouped here with nurserymen because of their unique place in the development of plants for the retail market. The part they play in horticultural societies and shows is described in Chapter Six.
2. *Gardener's Magazine*, January 1826, p. 1.
3. Ward published his findings in *On the Growth of Plants in Closely Glazed Cases* (John van Voorst, 1842).
4. See George Drower, *Gardeners, Gurus and Grubs: The Stories of Garden Inventors and Innovations* (Sutton Publishing, 2001), p. 238.
5. Further details about Williams and his work can be found in Brent Elliott, 'Proprietor of Paradise', *The Garden*, June 1992, p. 273.
6. The catalogue for 1884 is available in the John Johnson collection, Horticultural Boxes, at the Bodleian Library, Oxford.
7. Also available in the John Johnson collection.
8. *Ibid.*
9. Shirley Hibberd, *Town Garden* (2nd edn, 1859), p. 99.
10. See Chapter Eleven.
11. See Chapter Fourteen.
12. Letter to Miss Jepson, quoted in Robyn Marsack, *My Garden: A Nineteenth-Century Writer on her English Cottage Garden* (Sidgwick & Jackson, 1990), p. 120.
13. *Ibid.*, p. 81.
14. See *Gardener's Magazine*, 31 January 1874, p. 51; 8 January 1876, p. 15; 3 June 1876, pp. 285, 286.
15. A quart is two pints, which is equivalent to 1.1 litres. An ounce is equivalent to 28 grams.
16. Watts, *Modern Practical Gardening*, p. 74.
17. J.H. Clark, *The Cottager's Kitchen, Fruit and Flower Gardens* (Milner and Company, c. 1850), pp. 29–30.
18. See Anna Pavord, *The Tulip* (Bloomsbury, 1999), pp. 222–3.
19. Information on florists generally can be found in Ruth Duthie, *Florists' Flowers and Societies* (Shire Publications Ltd, 1988); Ruth E. Duthie, 'English Florists' Societies and Feasts in the Seventeenth and First Half of the Eighteenth Centuries', *Garden History*, Spring 1982, p. 17; Ruth Duthie, 'Florists' Societies and Feasts after 1750', *Garden History*, Spring 1984, p. 11; Miles Hadfield, *A History of British Gardening* (Penguin, 1985), pp. 261–7; and Tom Carter, *The Victorian Garden*, ch. 6.

20. He reports this happening at Reading, Hull and Hereford: see *Gardener's Magazine*, February 1834, pp. 56–8.
21. *Midland Florist*, 1849, p. 152.
22. See *Gardener's Magazine*, July 1826, p. 349.
23. Jane Loudon, *The Ladies' Companion to the Flower Garden* (Bradbury, Evans & Co., 8th edn, ed. Charles Edmonds, 1864), p. 120.
24. Watts, *Modern Practical Gardening*, p. 249.
25. *Beeton's All about Gardening* (new edn, Ward, Lock & Co. Ltd, c. 1902), p. 178.
26. Alfred Smee, *My Garden* (2nd edn, Bell and Daldy, 1872), p. 226.
27. *Ibid.*, p. 229.
28. See *The Victorian Garden Catalogue: A Treasure Trove of Horticultural Paraphernalia* (Studio Editions, 1995), pp. 24–9.

Chapter Five

1. Advertisement from the Gutta Percha Company of City Road, London, July 1851, in the John Johnson Collection, Horticultural Boxes, at the Bodleian Library, Oxford.
2. Advertisement in the John Johnson Collection, 17 March 1866.
3. Advertisement from Prentice Bros Chemical Laboratories, Stowmarket, June 1879, in the John Johnson Collection.
4. Shirley Hibberd, *The Rose Book* (Groombridge and Sons, 1864), p. 204.
5. See *Amateur Gardening*, 14 March 1885, p. 551.
6. Watts, *Modern Practical Gardening*, p. 199. Unless otherwise quoted, all references to Watts on tools come from pp. 198–204.
7. Smee, *My Garden*, p. 58. Unless otherwise quoted, all references to Smee on tools come from pp. 56–66.
8. Mrs C.W. Earle, *Pot-Pourri from a Surrey Garden* (Smith, Elder & Co., 1897; repr. Century and The National Trust, 1988), p. 90.
9. *Thompson's Gardener's Assistant*, ed. William Watson (Gresham Publishing Co., new edn, 1904), vol. I, p. 180.
10. For further details of secateurs, see Drower, *Gardeners, Gurus and Grubs*, pp. 7–10; Brent Elliott, 'Shear Diversity', *The Garden*, March 1996, p. 138.
11. Jane Loudon, *Ladies' Companion*, p. 269.
12. Similarly, in the early days of typewriters, 'typewriter' meant the typist, not the machine.
13. Cobbett, *English Gardener*, p. 235.
14. For details of the history of lawn mowers, see Brent Elliott, 'At the Cutting Edge', *The Garden*, May 1996, p. 289.

15. *Amateur Gardening*, 11 May 1889, p. 15.
16. See further Drower, *Gardeners, Gurus and Grubs*, pp. 68–73.
17. Jane Loudon, *Ladies' Companion*, p. 350. Stooping is difficult, if not impossible, in corsets.
18. 'Truck' here comes from a word meaning transport, whereas the dictionary gives the origin of trug as coming from the word 'trough'.
19. *Beeton's All about Gardening*, p. 386.
20. Shirley Hibberd, *Amateur's Flower Garden*, pp. 57–9.
21. Smee, *My Garden*, p. 59.
22. *Beeton's Gardening*, p. 118.
23. There are frequent mentions of 'road grit' in the books. It is not clear whether you were expected to gather the grit from the road, or whether it is simply a description of the type of grit, i.e. the sort of grit that is used on roads. Presumably taking it off the road would be stealing.
24. *Agricultural Gazette*, 8 May 1858.
25. Shirley Hibberd, *Profitable Gardening* (Groombridge and Sons, 1884), p. 30.
26. *Gardener's Magazine*, 6 June 1874, p. 293.
27. *Ibid.*, 26 September 1874, p. 513.
28. See further *ibid.*, 1877, p. 657, and *Amateur Gardening*, 16 August 1884, on collecting house sewage.
29. See Drower, *Gardeners, Gurus and Grubs*, pp. 156–61.
30. See *Thompson's Gardener's Assistant*, vol. I, p. 189.
31. Shirley Hibberd, *Profitable Gardening*, p. 99.
32. *Amateur Gardening*, 7 June 1884, p. 72.
33. *Thompson's Gardener's Assistant*, vol. I, p. 130.
34. *Florist*, February 1856, pp. 46, 47; March 1856, pp. 87–9.
35. *Amateur Gardening*, 17 August 1889, p. 183.
36. *Thompson's Gardener's Assistant*, vol. I, p. 122.
37. For a description of the range of glasshouses in a professional garden, see Susan Campbell, *Charleston Kedding: A History of Kitchen Gardening* (Ebury Press, 1996), pp. 179–91.
38. Shirley Hibberd, *Profitable Gardening*, pp. 281–3.
39. *Thompson's Gardener's Assistant*, vol. I, p. 195.
40. *Floral World*, 1867, p. 193.
41. *Ibid.*, 1876, p. 172.
42. Shirley Hibberd, *Profitable Gardening*, p. 127.

Chapter Six

1. See an advertisement dated 3 February 1829, held in the John Johnson Collection, Horticultural Boxes, at the Bodleian Library, Oxford.
2. *Gardener's Magazine*, July 1826. For further details on florists and their shows, see *Florists' Flowers* and Ruth Duthie's papers on florists' societies in *Garden History*, Spring 1982, p. 17; Spring 1984, p. 11.
3. *Gardener's Magazine*, October 1830, p. 598, quoting the *Stockport Advertiser* of 5 March 1830.
4. *Turner's Hackney Directory 1849*, p. 255.
5. *Gardeners' Chronicle*, 20 June 1846, p. 40.
6. *Midland Florist*, November 1847, p. 373.
7. *Ibid.*, April 1848, pp. 53, 126.
8. See *Gardener's Magazine*, July 1826, p. 347.
9. The rules of the society can be found in the Berkshire Record Office, ref. D/Ex610/2.
10. See documents in the John Johnson Collection.
11. *Gardeners' Chronicle*, 5 November 1859, p. 887.
12. See *ibid.*, 31 May 1856, p. 374; 28 June 1856, p. 438; and 13 September 1856, p. 614.
13. *Ibid.*, 28 April 1860, p. 387.
14. *Ibid.*, 2 June 1860, p. 505.
15. *Floral World*, July 1860, p. 142.
16. See *Gardeners' Chronicle*, 31 May 1856, p. 374; 7 June 1856, p. 390; and 14 June 1856, p. 406.
17. *Gardener's Weekly Magazine*, 10 September 1860, p. 160.
18. *Floral World*, October 1860, p. 222.
19. For further details of this society, see Julia Matheson's unpublished MA dissertation for the Open University, 'Popular Gardening in London 1860–1900', submitted September 2001.
20. See Anne Wilkinson, 'Stoke Newington and the Golden Flower', *Hackney History*, 1999, p. 22.
21. *Gardener's Magazine*, 25 November 1876, p. 629.
22. *Ibid.*, 1 November 1890, p. 693.
23. Further details of the societies and their shows can be found in the John Johnson Collection.
24. *Amateur Gardening*, 11 May 1889, p. 13.

Chapter Seven

1. See H.J. Dyos, *Victorian Suburb* (Leicester University Press, 1961).
2. Shirley Hibberd, *Rustic Adornments*, pp. 361–2.
3. *Ibid.*, p. 362.
4. *Ibid.*, pp. 362–3.
5. *Amateur Gardening*, 21 June 1884, p. 90, which shows the same Jardinet, described as a 'chameleon garden-bed' because of its frequent changes.
6. *Ibid.*, 27 October 1888, p. 306.
7. *Cassell's Popular Gardening*, vol. 1, p. 13. It seems that a patent was taken out in 1873 by T.L. Phipps for a lawnmower using horse-clipper blades: see Brent Elliott, 'At the Cutting Edge', *The Garden*, May 1996, p. 290.
8. Earle, *Pot-Pourri from a Surrey Garden*, p. 170.
9. *Floral World*, June 1871, p. 229.

10. *Ibid.*, p. 231.
11. *Gardening Illustrated*, 13 December 1879, p. 625.

Chapter Eight

1. Information on the Butters family and their gardens is available in the Hackney Archives Department, 43 De Beauvoir Road, London N1 5SQ. Several photographs appear in David Mander and Jenny Goolden, *The London Borough of Hackney in Old Photographs 1890–1960* (Alan Sutton, 1991).
2. See Shirley Hibberd, *Town Garden* (2nd edn), ch. IV.
3. See *Floral World*, February 1858, pp. 36–41.
4. See the *Gardener's Magazine*, July 1838, and Chapter One. Some illustrations can also be found in John Claudius Loudon, *In Search of English Gardens: The Travels of John Claudius Loudon and his Wife, Jane* (repr. National Trust and Century, 1990), pp. 91–3; the garden is also described in M. Hadfield, *A History of British Gardening* (Penguin, 1985), pp. 259–60.
5. See David Robinson and Christopher Sturman, *William Brown and the Louth Panorama* (Louth Naturalists', Antiquarian and Literary Society, and Louth Town Council (Panorama Paintings), 2001).
6. Watts, *Modern Practical Gardening*, preface. This book was a collective reprint of three books: *Vegetables: How to Grow Them, Flowers and the Flower Garden* and *The Orchard and Fruit Garden* (all published by Frederick Warne at a shilling each).
7. *Ibid.*, pp. 186–7.
8. *Ibid.*, p. 188.
9. *Amateur Gardening*, 28 March 1885, p. 566; 4 April 1885, p. 578.
10. *Modern Practical Gardening*, pp. 7, 8.
11. *Town Garden* (2nd edn), p. 30.
12. Shirley Hibberd, *Amateur's Flower Garden*, p. 262.
13. *Ibid.*, p. 263.
14. *Town Garden* (2nd edn), p. 80.
15. For those used to the metric system, a foot (12in) is about 30cm, a yard (3ft) just under a metre, and an inch about 2.5cm.
16. Watts, *Modern Practical Gardening*, p. 196.
17. Shirley Hibberd, *Amateur's Flower Garden*, pp. 264–5.
18. *Ibid.*, pp. 266–7.
19. Brent Elliott, 'A Novelist in the Fruit Garden', *The Garden*, 1992, p. 490. Dr Elliott refers to Blackmore's novel, *Cradock Nowell*, published in 1866.
20. Watts, *Modern Practical Gardening*, p. 197.
21. *Floral World*, January 1863, pp. 4–8. This is the illustration that also features the small fern house:

see Shirley Hibberd, *The Fern Garden* (Groombridge and Sons, 9th edn, 1881), p. 35.
22. Shirley Hibberd, *Amateur's Flower Garden*, p. 12.
23. Watts, *Modern Practical Gardening*, p. 194.
24. For trees and evergreens, see *ibid.*, pp. 204–10.
25. *Ibid.*, p. 221.
26. *Floral World*, May 1875, pp. 137–40.
27. See Judith Flanders, *The Victorian House* (Harper Perennial, 2004), p. 268.

Chapter Nine

1. Paterson, *Manse Garden*, pp. 115–16.
2. Watts, *Modern Practical Gardening*, p. 78.
3. Smee, *My Garden*, p. 112.
4. *Gardener's Magazine*, 9 May 1874, p. 244.
5. See *Floral World*, February 1869, p. 50; January 1871, p. 13.
6. Shirley Hibberd, *Profitable Gardening*, pp. 50–64.
7. *Ibid.*, pp. 64–6.
8. *Gardeners' Chronicle*, 3 April 1858, p. 263. The yam was the subject of prolonged correspondence during 1858: see the index to that volume, under Chinese yam.
9. Earle, *Pot-Pourri from a Surrey Garden*, p. 13.
10. Watts, *Modern Practical Gardening*, pp. 48, 49.
11. *Ibid.*, p. 47.
12. *Ibid.*, pp. 48–51.
13. Paterson, *Manse Garden*, p. 118.
14. See *Beeton's Book of Household Management* (1861; repr. Jonathan Cape, 1977), p. 768.
15. Watts, *Modern Practical Gardening*, p. 45.
16. *Thompson's Gardener's Assistant*, vol. VI, pp. 393–402.
17. Shirley Hibberd, *Profitable Gardening*, p. 139.
18. Blanching sometimes accompanied forcing, as plants were covered to protect them and force them into growth, but it was also used to make plants sweeter and more tender. Seakale was forced under large terracotta pots, like rhubarb, and as it was so hardy it could be produced early. It was recommended by Mrs Beeton as being easily digested and therefore good for those with delicate appetites.
19. Watts, *Modern Practical Gardening*, p. 92.
20. Paterson, *Manse Garden*, p. 138.
21. Shirley Hibberd, *Profitable Gardening*, p. 118.
22. This must not be confused with a completely different vegetable called the asparagus pea, or the winged pea, which is a plant of the vetch family with small knobbly pods. When picked at the right time (about 2cm long) they can be used like mangetout or sugar peas and are supposed to taste

like asparagus. However, if allowed to grow any longer, they become stringy and tasteless, but they do have attractive dark red flowers. Winged pea seeds were offered as a free gift to readers of the *Floral World* in 1858. They were asked to send in a stamped addressed envelope, and the offer was so popular that the number of seeds had to be reduced from six to three or four: see *Floral World*, April 1858, p. 80; May 1858, p. 118.

23. *Gardener's Magazine*, 8 June 1878, p. 287.
24. See Shirley Hibberd, *Profitable Gardening*, p. 126, quoting an article first appearing in the *Gardeners' Chronicle*. Pea tops or 'shoots' appeared as a novelty in supermarkets in 2004, no one apparently realising that they had been around for over a century: see *The Times*, 5 November 2004, p. 20.
25. Paterson, *Manse Garden*, p. 113.
26. *Ibid.*, p. 128.
27. Watts, *Modern Practical Gardening*, p. 100.
28. Shirley Hibberd, *Profitable Gardening*, pp. 137–8.
29. Even the *Shorter Oxford Dictionary* does not define a 'towit'.
30. All the recipes come from the *Gardener's Magazine*, July 1826, p. 353, and were supplied by 'an eminent French cook, lately in the service of the Earl of Essex'.
31. Earle, *Pot-Pourri from a Surrey Garden*, p. 175.
32. *Gardener's Magazine*, 21 April 1877, p. 177.
33. *Ibid.*, p. 178.
34. Paterson, *Manse Garden*, pp. 122, 124, 125, 130.
35. Published by E.W. Allen.
36. *Beeton's Household Management*, p. 795.
37. See J.H. Clark, *The Cottager's Kitchen, Fruit and Flower Gardens* (Milner and Co., *c.* 1850), pp. 118–27.
38. Watts, *Modern Practical Gardening*, pp. 142–54.
39. Smee, *My Garden*, pp. 134–5.
40. *Ibid.*, pp. 124–35.

Chapter Ten

1. Paterson, *Manse Garden*, pp. 132–3.
2. *Gardener's Magazine*, 21 April 1877, p. 178.
3. *Floral World*, February 1866, p. 36.
4. *Ibid.*, November 1863, p. 242.
5. *Gardener's Magazine*, 15 September 1877, pp. 455–6.
6. *Ibid.*, 29 September 1877, pp. 478–9.
7. Watts, *Modern Practical Gardening*, pp. 516–17.
8. *Ibid.*, p. 515.
9. *Ibid.*, p. 427.
10. *Ibid.*, p. 385.
11. *Floral World*, March 1876, p. 86.
12. *Ibid.*, June 1872, p. 169.
13. Cobbett, *English Gardener*, para. 274.
14. *Beeton's Household Management*, pp. 631, 767.
15. Henry A. Bright, 'A Year in a Lancashire Garden', *Gardeners' Chronicle*, 4 September 1874.
16. *Ibid.*, 15 October 1874.
17. *Floral World*, January 1868, pp. 7, 8.

Chapter Eleven

1. For an explanation of colour theory, see Brent Elliott, *Victorian Gardens* (B.T. Batsford, 1986), pp. 123–8, 148–52.
2. *Floral World*, July 1866, p. 193.
3. Watts, *Modern Practical Gardening*, p. 279.
4. *Cassell's*, vol. I, p. 133.
5. Shirley Hibberd, *Amateur's Flower Garden*, pp. 16–17.
6. See Mary E. Campbell, *Fancy-Leaved Pelargoniums: Peter Grieve and After* (British Pelargonium and Geranium Society, 1990).
7. *Floral World*, July 1864, p. 150.
8. David Thomson, *Handy Book of the Flower Garden* (William Blackwood and Sons, 1871), p. 363.
9. Shirley Hibberd, *Amateur's Flower Garden*, p. 17.
10. *Gardener's Magazine*, 23 September 1874, p. 513.
11. *Ibid.*, 28 March 1874, p. 157.
12. Henry A. Bright, 'A Year in a Lancashire Garden', *Gardeners' Chronicle*, 25 April 1879.
13. Henry N. Ellacombe, *In a Gloucestershire Garden* (Edward Arnold, 1906), p. 96.
14. I have found exactly the opposite: violets grew like weeds in my garden in Hackney, while lilies of the valley never would.
15. Ellacombe, *Gloucestershire Garden*, pp. 54–5.

Chapter Twelve

1. H.J. Bidder, *A Handlist of Alpine and Other Plants . . . in the Gardens of St John's College, Oxford* (Oxford, St John's College, 1913), note.
2. Shirley Hibberd, *Fern Garden*, p. 37.
3. Shirley Hibberd, *Rustic Adornments*, pp. 403–9.
4. *Ibid.*, p. 412.
5. *Ibid.*, p. 413.
6. 'Cockney' was often used as an insult in gardening. It is usually meant to describe someone born within the sound of Bow bells in London, in other words a city person who would know nothing of the countryside, and hence gardening. But it also has connotations with the mythical Land of Cockaigne, which exemplified easy living, and also therefore inappropriate to anyone who claimed to be capable

of the hard work of gardening. The feud between Shirley Hibberd and William Robinson in the 1880s culminated in Robinson claiming Hibberd's place of birth as 'unmistakenly Cockaigne', and inaccurately naming it as Whitechapel.

7. Watts, *Modern Practical Gardening*, pp. 327–8.
8. *Ibid.*, p. 332.
9. See Bidder, *A Handlist of Alpines and Other Plants*.
10. *Amateur Gardening*, 10 January 1885, pp. 438–9.
11. Shirley Hibberd, *Fern Garden*, p. 8.
12. *Floral World*, September 1867, p. 287.
13. Shirley Hibberd, *Rustic Adornments*, pp. 429–30.
14. *Ibid.*, pp. 432–3.
15. Henry A. Bright, 'A Year in a Lancashire Garden', *Gardeners' Chronicle*, 4 April, 24 October 1984.
16. Watts, *Modern Practical Gardening*, p. 332.
17. *Amateur Gardening*, 17 May 1884, p. 35.
18. *Floral World*, July 1858, p. 152.
19. *Amateur Gardening*, 14 June 1884, p. 78.
20. Smee, *My Garden*, p. 267.
21. See *Floral World*, July 1873, p. 200.
22. Shirley Hibberd, *Rustic Adornments*, p. 496.
23. *Ibid.*, p. 498.
24. Earle, *Pot-Pourri from a Surrey Garden*, p. 170.
25. *Ibid.*, p. 90.

Chapter Thirteen

1. See Thompson, *Lark Rise to Candleford*, p. 78.
2. S. Reynolds Hole, *A Book about Roses* (J.M. Dent and Sons Ltd, repr. 1932), p. 144.
3. See Chapter Nine. He was the inventor of the orchard house for growing small-sized potted fruit trees indoors.
4. Shirley Hibberd, *Amateur's Flower Garden*, p. 202.
5. *Ibid.*, p. 201.
6. To identify the roses named in the books referred to in this chapter, I used *The Graham Stuart Thomas Rose Book* (John Murray, 1994) and the catalogues from nurserymen David Austin and Peter Beales (see Appendix 2).
7. The noisette rose he names as 'Fellenberg', which does not appear in present-day catalogues, although David Austin lists a 'Fellemberg' as a climbing China rose, dated 1857.
8. The 'crimson miniature rose' is probably Slater's Crimson China, now known as Old Crimson China.
9. That is, 10p.
10. Shirley Hibberd, *Amateur's Flower Garden*, p. 205.
11. Shirley Hibberd, *Rose Book*, preface.
12. Sometimes referred to as Félicité Perpétuelle or other similar names.
13. See *Gardener's Magazine*, 17 January 1874, p. 27.

14. *Ibid.*, p. 28.
15. Reynolds Hole, *Book about Roses*, pp. 93–5.
16. See William Robinson, *The English Flower Garden and Home Grounds* (John Murray, 1883; repr. Bloomsbury Gardening Classics, 1996), ch. XVII.
17. *Ibid.*, p. 64.
18. *Amateur Gardening*, 31 January 1891, p. 407.

Chapter Fourteen

1. *Cassell's*, vol. III, p. 27.
2. According to the Preface, John Loudon wrote the section on Water.
3. Jane Loudon, *Ladies' Companion*, p. 348.
4. Shirley Hibberd, *Rustic Adornments*, p. 384.
5. *The Book of the Marine Aquarium*, *The Book of the Freshwater Aquarium* and *The Book of the Water Cabinet*, all published by Groombridge and Sons, and collected into *The Book of the Aquarium*, published by them in 1860.
6. Shirley Hibberd, *Rustic Adornments*, p. 385.
7. *Ibid.*, p. 391.
8. *Cassell's*, vol. III, p. 137.
9. Thomson, *Handy Book*, p. 241.
10. *Ibid.*, p. 242.
11. *Amateur Gardening*, 19 July 1884, p. 135.
12. *Ibid.*, 27 June 1885, p. 102.

Chapter Fifteen

1. A stove produced heat and humidity throughout the year; a greenhouse might not be heated at all.
2. Smee, *My Garden*, p. 295.
3. *Beeton's All about Gardening*, p. 352. A description of Williams' Paradise Nursery appears in the *Gardeners' Chronicle*, 1 February 1862.
4. Shirley Hibberd, *The Amateur's Greenhouse and Conservatory* (W.H. and L. Collingridge, rev. T.W. Sanders, 1897), p. 220.
5. See Brent Elliott, 'A Political Family', *The Garden*, January 1992, p. 37.
6. Earle, *Pot-Pourri from a Surrey Garden*, p. 249.
7. Hibberd, *Amateur's Greenhouse and Conservatory*, pp. 225–6.
8. *Floral World*, January 1868, p. 6.
9. Osborne was Queen Victoria's home on the Isle of Wight, which probably had a milder climate than most parts of the British Isles.
10. Shirley Hibberd, *Amateur's Greenhouse*, pp. 215–17.
11. *Ibid.*, p. 218.
12. *Ibid.*, p. 206.
13. *Ibid.*, p. 197.

14. Shirley Hibberd, *Amateur's Flower Garden*, p. 222.
15. Thomson, *Handy Book*, p. 208.
16. *Ibid.*, pp. 216–17.

Chapter Sixteen

1. *Floral World*, November 1872, p. 327.
2. *Ibid.*, April 1874, pp. 110–11.
3. *Ibid.*, p. 112.
4. *Ibid.*, p. 105.
5. *Amateur Gardening*, 6 October 1888, p. 270.
6. People sometimes wonder why these shutters often leave a gap at the top of the window: this is the space where the blind would be pulled up at night.
7. Shirley Hibberd, *Rustic Adornments*, p. 137.
8. *Ibid.*, p. 148.
9. Shirley Hibberd, *The Ivy: its History, Uses and Characteristics* (Groombridge and Sons, 1871), p. 35.
10. Shirley Hibberd, *Rustic Adornments*, p. 171.
11. Letter from Shirley Hibberd, *Gardeners' Chronicle*, 2 April 1895, p. 290.
12. Earle, *Pot-Pourri from a Surrey Garden*, pp. 8–9.
13. Shirley Hibberd, *Ivy*, p. 46.
14. Earle, *Pot-Pourri from a Surrey Garden*, pp. 12–13.
15. *Floral World*, 1871, p. 366.
16. *Ibid.*, p. 369.
17. Shirley Hibberd, *Rustic Adornments*, p. 178.
18. *Ibid.*, p. 182.
19. *Thompson's Gardener's Assistant*, vol. III, p. 651.
20. Advertisement found in the John Johnson Collection, Horticultural Boxes, in the Bodleian Library, Oxford.
21. *Floral World*, 1871, p. 188.
22. Shirley Hibberd, *Field Flowers: A Handy Book for the Rambling Botanist* (W.H. and L. Collingridge, 1894), p. 154.

Epilogue

1. *The Leisure Hour*, 21 December 1872.
2. *Amateur Gardening*, 3 January 1891, p. 372.
3. Shirley Hibberd, *Rustic Adornments*, p. 508.

Bibliography

The place of publication is London unless otherwise stated.
For nineteenth-century periodicals and where they can be found, see Appendix 1.

Abercrombie, J. *Every Man his own Gardener*, attr. T. Mawe, W. Griffin, 1767

Alfrey, N., ed. *Art of the Garden*, Tate Publishing, 2004

Allan, M. *William Robinson 1838–1935*, Faber and Faber, 1982

Barber, L. *The Heyday of Natural History 1820–1870*, New York, Doubleday & Co., 1980

Beeton's Book of Household Management, 1861, facsimile edn; repr. Jonathan Cape, 1977

Beeton's All about Gardening, new edn, Ward Lock & Co., *c.* 1902

Best, G. *Mid-Victorian Britain 1851–75*, Fontana Press, 1985

Bidder, H.J. *A Handlist of Alpine and other Plants . . . in the Gardens of St John's College, Oxford*, Oxford, St John's College, 1913

Birkenhead, J. *Ferns and Fern Culture*, Manchester, John Heywood, 1892

Briggs, A. *The Age of Improvement*, Longman, 1996

——, *Victorian Cities*, Penguin Books, 1968

——, *Victorian Things*, Penguin Books, 1990

Bright, H.A. *A Year in a Victorian Garden*, 1879; repr. Pyramid Books, 1989

Brown, J. *The Pursuit of Paradise: A Social History of Gardens and Gardening*, HarperCollins, 1999

Brown, L. *Victorian News and Newspapers*, Oxford, Clarendon Press, 1985

Burchardt, J. *The Allotment Movement in England 1793–1873*, The Royal Historical Society and The Boydell Press, 2002

Burn, W.L. *The Age of Equipoise*, George Allen and Unwin, 1964

Burnett, J. *A Social History of Housing*, Methuen, 1980

Campbell, M.E. *Fancy-Leaved Pelargoniums: Peter Grieve and After*, British Pelargonium and Geranium Society, 1990

Campbell, S. *Charleston Kedding: A History of Kitchen Gardening*, Ebury Press, 1996

Carter, T. *The Victorian Garden*, Bell & Hyman, 1984

Cassell's Popular Gardening, ed. D.T. Fish, 3 vols, Cassell & Co., *c.* 1892

Clark, J.H. *The Cottager's Kitchen, Fruit and Flower Gardens*, Milner and Co., *c.* 1850

Clayton-Payne, A. *Victorian Flower Gardens*, Weidenfeld & Nicolson, 1988

Cobbett, W. *The English Gardener*, 1829; repr. Bloomsbury Gardening Classics, 1996

Constantine, S. 'Amateur Gardening and Popular Recreation in the 19th and 20th Centuries', *Journal of Social History* (Spring 1981), 387.

Conway, H. *People's Parks: The Design and Development of Victorian Parks in Britain*, Cambridge, Cambridge University Press, 1991

Crouch, D. and C. Ward, *The Allotment: Its Landscape and Culture*, Nottingham, Mushroom Bookshop, 1994

Crowley, D. *Introduction to Victorian Style*, Mallard Press, 1990

Cunningham, H. *Leisure in the Industrial Revolution 1780–1880*, Croom Helm, 1980

Davies, J. *The Victorian Flower Garden*, BBC Books, 1991

——, *The Victorian Kitchen Garden*, BBC Books, 1991

Delamer, E.S. *The Flower Garden*, Routledge & Co., 1856

Desmond, R. 'Victorian Gardening Magazines', *Garden History* (Winter 1977), 47

Dictionary of British and Irish Botanists and Horticulturalists, R. Desmond Taylor and Francis and The Natural History Museum, 1994

Drower, G. *Gardeners, Gurus and Grubs: The Stories of Garden Inventors and Innovations*, Stroud, Sutton Publishing, 2001

Duthie, R. *Florists' Flowers and Societies*, Princes Risborough, Shire Publications Ltd, 1988

——, 'English Florists' Societies and Feasts in the Seventeenth and First Half of the Eighteenth Centuries', *Garden History* (Spring 1982), 17

——, 'Florists' Societies and Feasts after 1750', *Garden History* (Spring 1984), 11

Dyos, H.J. *Victorian Suburb*, Leicester, Leicester University Press, 1961

Earle, C.W. *Pot-Pourri from a Surrey Garden*, Smith, Elder & Co., 1897; repr. Century and The National Trust, 1988

Ellacombe, H.N. *In a Gloucestershire Garden*, Edward Arnold, 1906

Elliott, B. *Victorian Gardens*, B.T. Batsford, 1986

——, *The Royal Horticultural Society: A History 1804–2004*, Phillimore, 2004

——, 'A Novelist in the Fruit Garden', *The Garden* (1992), 488

——, 'A Political Family', *The Garden* (1992), 37

——, 'At the Cutting Edge', *The Garden* (1996), 289

——, 'Gardening Times', *The Garden* (1993), 411

——, 'Proprietor of Paradise', *The Garden* (1992), 273

——, 'Robert Hogg: Standard Setter', *The Garden* (1992), 427

——, 'Shear Diversity', *The Garden* (1996), 138

Fearnley-Whittingstall, J. *Rose Gardens*, Chatto and Windus, 1989

Flanders, J. *The Victorian House*, Harper Perennial, 2004

Fletcher, H. *The Story of the Royal Horticultural Society 1804–1968*, Oxford, Oxford University Press, 1969

Galinou, M., ed. *London's Pride: The Glorious History of the Capital's Gardens*, Anaya Publishers, 1990

Gaskell, S.M. 'Gardens for the Working Class: Victorian Practical Pleasure', *Victorian Studies* (Summer 1980), 479

Golby, J. and A.W. Purdue, *The Civilisation of the Crowd: Popular Culture in England 1750–1900*, Stroud, Sutton Publishing, 1999

Grieve, P. *A History of Ornamental-Foliaged Pelargoniums*, 1869; repr. The British Pelargonium and Geranium Society, 1977

Hadfield, M. *A History of British Gardening*, Penguin, 1985

Handbook of Town Gardening by a Lady, Orr & Co., 1847

Hibberd, S. *Field Flowers: A Handy Book for the Rambling Botanist*, 1870; new edn, W.H. and L. Collingridge, 1894

——, *Profitable Gardening*, 2nd edn, Groombridge and Sons, 1884

——, *Rustic Adornments for Homes of Taste*, 1857; repr. Century and The National Trust, 1987

——, *The Amateur's Flower Garden*, 1871; repr. Croom Helm, 1986

——, *The Amateur's Greenhouse and Conservatory*, rev. T.W. Sanders, W.H. and L. Collingridge, 1897

——, *The Book of the Aquarium*, Groombridge & Sons, 1860

——, *The Fern Garden: How to Make, Keep and Enjoy It*, 9th edn, Groombridge and Sons, 1881

——, *The Ivy: Its History, Uses and Characteristics*, Groombridge and Sons, 1871

——, *The Rose Book*, Groombridge and Sons, 1864

——, *The Town Garden*, Groombridge and Sons, 1855; 2nd edn, Groombridge and Sons, 1859

Hobsbawm, E. *The Age of Capital 1848–1875*, Abacus, 1998

Hole, S.R. *A Book about Roses*, ed. E.F. Daglish, Open-Air Library, J.M. Dent and Sons, 1932

——, *A Book about the Garden and the Gardener*, Thomas Nelson & Sons, 1892

——, *The Memories of Dean Hole*, Edward Arnold, 1892

Horn, P. *The Rise and Fall of the Victorian Servant*, Stroud, Sutton Publishing, 1995

James, L. *Print and the People*, Allen Lane, 1976

Kemp, E. *How to Lay Out a Small Garden*, Bradbury & Evans, 1855

Kitson Clark, G. *The Making of Victorian England*, Methuen, 1962

Laws, B. *Spade, Skirret and Parsnip: The Curious History of Vegetables*, Stroud, Sutton Publishing, 2004

Lee, A.J. *The Origins of the Popular Press 1855–1914*, Croom Helm, 1976

Longstaffe-Gowan, T. *The London Town Garden 1740–1840*, New Haven, Yale University Press, 2001

Loudon, J.C. *The Suburban Gardener and Villa Companion*, Longman, Orme, Brown, Green and Longmans, 1838

——, *The Suburban Horticulturalist*, William Smith, 1842

——, *In Search of English Gardens: The Travels of John Claudius Loudon and his Wife Jane*, National Trust Classics, 1829–1842; repr. Century, 1990

—— and J. Loudon, *The Villa Gardener*, William S. Orr & Co., 1850

Loudon, J.W. *Gardening for Ladies*, John Murray, 1840

——, *The Ladies' Companion to the Flower Garden*, ed. Charles Edmonds, 8th edn, Bradbury, Evans & Co., 1864

MacDougall, E.B., ed. *John Claudius Loudon and the Early Nineteenth Century in Great Britain*, Washington, DC, Dumbarton Oaks, Trustees for Harvard University, 1980

Mander, D. and J. Goolden, *The London Borough of Hackney in Old Photographs 1890–1960*, Stroud, Alan Sutton, 1991

Marcus, S.T. 'Town Gardens in London 1820–1914', unpublished thesis for the Architectural Association

Marsack, R. *My Garden: A Nineteenth-Century Writer on her English Cottage Garden*, Sidgwick & Jackson, 1990

Marshall, J. and I. Wilcox, *The Victorian House*, Sidgwick & Jackson, 1986

Matheson, J. 'Popular Gardening in London 1860–1900', unpublished M.A. dissertation for Open University, September 2001

May, W.J. *Villa Gardening*, The Bazaar Office, 32 Wellington Street, undated

M'Intosh, C. *The Flower Garden*, William S. Orr & Co., 1844

Morgan, J. and A. Richards, *A Paradise out of a Common Field: The Pleasures and Plenty of the Victorian Garden*, Century, 1990

Musgrave, T., C. Gardner and W. Musgrave, *The Plant Hunters*, Ward Lock, 1998

Muthesius, S. *The English Terraced House*, New Haven, Yale University Press, 1982

Newsome, D. *The Victorian World Picture*, Fontana Press, 1998

Olsen, D.J. *The Growth of Victorian London*, B.T. Batsford, 1976

Pankhurst, A. *Who Does Your Garden Grow?*, Colchester, Earl's Eye Publishing, 1992

Paterson, N. *The Manse Garden*, James Blackwood & Co., *c.* 1837

Paul, W. *The Hand-Book of Villa Gardening in a Series of Letters to a Friend*, Piper, Stephenson and Spence, 1855

Pavord, A. *The Tulip*, Bloomsbury, 1999

Perkin, H. *Origins of Modern English Society*, Routledge, 1994

Quest-Ritson, C. *The English Garden: A Social History*, Viking, 2001

Read, D. *The Age of Urban Democracy: England 1868–1914*, Longman, 1994

Reed, D. *The Popular Magazine in Britain and in the United States 1880–1960*, The British Library, 1997

Roberts, J. *Cabbages & Kings: The Origins of Fruit and Vegetables*, HarperCollins, 2001

Robinson, D. and C. Sturman, *William Brown and the Louth Panorama*, Louth, Louth Naturalists', Antiquarian and Literary Society, and Louth Town Council (Panorama Paintings), 2001

Robinson, W. *Alpine Flowers for English Gardens*, John Murray, 1870

——, *The English Flower Garden and Home Grounds*, John Murray, 1883; repr. Bloomsbury Gardening Classics, 1996

——, *The Wild Garden*, 1871; repr. Century Paperbacks, 1983

Scott-James, A. *The Cottage Garden*, Allen Lane, 1981

Smee, A. *My Garden*, 2nd edn, Bell and Daldy, 1872

Solman, D. *Loddiges of Hackney: The Largest Hothouse in the World*, The Hackney Society, 1995

Stuart Thomas, G. *The Graham Stuart Thomas Rose Book*, John Murray, 1994

Thompson, F. *Lark Rise to Candleford*, Penguin Books, 1973

Thompson, F.M.L. *The Rise of Respectable Society: A Social History of Victorian Britain 1830–1900*, Fontana Press, 1988

Thompson's Gardener's Assistant, ed. W. Watson, new edn, 6 vols, Gresham Publishing Co., 1904

Thomson, D. *Handy Book of the Flower Garden*, 2nd edn, William Blackwood & Sons, 1871

Tindall, G. *The Fields Beneath: The History of One London Village*, Temple Smith, 1977

Tjaden, W. 'George Glenny, Horticultural Hornet', *The Garden* (1986), 318

——, 'The Gardener's Gazette 1837–1847 and its Rivals', *Garden History* (Spring 1983), 70

Turner's Hackney Directory, Turner, 1849

The Victorian Garden Album, ed. E. Drury and P. Lewis, Collins & Brown, 1993

The Victorian Garden Catalogue: A Treasure Trove of Horticultural Paraphernalia, Studio Editions, 1995

The Virago Book of Women Gardeners, ed. D. Kellaway, Virago Press, 1996

Ward, N.B. *On the Growth of Plants in Closely Glazed Cases*, John van Voorst, 1842

Watson, I. *Gentlemen in the Building Line*, Padfield Publications, 1989

Watts, E. *Modern Practical Gardening, Vegetables, Flowers and Fruit: How to Grow Them*, Frederick Warne & Co, *c.* 1865

Wiener, M.J. *English Culture and the Decline of the Industrial Spirit 1850–1980*, Penguin Books, 1992

Wilkinson, A. 'Stoke Newington and the Golden Flower', *Hackney History* (1999), 22

——, 'The Preternatural Gardener: The Life of James Shirley Hibberd (1825–90)', *Garden History* (Winter 1998), 153

Index

References in italics are to illustrations.
References in bold type are principal references.